MW00559315

Becoming Buddha

*A Buddha's Timeless Path
of Meditation, Mindfulness
and Profound Wisdom*

Becoming Buddha

A Buddha's Timeless Path
of Meditation, Mindfulness
and Profound Wisdom

John Haspel

Copyright © 2017 John Haspel

1329 Leddys Lane

Upper Black Eddy

Pennsylvania 18972

Paperback Edition

ISBN-13: 978-0-9853403-7-7

Kindle and Electronic Editions

ISBN-13: 978-0-9853403-8-4

Questions or comments please use the contact form at Becoming-Buddha.com

Dedication

To Siddartha Gotama, a human being who through his own efforts awakened and spent the rest of his life teaching what he understood so that all interested can do the same.

To my Sangha at Cross River Meditation Center in Frenchtown New Jersey. Thank you all for your mindful presence, enlightening discussions, and for the precious honor of being your teacher.

To my online Sangha, thank you all for your mindful presence, enlightening emails, and for the precious honor of being your teacher.

To Moira, for being Moira.

To my friend Matthew Branham, thank you for your insight, generosity, and persevering commitment to the truth.

Also By John

The Truth Of Happiness

A personal study guide to Becoming Buddha and Correspondence Course

5.0 out of 5 *stars A path to a happier life.* This book has the potential to change your life for the better. You'll be introduced to a way of thinking that can calm your mind, bringing both contentment and peace, as well as understanding. Lynn A.

5.0 out of 5 stars I highly recommend this book to anyone serious about this path. If you are interested in what the Buddha actually taught, this book will provide the answers. *Joan E*

5.0 out of 5 stars *The Best Book of its Type.* John has a clear, concise way of explaining the Buddha's teachings. John is a very special man - clearly insightful, kind and walking the talk. Amazon Customer

5.0 out of 5 stars An absolute gem. John strips away unnecessary ritual, religion and cultural. This is a book that anyone interested in Buddhism and meditation will find full of insight, clarity and wisdom. I have been practicing meditation for 25+ years. It would have been very helpful to have had this book at hand back in 1990 when I first realized that the path to freedom was an 'inside job'. Jackie

Available at Amazon.com and other retail outlets.

Contents

About Becoming Buddha

Becoming Buddha is the culmination of an unfinished life's engagement with Buddhism. For the past 36 years - I'm 61 as of this writing - I have been practicing Buddhism. The Buddha's teachings as preserved in the Sutta Pitaka, the second book in the Pali Canon, guide my practice and my teaching. The suttas from the Pali Canon are the foundation for this book.

A complete explanation of the preservation of the Buddha's teachings in the Pali Canon follows the Introduction in the next chapter.

My purpose in writing Becoming Buddha is to provide clarity and consistency about what the Buddha actually taught, and his direct path to becoming awakened, to Becoming Buddha. Throughout this book I will occasionally make note of the differences and contradictions between the Buddha's teachings as preserved in the Sutta Pitaka, and what has developed since the Buddha's passing. This is necessary for clarity, consistency, contextual relevancy, for respect to an awakened human being, Siddartha Gotama, and his Dhamma.

I have found no useful or practical reason to alter or adapt the teachings of an awakened human being. Doing so has led to often ineffective and confusing modern Buddhist practices inaccessible to many who would hope to develop understanding.

A more complete description of my interest in Buddhism and the development of my practice is included at the end of this book.

There are many well established Buddhist religions - authentic to their own philosophy and lineages. If the reader has found a Buddhist practice that is bringing understanding and a calm and peaceful mind, free of craving and clinging, please continue wholeheartedly. My intention is not to disparage any individual or lineage, or to persuade anyone to abandon their religion.

If the reader is a modern Buddhist practitioner interested in the Buddha's teachings as preserved in the Sutta Pitaka, please continue with an open mind.

14

You will, at the very least, gain a new perspective of the teachings of an awakened human being.

If the reader is new to modern Buddhism, or new to meditation and mindfulness practices, please continue. You will find the direct teachings of an awakened human being presented in the context in which the Buddha intended.

Many modern teachers are too eager to ignore, rather than recognize and explain clearly, the contradictions and inconsistencies common in modern Buddhism.

The Buddha never shied away from clearly pointing out the significant contradictions between what he taught and what other's taught. He understood the importance of this one thing - establishing and maintaining integrity with the Dhamma. This is true compassion informed by awakened wisdom strengthened by the courage that comes from profound Right View. A Buddha is an ongoing example of these qualities.

The first twenty years of my Buddhist practice, perhaps a bit longer, I studied and practiced in many of the modern Mahayana schools of Buddhism. Much of my practice was in the Kagyu lineage of Tibetan Buddhism, in which I took vows. I have also studied and practiced in the various modern "Zen" schools.

At times I became pleasantly comfortable in my practice and associations. I met many wonderful and sincere teachers and supportive fellow practitioners. I found Buddhist religions rich with history, tradition, and established teachings. Eventually, these modern dharmas and associations proved increasingly confusing and disappointing. I now understand that my confusion and disappointment was the result of not developing the Buddha's direct teachings.

My experience with most of the modern Buddhist schools is that the contradictions between their particular form of Buddhism and what the Buddha actually taught are explained away without realistic foundation.

One modern Buddhist religion that I know of - Won Buddhism - is clear that they practice a reformed Buddhism, and for entirely altruistic reasons.

There certainly may be other modern Buddhist religions that clearly state that their form of Buddhism differs in some way from what the Buddha taught.

What I have found is that most claim a direct connection to the historical Buddha. When compared to the Sutta Pitaka the contradictions in both purpose and practice are obvious and significant. This is where much of the confusion arises.

There is no question that the Buddha's original teachings have been adapted and accommodated over the past two-thousand six-hundred years to fit charismatic individual views and cultural and established religious influences. This should be expected and has occurred to every religion.

It seems unique to Buddhism that the fundamental differences between what the Buddha taught and what has developed are "religiously" overlooked. This has led to a modern "thicket of views" within Buddhism that confuses, distracts, and disappoints many who might otherwise find true refuge in the Buddha's Dhamma.

The past sixteen years I have been studying, practicing, writing, and teaching the Buddha's Dhamma as preserved in the Sutta Pitaka. This direct inquiry into the Buddha's Dhamma has proven to be highly effective in developing what the Buddha taught

17

in the context that he taught. The Buddha taught that it is ignorance of Four Noble Truths that gives rise to confusion, deluded thinking, and ongoing stress and suffering.

In studying the suttas I came to understand that I alone am responsible for continuing ignorance although ignorance in this context is the common human problem. It became clear that the Buddha taught Four Noble Truths to recognize and abandon ignorance. The path that he taught to do so is an Eightfold Path. It is the Eightfold Path that provides the framework and guidance necessary to empty one's self of ignorance - to Become Buddha.

Dhamma (Sanskrit: dharma) is a Pali word with many meanings. In this context Dhamma refers to the Buddha's teachings as preserved in the Sutta Pitaka. I use the word "Dharma" to refer to later-developed Buddhist teachings.

Direct inquiry into the suttas ended all the confusion and contradictions prevalent in modern Buddhism. This direct inquiry developed an accessible, useful, understandable, applicable, relevant, and highly effective Buddhist practice. I now understand this is what the founder intended.

Common in modern Buddhism is the claim that the Buddha taught to "question everything" as if questioning the Buddha's actual teachings is an expected, even sacred part of modern dharma. The contradictions in modern Buddhism are often presented to be followed without question, but the Buddha's teachings could and should be questioned and accommodated, rather than developed as intended.

The final chapter in this book is the Buddha's teaching to the Kalama's, a group confused by the many competing and contradictory "dharma's" prevalent even during the Buddha's teaching career.

This sutta has been altered by many modern teachers, and then commonly cited to support the "question everything" doctrine. The Buddha teaches just the opposite.

In the Kalama Sutta, the Buddha teaches the Kalama's how to know if a Dhamma is authentic to his teaching, and useful: Through direct experience of actually developing his Dhamma separately from other

19

dharmas. If, after direct involvement with his Dhamma there are questions, the Buddha then suggests that he should be questioned directly so that he could provide additional clarity.

Questioning the Buddha directly is no longer possible but we can look to the suttas which are an authentic, consistent, and clear presentation of the Buddha's Dhamma. It is foolish to disregard the Buddha's teachings simply because of ignorance or confusion. Ignoring the Dhamma, ignoring Four Noble Truths, to fit confused and deluded views leads to all manner of disappointment and ongoing confusion.

As shown in Dependent Origination it is ignorance of Four Noble Truths that the Buddha's Dhamma addresses and remedies. The framework of the Eightfold Path provides the context and direction to recognize ignorance and avoid confusion and distracting adaptations to the Dhamma.

Beginning with the story of Siddhartha Gotama's life, this book presents a comprehensive explanation of the foundational themes of the Buddha's Dhamma.

Following the introduction is a chapter on the Pali Canon that presents the remarkable story of how the Buddha's teachings came to be authenticated and preserved over time beginning at the First Buddhist Council. The first Buddhist council convened about a month after the Buddha's passing.

As will be seen, the Buddha's teachings have survived intact and authentic due to a remarkably skillful method rooted directly in his Dhamma. The Buddha's Dhamma continues in relevancy and effectiveness to this day due to this careful maintenance. Included in this chapter is an explanation of how the various modern Buddhist religions developed, tracing back to a dissatisfied group at the Second Buddhist Council about one hundred years after the first council.

The chapter on Impermanence, Not-Self, and Dukkha explains the environment that confusion and suffering arise and the cause of the personal experience of suffering.

The Buddha's awakening is described in his own words in the Nagara Sutta. This is followed by an

21

explanation of what Siddhartha awakened to - Dependent Origination.

Dependent origination clearly shows that it is ignorance of these Four Noble Truths that the conditions of confusion, deluded thinking, and ongoing disappointment originate in, and are dependent on.

Upon his awakening, he became known as a Buddha to describe his "awakened" quality of mind. As far as can be found Siddartha never referred to himself as The Buddha although I will in this book. He refused ceremonial titles and simply referred to himself as the "Tathagatha." Tathagatha describes a human being who, through their own efforts, "awakened" and became mindfully and continually established in reality.

"Buddha" describes the quality of an awakened, fully mature mind. The Buddha spent the final forty-five years of his life as a teacher so that others could learn from an awakened human being to do the same: Become Awakened, Become Buddha.

Each section in Becoming Buddha introduces a specific theme, or topic, that is related to the themes introduced in the following sections. Some of these themes are repeated as they are best understood in different but relevant contexts. This is how the Buddha taught the Dhamma - relevant to the situation and always in context of Four Noble Truths.

An explanation of what may be the most misunderstood single word in all of Buddhism follows the chapter on Dependent Origination - the meaning of "becoming" in the context of the main themes of the Dhamma.

The personal experience of stress and suffering - The Five Clinging-Aggregates - is explained in detail in different but similar contexts.

The Buddha's first three discourses, known as "The Cardinal Discourses" to signify their primary importance follows the section on The Five Clinging-Aggregates. These suttas relate directly to the central themes of Dependent Origination, The Three Marks of Human Experience, and ongoing Stress and Suffering. It can truly be said that The Buddha presented the foundation and context of his entire Dhamma in these first three discourses.

Following the section on the Buddha's first three discourses is a section explaining the practical understanding of The Four Noble Truths and the method of cultivating the Buddha's path to Becoming Buddha. This path is the Eightfold Path.

As stated, The Buddha awakened to the understanding that the problem of human suffering is rooted in ignorance of Four Noble Truths. Every teaching the Buddha presented was presented in the context of this very first teaching, the Dhammacakkappavattana Sutta. In this sutta the Buddha presents Four Noble Truths to explain what he awakened to - Dependent Origination.

The First Noble Truth describes the common human problem of ongoing disappointing and unsatisfactory experiences as Dukkha. Dukkha is an ancient word from the Pali language that means unsatisfactory, uncertain, disappointing, stressful, confusing, and all manner of mental and physical suffering.

The Second Noble Truth describes the personal experience of suffering that arises from misunderstanding Dependent Origination and the Three Marks of Human Experience.

The Third Noble Truth shows the possibility of individual awakening.

The Fourth Noble Truth is the truth of the path developing the cessation of confusion, deluded thinking, and ongoing disappointment - the Eightfold Path. The Buddha taught the Eightfold Path so that all who are interested could empty themselves of ignorance in this present lifetime and develop calm and peaceful minds and lives of lasting happiness.

Included in this section is the Buddha's simple meditation method as one factor of the Eightfold Path, and the two specific applications of refined mindfulness. The Buddha taught mindfulness to support the integration of the Eightfold Path as the framework for one's life.

If you have been using a meditation method other than Shamatha-Vipassana meditation, please learn and practice this simple method and then decide for yourself its effectiveness. Keep in mind that Shamatha-Vipassana meditation is the only meditation method taught by the Buddha and is the eighth factor of the Eightfold Path.

Also in this section is clarification on the meaning of Karma and Rebirth in the context of Dependent Origination, Four Noble Truths, Three Marks of Human Experience, and Five Clinging-Aggregates.

Becoming Buddha concludes with suttas supportive and contextually relevant to the themes of the Buddha's Dhamma.

Much of the confusion and contradictions present in modern Buddhism has occurred from losing or ignoring the context that an awakened human being intended. This has led to a modern thicket of views that alters, accommodates, complicates, and obscures what was originally a direct, accessible, and effective path towards awakening, towards full human maturity, towards Becoming Buddha.

Throughout this book I have made contextual edits from scholarly translations of the suttas from the original Pali for further clarity, to minimize repetition, to modernize wording and phraseology, and maintain contextual relevancy to The Four Noble Truths. The purpose, intent, and meaning of these teachings are not altered in any way.

Within the suttas my commentary is italicized, and otherwise to provide emphasis.

Introduction - Siddartha Gotama Becomes Buddha

"Abandon unskillful thoughts, words, and actions, develop skillful thoughts, words, and actions, and purify one's mind, this is the purpose of the Buddha's teachings." (Dhammapada 183)

Siddhartha Gotama was born in Kapilavastu in what is now southern Nepal on the Indian border. Current research places his birth between 563 BCE and 463 BCE. His father was King Suddhodana, the leader of the Shakya clan. Upon his birth, his mother, Queen Maha Maya, and the king were told by visiting holy men that he would either be a great king or a great holy man.

Queen Maha Maya died shortly after giving

birth to Siddhartha and he was raised by his aunt, Maha Prajapati.

A traditionally arranged marriage at the age of 16 to Yasodharā, a distant cousin, bore a son, Rahula. Prajapati and Yasodharā would later become nuns and Rahula a monk, following the Buddha's teaching.

Siddhartha had all the comforts of being a prince and heir to his father's throne. Despite this, restlessness and dissatisfaction caused him to begin to question his values and his view of the world. At the age of twenty-nine, Prince Siddhartha left the palace grounds. For the first time in his life, he observed a sick person, and then an old person, and finally a corpse. Later he came across a wandering mendicant.

In stark contrast to his life of wealth and comfort, he noticed the stress that other's experience in their daily lives. He noticed the aggression and competitiveness that occurred as a result of stress.

This experience left Siddhartha greatly confused about the purpose and meaning of life. If everyone is subject to the uncertainty of physical life and the struggle to simply survive, is there any meaning to life?

If disappointment, sickness, aging, and death are certain, is there a way of living free of the consequences of these experiences? Is there a way to liberate himself and others from these common problems?

Is there a way of living in the world and yet not be affected by the seemingly random events of life? What are the individual contributions to stress, disappointment, disillusionment, and suffering? Is it possible to escape stress and suffering for good?

The future Buddha left his wife and child, and his life of riches, comfort, and power, seeking answers to these questions. As was common to the men in his culture, he became a mendicant. He relied on the charity of others as he wandered and studied with the spiritual leaders of his time.

He encountered two teachers whose teachings were developed from the Vedas. The Vedas are the foundational scripture for modern Hinduism.

He first studied with Alara Kalama who taught a philosophy and meditation method in what would be called today "Yogic" meditation. (The "yoga" of today

31

would not become a cohesive philosophy for at least another 1,500 years)

The future Buddha grasped these techniques quickly. He was able to enter "the sphere of nothingness," the goal of this meditation.

Another teacher, Uddaka Ramaputta, taught a meditation technique developing neither-perception-nor-non-perception, a kind of non-dualistic view. Siddhartha quickly mastered this technique as well.

These meditation techniques were recognized as the most advanced meditation techniques available. Similar methods that both teachers used are still taught today.

Siddhartha rejected both of these teachings and their meditation methods. He realized they were only an escape and diversion from the understanding he sought. Siddhartha stated that Alara Kalama's teachings "leads not to disenchantment, dispassion, cessation, stilling, direct knowledge, awakening, or to unbinding. These teachings lead only to reappearance in the (mentally fabricated) dimension of nothingness."

He stated that Uddaka Ramaputta's teachings "lead not to disenchantment, dispassion, cessation, stilling, direct knowledge, awakening, or to unbinding. These teachings lead only to reappearance in the (mentally fabricated) dimension of neither-perception-nor-non-perception."

These mind states are still taught as a goal today in most modern Buddhist schools. Popular doctrines of achieving or revealing an inner "Buddha-nature" or "Buddhahood," or abiding in environments of nothingness or emptiness are examples of modern non-dual doctrines.

Siddhartha understood how these philosophies, regarded as highly advanced, only led to continued establishment of a fabricated "self." Though not yet fully developed in his mind, Siddhartha understood that any proliferation of an impermanent "self" in any real or imagined realm could only lead to more confusion, deluded thinking, and suffering.

Both of these teachers were highly respected. Siddhartha understood that their doctrines only developed self-referential wrong views rooted in ignorance. This is significant as this understanding would coalesce as Dependent Origination.

Both teachers asked the Buddha to join them as a senior teacher. Siddhartha, with great courage and conviction, rejected both of these teachers and their teachings. He understood that lineage, popularity, power, or prestige alone did not qualify a teacher or their teachings. If their teachings did not bring an end to clinging to ignorant views, they must be abandoned. He joined with five other mendicants and began severe ascetic practices. Their belief was that by denying the needs and pleasures of the body they could overcome the desires and cravings of the body and free their minds.

Siddhartha was so intent and adept at ascetic practices he would only eat a few beans or a few grains of rice a day. He became so emaciated that he later told that he could feel his spine by touching his belly. Siddhartha and his group also practiced breath-control and manipulation. Siddhartha became able to slow his breath to an almost imperceptible level.

One day, while bathing in a river, he collapsed and nearly died. He realized then that severe asceticism was not the way of liberation and freedom.

He realized that asceticism was only self-inflicted suffering.

Siddhartha became deeply frustrated. Six years of study with highly regarded teachers and many years of asceticism brought him no closer to the understanding he sought. The soon-to-be Buddha was beginning to understand what he would call "The Middle Way."

In describing the middle way between extreme views and resulting actions the Buddha stated:

"These two extremes are to be abandoned:

The compulsion to indulge and gain pleasure from objects of sensual desire which is inferior, low, vulgar, ignoble.

The compulsion to indulge in self torment, (asceticism) which is painful and ignoble.

These (practices) only lead to more delusion."

Many ascetic practices continue today in the form of extreme periods of forced silence, lengthy repetitive chanting, and ritualistic bowing. Extremely long meditation sessions is also a modern form of asceticism.

35

Siddhartha remembered a time as a youth when he was also frustrated. He developed a measure of calm and focus by sitting under the shade of a tree and placing his attention on his breathing.

He decided to try this simple meditation method again with the strong resolve to finally develop the understanding he sought. Over the next forty days Siddhartha engaged in Shamatha-Vipassana meditation.

The significance here is that Siddhartha developed the strong resolve or Right Intention (the second factor of The Eightfold path) to awaken.

As agitating and distracting thoughts arose, he recognized that the origination of these thoughts were rooted in ignorance. (In the more mystical accounts of this story the effects of ignorance is portrayed metaphorically as the malevolent god Mara)

As his concentration increased, he noticed that these thoughts were clinging to impermanent objects. He noticed how one thought immediately followed the next - one thought clinging to the next.

Siddhartha used this simple meditation method to quiet his mind and increase his concentration. As his mind quieted and his concentration increased, he was able to develop insight into The Three Marks of Existence.

The Three Marks of Existence - Anicca, Anatta, Dukkha - is explained further on.

As desire, fear, and aversion arose in the Buddha's mind, he recognized that he was joined to these thoughts. As he continued he realized the impermanence of these conditioned views.

With great conviction he recognized and abandoned all views rooted in ignorance. With gentle determination, he put every conditioned thought aside, always returning to his breath.

A great peace arose within Siddhartha. As his concentration increased he recognized self-referential mental fabrications. He understood the effect these fabrications had on his thoughts and views.

Through his own efforts he developed a profound understanding of the nature of confusion and suffering. He understood the confusing interplay between the impermanent phenomenal world and a misunderstanding of what he assumed as a "self." His

37

mind cleared and Siddhartha awakened. Siddhartha became Buddha.

He was now able to view life through profound Right View. He was an Arahant, a rightly self-awakened human being.

Siddhartha recognized the process originating in ignorance that resulted in mental fabrications. These fabrications were masking the confused and deluded nature of his mind.

In the Nagara Sutta he described becoming stuck in the feedback loop of fabrications: "This consciousness turns back at name-&-form, (self-referential views) and goes no farther."

The Nagara Sutta is included further on.

He now understood what an effective meditation technique would provide. Siddhartha realized that attempting to enter a mental state where all thought was denied, or masked by objects or suggestion was only furthering distraction. This would only avoid what was singularly important.

He understood the nature of distraction arising from fabrications. He understood that increasing concentration was primary in ending distraction. He understood that a well-concentrated mind was necessary in gaining insight into the qualities of his own mind and the impermanence of all things. Most importantly he gained a profound understanding of the fleeting nature of his own thoughts.

Upon his awakening the now Buddha realized that the confusion, deluded thinking, and individual contributions to suffering were the result of ignorance. He came to understand that it was ignorance of four truths, Four Noble Truths, as the common human problem.

This often misunderstood and often intentionally misapplied understanding that Siddhartha awakened to is known as Dependent Origination. Dependent Origination states that from ignorance of Four Noble Truths, through twelve observable causative links, all manner of confusion, delusion, and suffering arises.

Dependent Origination is not a creation myth nor does it establish a doctrine of interdependence, inter-connectedness, or "inter-being." These are modern adaptations when seen in the context of The

39

Four Noble Truths only encourage continued fabrications.

An explanation of how this singularly important teaching has been altered is included in the chapter on The Pali Canon.

As a practical matter an authentic Dhamma practice rests on a clear understanding of Dependent Origination. From this understanding the importance of Four Noble Truths will not be diminished or ignored further.

The Buddha's great realization was his insight into the human problem, the human dis-ease. It is due to initial ignorance of Four Noble Truths that an ongoing strategy is developed to ignore the causes that continue dukkha. This is conditioned thinking and it is the purpose of the Eightfold Path to recognize and abandon conditioned thinking.

The Buddha now understood that self-referential clinging to objects, events, views, and ideas develops greed, aversion, and deluded thinking. He understood that greed, aversion, and deluded thinking arose from this specific ignorance of Four Noble

Truths. He understood that these three defilements continue to mask ignorance.

The Buddha describes his awakening in relation to Dependent Origination and in the context of Four Noble Truths in the chapter on The Nagara Sutta.

In his first teaching after his awakening the Buddha presented the Dhammacakkappavattana Sutta to the five mendicants he befriended earlier. This sutta established Four Noble Truths and "set the (only) wheel of truth in motion."

The Buddha would spend the next 45 years of his life instructing all that were interested, from the most powerful rulers to the most shunted and ignored, that stress and suffering originated in, and was dependent on, ignorance of Four Noble Truths.

It was never the Buddha's intention to create a religion based on dogma, intellectual scriptural study, or ritualistic worship. He did not teach to worship a supreme being or disincarnate deities or disincarnate past, present, or future "Buddha's."

He never viewed himself as a savior or his Dhamma as salvific.

41

He presented his teachings to those that were interested in developing understanding and renunciation of the nature of their own confusion and suffering. He taught an Eightfold Path leading to the cessation of all delusion, confusion and suffering.

Near the end of his life when asked by the attending monks who would be their teacher when he passed. The Buddha replied that he had taught all that was necessary for each person to work out their own liberation. His final words were "Behold my dear friends, impermanence and decay is relentless, work diligently for your own liberation." (Digha Nikaya 16)

At the age of 80 the Buddha left this world awake and at peace.

There is nothing esoteric or mystical about the Buddha's Dhamma. The Buddha held nothing back. The Buddha said that his teachings "are not like that of a teacher with a closed fist who keeps something back." He taught that "his teachings are the same (in practice) for monks and lay people." (Digha Nikaya 16)

No special abilities or "good karma" or encounters with other "enlightened" beings are necessary to develop the Buddha's Dhamma. There are no magical transmissions, special rituals, or special empowerments taught by the Buddha as necessary for awakening to occur.

The only requirement is to develop his direct teachings wholeheartedly. He taught the Eightfold Path as the direct path to awakening, to full human maturity.

There is nothing that can be added to or imposed on Dhamma practitioners that are necessary to awaken. Awakening is not bestowed based on grace or the accumulation of "good works" or merit. The only merit to be gained is the understanding gained by direct engagement with the Eightfold Path.

Awakening is developed by systematically recognizing and abandoning ignorance. Awakening is developed through practical insight and wisdom developed from the Eightfold Path.

The Buddha described an awakened human being as "released" or "unbound" as in released or unbound from clinging to self-referential views rooted in ignorance of Four Noble Truths. He taught the Eightfold Path to "empty" oneself of ignorance. The Buddha described the quality of mind of an awakened human being as "calm."

43

The Buddha taught an Eightfold Path to be developed by each individual by becoming familiar with the present nature of their own minds. The Buddha taught a path of virtue, concentration and wisdom. This path develops liberation from the stress, disappointment, disillusionment, and suffering of day-to-day life. This path develops lives of lasting peace and contentment.

The Buddha often used the word "Ehipassiko" which means "come and see for your self" in describing how to develop understanding. His Dhamma is to be individually developed leading to an individual experience of the cessation of craving and clinging and ongoing Dukkha originating in, and dependent on, ignorance of Four Noble Truths.

The purpose of the Buddha's teachings is to recognize and abandon ignorance of Four Noble Truths. The purpose of the Buddha's teachings is to become empty of ignorance and the resulting suffering that follows from craving and clinging.

The Buddha's second discourse is the Anatta-Lakkhana Sutta. Here he teaches the confusion and contradictions of conceit, or "I-making" that results from ignorance of Four Noble Truths.

His third discourse was the Adittapariyaya Sutta, The Fire Discourse. In this sutta the Buddha describes how conceit is reinforced by craving and clinging, the fires of passion, resulting in continued Dukkha.

The Buddha's first three discourses relate very closely to Dependent Origination in what may at first be overlooked. The Buddha's first discourse teaches the common human problem of disappointment- Dukkha. He teaches that Dukkha originates in craving and clinging. He teaches that disappointment is an impermanent though persistent experience dependent on certain conditions.

His next discourse explains Anatta, the Not-Self characteristic, and its impermanent nature. This discourse explains the conditions required to end confusion and deluded views.

The third discourse is on disappointment and suffering arising within an environment of impermanence and the fabricated "self" that experiences disappointment.

45

The three underlying themes of these first three teachings describe the Three Marks of Existence. These three common experiences are:

1. Anicca, impermanence.

2. Anatta, the not-self characteristic.

3. Dukkha, confusion, deluded thinking, disappointment, dissatisfaction, suffering.

Immediately the practicality of Buddha's teaching can be seen. His first three teachings directly address the problem of human disappointment and suffering. He explains the environment that allows for the arising and cessation of suffering. He then shows where understanding is to be applied: to individual wrong or ignorant views.

Wrong or ignorant views result in craving for self-referential existence. This is conceit or "I-Making. The personal experience of I-Making is the Five Clinging-Aggregates. The Buddha teaches that the Five Clinging-Aggregates. is Dukkha. The defining characteristic of Dukkha is clinging to the formation of self-referential existence.

It is ignorance that initiates the formation of the 12 links of Dependent Origination. The Eightfold Path provides the framework to recognize and abandon conditioned wrong views rooted in ignorance.

Please keep in mind that everything the Buddha taught for his entire teaching career was taught in the context of Four Noble Truths. Developing Right View unravels the links of the twelve-link chain of dependencies rooted in ignorance. This brings confusion, deluded thinking, and resulting Dukkha to cessation.

The Eightfold Path is a practical and direct way to develop understanding of results of ignorance of Four Noble Truths. The Eightfold Path is a practical and direct way to develop profound wisdom and end confusion and experience the cessation of stress and confusion.

The Buddha taught that anything that could not be observed and experienced individually should be abandoned. He taught that anything that did not directly lead to becoming empty of ignorance should be abandoned.

47

As different cultures adapted these basic teachings, it became more and more difficult to understand what was essential to awakening. The Eightfold Path leads to awakening, free of craving, aversion, and deluded thinking.

The Buddha did not teach any specific type of physical conditioning, or a focus on any particular part of our bodies, whether physically apparent or imagined, or vague "mindfulness" techniques. The Buddha did not teach to follow speculative or conceptual scripture blindly or to develop rituals as a way of gaining some type of merit that would have a reward at some future time.

The Buddha did not offer any ritual or practice for the purpose of accumulating good will or favor from an external being or beings.

The Buddha did not teach anything that could not be verified by direct and mindful experience.

He taught that awakening took place here in this present life unencumbered by conditioned thinking of any kind. The Buddha taught that our awakening develops within our own minds.

Rooted in ignorance, we alone are responsible for the conditions that lead to confusion, deluded thinking, and ongoing disappointment. By developing wisdom and understanding, we alone are responsible for creating the conditions of our own liberation by first gaining insight to the nature of stress.

The Buddha's teaching is free of any dogma, superstition, or time constraints. Through wholehearted practice awakening can and does occur within the present lifetime. Awakening is dependent on becoming empty of ignorance and creating the conditions of awakening, the conditions for Becoming Buddha.

As the teachings of The Buddha spread and were integrated by different cultures, many changes to his teachings took place. Shamatha-Vipassana meditation became altered and embellished.

Some traditions will present koan or hwadu practice as superior to Shamatha-Vipassana meditation. Some traditions will teach a form of modified shamatha but not recognize the need for vipassana. Some traditions will teach an analytical form of vipassana - insight - without a continually effective method of quieting the mind. Often shamatha is taught as a preliminary practice to vipassana rather than that the two aspects are a part of cohesive and effective practice requiring both.

The Yuganaddha Sutta, included in the section on meditation and mindfulness, shows the importance of practicing Shamatha-Vipassana in tandem. It is through deepening concentration developed in a proper Shamatha-Vipassana meditation practice that supports the refined mindfulness necessary to develop the framework and guidance of the entire Eightfold Path.

It is from the framework and guidance of the Eightfold Path that true and useful "vipassana," insight, is gained into The Three Marks of Existence and brings to cessation ignorance of Four Noble Truths.

Some modern Buddhist traditions even discard meditation entirely and focus on scriptural study, intricate visualization, or invoking the Buddha's image or name. Chanting and the use of mantra or other techniques to gain favor or induce a trance are also attributed to the Buddha's teaching erroneously.

Breath manipulation techniques, often characterized as "mindfulness" practices, are also best to avoid as these will only distract from developing Shamatha-Vipassana meditation within the framework of the Eightfold Path.

There is no intention here to disparage other wholesome practices, merely to emphasize the direct teachings of the Buddha.

Engage with these teachings with a soft and gentle mind and open heart. Do not "try" too hard to fully understand these teachings immediately. It is enough to begin to integrate these teachings and to continue to engage Right Effort and develop the entire Eightfold Path.

As the Eightfold Path is developed, profound insight into The Three Marks will arise and abandonment of ignorant (wrong) views will naturally occur.

Some, like Kondanna, will fully understand quickly. Others, the Buddha's cousin Ananda comes to mind, who heard every teaching the Buddha presented over the last twenty-five years of his teaching career,

51

did not fully awaken until a month after the Buddha's passing.

The Buddha presented an Eightfold Path so that these teachings could be developed by anyone who would wholeheartedly engage with them and develop a life of lasting peace and happiness. Take refuge in this understanding and the true lineage of the Dhamma.

The chapter on the Ratana Sutta near the end of this book explains the meaning of taking refuge in The Buddha, his Dhamma, and a well-focused Sangha in the context of Four Noble Truths.

The Buddha consistently described his teachings as "I teach understanding suffering (dukkha) and the cessation of suffering. Nothing more." When describing dukkha the Buddha teaches that "birth is suffering, sickness is suffering, aging is suffering, death is suffering. Being separated from what is desired is suffering. Associating with the un-desired is suffering. In short, the Five Clinging-Aggregates are suffering."

Even though by clinging these five disparate aggregates together to establish a "self" seems to provide an argument for a self, the argument cannot be sustained. The Buddha never answered the questions "is there a self" or "is there not a self," he simply taught that what is commonly viewed as a self is not a self. The view that would establish a self is a wrong view rooted in ignorance.

As the question itself is rooted in ignorance (of Four Noble Truths) when asked, the Buddha would often simply remain silent to indicate that the question itself did not deserve an answer. At other times the Buddha would answer "holding this question is the cause of your confusion, let the question go."

In the Panha Sutta (Anguttara Nikaya 4.42) the Buddha teaches that there are four skillful ways to answer questions:

- Questions that are suitable should be answered directly - yes, no, this, that.

- Questions that are suitable should be answered with a descriptive or defining answer.

- Questions that are suitable should be answered with another question.

- Questions that are unsuitable to developing understanding should be put aside.

Further on in this sutta the Buddha calls those that understand how to answer questions properly as "one who has broken through to what is worthwhile, prudent and wise."

Many modern Buddhists claim that it is the essence of Buddhist practice to question everything and if an answer is unsatisfactory that the Buddha's direct teachings should be abandoned in favor of what satisfies the ego.

Many modern Buddhist teachers insist that if the Dhamma cannot be supported by ever-changing "science" then the Dhamma itself should be altered or abandoned.

The Buddha did not spend the last forty-five years of his life teaching a Dhamma that should be altered or discarded simply because his Dhamma does not support established views rooted in ignorance.

Wisdom is challenging clinging views rooted in ignorance. It is Anatta, what the Buddha teaches is not-a-self, that insists on satisfactory answers to all questions. It is Anatta that will alter and accommodate "answers" to allow for continuation of deluded self-referential views.

This is the result of thinking that has been "conditioned" by ignorance and dependent on ignorance of Four Noble Truths. Modern psychology calls conditioned thinking "confirmation bias." Conditioned thinking can only produce views that are biased towards confirming established conditioned views.

It is an aspect of ignorance to ignore or adapt anything that would challenge established ignorance.

Common in modern Buddhism and in modern "new age" thought in general is the notion of non-duality. This is the belief that the individual is a part of one grand cosmic entity attached (clinging) to others and to all phenomena. This is simply an extreme view of establishing the Five Clinging-Aggregates in all phenomena. This belief only continues the confusion, delusion, and suffering inherent in ignorance of Four Noble Truths.

The Five Clinging-Aggregates is the personal experience of suffering arising from clinging to ignorant views. The Five Clinging-Aggregates is explained in different contexts throughout this book.

The Buddha taught to see phenomenal reality clearly and to see the discrete, separate, and impermanent nature of all things in the world. In describing an Arahant, an awakened human being, he consistently used the words unbound or released as in unbound or released from all clinging views including the deluded view that individuals are part of one singular, substantial, sustainable, clinging universal existence.

He taught an Eightfold Path that develops the concentration and refined mindfulness necessary to recognize and abandon all confused and deluded views that would only continue confusion and delusion, and further individual human suffering.

When using the word anatta, the Buddha is not attempting to establish a true self or a cosmic self found in all things and connected to all living things. These are contradictory non-dual teachings of later developed Buddhist schools.

As shown earlier, the Buddha studied and rejected non-dual doctrines. Non-dual doctrines arise from a misunderstanding and misapplication of Dependent Origination.

The Buddha taught that what is commonly viewed as a "self" is an ignorant view. This view is the originating condition that confusion, deluded thinking, and ongoing suffering is dependent on. This view is "anatta," not-a-self worth establishing or defending.

He taught that these views are inherently impermanent as they are attached to impermanent objects, events, views, and ideas. He taught that whatever is impermanent is Dukkha.

He taught that craving for, or clinging to, impermanent objects, events, views, and ideas is rooted in ignorance of Four Noble Truths, including the insistence that a self can be established cosmically through inter-being, interconnectedness, or interdependence.

It is a profoundly wrong view that insists on establishing a self in any impermanent environment or cosmic or higher realm.

Any conditioned view that establishes or maintains a permanent sustainable self is based in ignorance of Four Noble Truths. This conditioned view of a self is anatta, not-a-self.

Any attempt to establish or maintain this confused view contradicts the Four Noble Truths and will only lead to more confusion, delusion, and suffering.

The Buddha's Eightfold Path develops freedom from clinging. This includes clinging to the view of the interdependence, interconnectedness, or the inter-being of all sentient beings.

The Eightfold Path develops a life of lasting peace and contentment through recognizing and abandoning all confused and deluded views clinging to the notion that a permanent "self" can somehow be established through commonly held beliefs or constantly repeated confused views.

Seeing these confused views clearly is the essence of useful insight and the essence of the Buddha's Dhamma. There is no great mystery to be solved. Human life is not a mystery to be endlessly contemplated or solved. There is an Eightfold Path to be wholeheartedly engaged with that will bring lasting peace and contentment in this lifetime.

There are audio and video recordings, including Sangha discussions, related to each of the topics in this book at Becoming-Buddha.com.

My companion book to Becoming Buddha, The Truth Of Happiness, is a ten-week personal study of the Buddha's fundamental teachings developing the Eightfold Path as the framework for understanding The Three Marks of Existence and release from ignorance, with the option for weekly correspondence. It is available at Amazon.com here: https://www.amazon.com/dp/B00NKV2ZZY

The Pali Canon and the Authenticity of the Sutta's

It is not my intent to disparage or diminish any Buddhist religion or practice. It is my intent to show the differences between what the Buddha taught and what has developed into the modern forms of Buddhism. My reference to the Buddha's teachings is the Sutta Pitaka, the second book of the Pali Canon.

More importantly, I hope to show that the Buddha's original teachings continue to be available and relevant today. The establishment and continuing careful maintenance of the authenticity of the Sutta is one of the most remarkable and important accomplishments in human history.

From heron when using the word "Sutta" I am referring to the Sutta Pitaka, the second book of the Pali Canon. "Sutra's" refers to texts that have become incorporated into modern Buddhism created after the Buddha's passing. I will use the word "Dhamma" when referring to the Buddha's teachings as preserved in the Pali Canon. I will use the word "dharma" when referring to the adapted and accommodated teachings that are not part of the original Sutta Pitaka.

Continued careful maintenance of the sutta's preserves these teachings for anyone interested in what the Buddha actually taught. It is as important to show the adaptations and accommodations made to the Dhamma. These came from many sources including charismatic individuals and cultural and religious influences.

It is often claimed that adapting and accommodating the Buddha's original teachings is reasonable as it is impossible to authenticate the Pali Canon. From this wrong view it is then seen as appropriate to rely solely on the adapted and accommodated dharma's that have followed.

I have spent the past thirty-six years of my life studying and practicing Buddhism in most of the modern schools. Prior to studying the sutta's I became increasingly confused and disappointed trying to make practical sense of the many modern "Dharma's," all claiming authentic origination in the Buddha.

While some of the modern schools of Buddhism continue to mention the Four Noble Truths, including the Eightfold Path. This fundamental teaching is often presented as preliminary or conceptual. The Buddha's entire teaching is taught in the context of Four Noble Truths. This is apparent when studying the sutta's.

It was not until studying the Sutta's that the Buddha's teachings become accessible and practical. I found that the Buddha awakened to Dependent Origination. Dependent Origination explains that the cause of all confusion, deluded thinking, and ongoing unsatisfactory experiences arise from ignorance.

Through the Sutta's I came to understand the primary importance of one of the most misunderstood and misapplied teachings - Dependent Origination - which clearly shows that it is through ignorance, through twelve observable causative links, all manner of confusion, deluded thinking, and ongoing disappointment and suffering arises.

Dependent Origination is one of the most misunderstood and misapplied teachings of modern Buddhism. Dependent Origination is also called Dependent Co-Arising.

Dependent Origination is taught in many sutta's and most significantly in Paticca-Samuppada-Vibhanga Sutta. In this sutta the Buddha clearly shows that it is ignorance of Four Noble Truths that originates all manner of suffering. In the Nagara Sutta the Buddha describes his own awakening in the direct context of Dependent Origination and the Eightfold Path.

Both Sutta's are included later in this book.

Comparing the Buddha's teaching on Dependent Origination and most modern presentations of Dependent Origination (or Dependent Co-Arising) clearly shows how the later-developed Buddhist doctrines have developed contradictory Dharma's through ignoring this foundational teaching.

Ignoring Dependent Origination and Four Noble Truths can only continue ignorance.

It is for this reason that I place great importance on understanding and acknowledging the significant differences in Buddhist practices that have developed in the twenty-six hundred years since the Buddha's passing.

It is for this reason that I refined my practice to only what can be found in the Sutta's.

It is for this reason that I teach only what can be found in the Sutta's.

This is the only way that I can practice all aspects of the Eightfold Path in all areas of my life with emphasis on Right Speech, Right Action, and Right Livelihood.

In this chapter (and this book) I will use Pali terms as much as possible. Pali is the language that is very similar to the language the Buddha spoke. Pali is the language used first in the oral tradition and later in the first written accounts of the Canon. Occasionally I wall use the more common Sanskrit terms solely to avoid confusion.

Much of my sources are listed at the end of this article and a link to a related article on Becoming-Buddha.com that is not part of this book. [1]

Modern Buddhism has developed from the practical and direct "path" taught by one awakened human being in his lifetime to multi-faceted and often contradictory religions. Many adaptations to the sutta's have been made to fit a view of "Buddhism" that accommodates individual, cultural, and religious predispositions.

These accommodations in no way diminish the many modern Buddhist religions or the individuals or cultures that have influenced Buddhist practice, but they have often diminished or dismissed entirely what the Buddha actually taught. Any study of religion is a study of adaptation and accommodation.

What has resulted from the many adaptations to the Buddha's original teachings is a modern "thicket of views." This modern thicket of views often contradicts in purpose, intent, and actual practice what the Buddha actually taught. [1]

The Buddha taught an easily understood and accessible path to awakening, to full human maturity. Buddhist practices not founded in the sutta's are often a confusing and inaccessible mix of mystical scriptures, intricate visualizations, mantras, repetitive physical exercise, deity and guru worship, and contemplative and analytical "meditation" and mindfulness practices that have little or no foundation in the actual teachings of the Buddha.

The Pali Canon consists of three distinct collections known today as Tipitaka, the three baskets. The first two, the Vinaya Pitaka and the Sutta Pitaka were recorded through an established oral tradition at the First Buddhist Council. This council convened about one month after the Buddha's passing. The third book, the Abhidhamma Piṭaka, contains intricate analysis of mundane phenomena and psychological and mystical teachings. The Abhidhamma Piṭaka developed over time beginning with the Second Buddhist Council. It will be shown that the Abhidhamma Piṭaka is not an authentic account of the Buddha's direct teachings.

The development of the Abhidhamma and its inclusion in the Pali Canon is explained in additional detail further on.

What is remarkable throughout the Sutta Pitaka is the consistency and relevancy of the sutta's to the Buddha's very first teaching - The Dhammacakkappavattana Sutta. Everything the Buddha taught during his forty-five year teaching career was taught in the context of this very first teaching and with the purpose of developing understanding of these Four Truths.

The Four Noble Truths are explained in the section on The Buddha's First Three Discourses.

It is when these teachings are taken out of the context intended that the Buddha's Dhamma becomes difficult to understand and practically apply. It is when these teachings are taken out of the context of what the Buddha awakened to - Dependent Origination - that overcoming ignorance of Four Noble Truths is diminished in importance, or entirely dismissed.

For many years as a "practicing Buddhist" I struggled with finding anything that I could apply practically. I became increasingly more confused from the many contradictions in modern Buddhism. It was not until I studied the Pali Canon directly and began to develop the Eightfold Path that the Buddha's teachings had any true relevance and usefulness to my life.

Development of the Pali Canon

The first book of the Pali Canon is the Vinaya Pitaka, a collection of rules for monastics. It is valuable in understanding the political and cultural climate within which the Buddha's teaching developed. As will be seen below, the preservation of the Vinaya Pitaka has followed the same course as the preservation of the Sutta Pitaka.

The second book of the Pali Canon is the Sutta Pitaka. It contains all the discourses, or sutta's, of the Buddha. There are over 10,000 sutta's in the five "nikayas" or smaller collections. The five nikayas are:

- The Digha Nikaya - The Long Discourses.

- The Majjhima Nikaya - The Middle Length Discourses.

- The Samyutta Nikaya - The Grouped Discourses, grouped by theme.

- The Anguttara Nikaya - The Expanded Discourses grouped by number of topics covered.

- The Khuddaka Nikaya - The Collection of "Short Books" consisting of 15 books. (The Burmese Tipitaka has 18 books)

The Suttas cited throughout this book list the "Nikaya" and location I.e. Samyutta Nikaya 56.11 from the Sutta Pitaka, the collection of Sutta's in the Pali Canon.

http://www.accesstoinsight.org/ is an excellent resource for study of the Sutta's.

The preservation of the authenticity of the direct teachings of the Buddha is due to the practical application of the Buddha's teachings themselves. Those that first preserved the Buddha's direct teachings through oral recitation had developed well-concentrated and well-focused minds through the Buddha's Dhamma.

The essence of the Buddha's teaching is a personal and direct experience of the Four Noble Truths. The Buddha's own teachings provided the integrity needed to maintain the authenticity of the Pali Canon.

First Buddhist Council

During his teaching career, the Buddha's discourses were memorized by senior monks and nuns contemporaneously and repeated in small groups to check for accuracy. These monks and nuns had extraordinary memories, likely due to their highly developed concentration. By repeating these memorized discourses, they were able to accurately maintain the teachings. Repetition is likely the beginning of Buddhist Chant and was not so much a religious ritual as it was a most skillful way to preserve and present the Dhamma.

This method of maintaining an accurate record of the teachings of the Buddha continued after the Buddha's passing. The First Buddhist Council was held one month after the Buddha's passing in Rajagaha. The purpose of this council, and some subsequent councils, was to maintain the authenticity of the Buddha's dhamma.

A well respected senior monk, Maha Kassapa, convened the first council. He was joined by approximately 500 other monks who had fully developed the Buddha's teachings.

It was decided that the recording of the Buddha's lifetime of teaching should be separated into the two general categories mentioned earlier. The Vinaya would be recounted by Upali, known for his thorough understanding of monastic discipline, and checked for accuracy from the others in attendance. This became the first book of the Pali Canon - the Vinaya Pitaka.

Ananda was the Buddha's cousin, and chief attendant during the last twenty-five years of the Buddha's teaching career. It was his responsibility to recount the Buddha's discourses. Ananda was known to have a word-perfect memory.

He was questioned on verifiable facts about the discourse he was reciting. Ananda would recount the subject being taught, the location, and the people present when the discourse was presented. It was accepted that Ananda retained a true, accurate, and complete recollection of the Buddha's teachings.

While there were written texts at the time of the Buddha, an oral recounting that could be directly verified by others was considered a much more accurate way of preserving the authenticity of the Vinaya Pitaka and the Sutta Pitaka.

Over the next seven months, the 500 monks recited their own memories of the Buddha's teachings. These recitations were compared for consistency and accuracy. It was then accepted by the entire council that what was presented was an accurate and complete presentation of the teachings of the Buddha. This became the Sutta Pitaka, the second book of the Pali Canon.

There was no mention at this first council of what would later be included in the Abhidhamma Pitaka.

Two important developments occurred at the first council. A question arose about relaxing some of the rules included in the Vinaya. Just prior to his passing the Buddha told Ananda that it would be acceptable if a few of the "minor" rules were relaxed but he passed before he could specify what rules he was referring to. It was decided by Maha Kassapa that since there was no way of knowing what rules could be relaxed that the Vinaya should be accepted as it was recounted.

It was also decided that the Sutta Pitaka be divided into sections very similar to the five nikayas (smaller collections) we have today. A group of senior monks and their pupils were given the responsibility to memorize these sections. The oral tradition was now established. Daily recitations of the Dhamma were then presented by various groups always verified by others in attendance.

The accuracy preserved in the Pali Canon to the earliest teachings is remarkable and a testament to this method of preserving the Sutta's and Vinaya. Most historians agree that an oral tradition shared and consistently verified by many is much more accurate than isolated individuals writing from their memory on what had occurred. As will be seen in future adaptations and accommodations to the Buddha's Dhamma, this will be proven entirely true.

Second Buddhist Council

The method of recitation and comparison continued through later Buddhist Councils. The second Buddhist Council met approximately 100 years after the first council. This was convened to continue to check for accuracy and authenticity and to again look at the Vinaya, the monastic rules. There continued to be a desire among some groups to relax some rules and to impose new rules.

During this second council a revisionist group known as the Mahasanghikas emerged. The Mahasanghikas protested some of the basic rules of discipline. The Mahasanghikas also desired a more visionary and mystical "Dharma" practice that would establish the Buddha as a god, and one of many Buddha-gods extending without limit to the past and future.

The Mahasanghikas created further divisiveness in the sangha and contradiction to Buddha's Dhamma by claiming that the Buddha's life as a human being was merely an apparition. This direct contradiction was necessary to support the "Buddha as one god among many god's" claim and to justify any and all adaptations and accommodations that would follow.

This is an excellent example of how an adaptation to the Buddha's Dhamma has resulted in dogmatic "fact."

Once the Buddha was established as a supernatural being then the "dharma" can be found in any realm and in any presentation with no authentication necessary. The initial adaptation creating a supernatural Buddha allows for any teaching that follows to be "authenticated" through supernatural speculation and common agreement. There is no way to disprove these adapted versions and of course what can't be disproved remains eternally "possible."

As will be shown further on when these supernatural teachings are compared to what the Buddha taught while in his physical body the many inconsistencies and contradictions become apparent.

Either the Buddha taught many contradictory "Dharma's" throughout history and prehistory, and in many realms, physical and otherwise, or he taught a cohesive, direct, useful, and accessible Dhamma preserved in the second book of the Pali Canon.

Whatever is believed to be true, these changes altered the Buddha's teaching in profoundly significant ways and would lead to the development of the modern Mahayana traditions.

Third Buddhist Council

During the reign of King Ashoka, approximately one hundred and twenty years after the Second Buddhist Council, the Third Buddhist Council convened. Following the license taken by the Mahasanghikas various sects had formed. Each sect had the desire to adapt and accommodate the Dhamma to fit their views of what the dharma should be.

The president of this council, Moggaliputta Tissa, compiled a book called the Kathavatthu. Tissa did this to refute some of the heretical and false teachings coming into vogue. He included in this book the more mystical practices that were becoming accepted as Dhamma practice. The Kathavatthu became one of the books included in the Abhidhamma.

Sponsored by the Theravadins, this established the Theravada sect separate from the Mahasanghika sect. The division between the Buddha's direct teachings and what followed from the split of these two sects was now distinct.

As far as can be found, the Kathavatthu became the first significant written document in Buddhist literature. The Kathavatthu is also the first written account of individual influences adapting the Buddha's direct teachings.

The oral tradition of recitation and confirmation preserving the Vinaya Pitaka and The Sutta Pitaka continued. The two original books of the Pali Canon now had an "accepted and authenticated" third book in the Kathavatthu. The Kathavatthu would later be included in the third book of the modern Pali Canon, the Abhidhamma. This explains why many scholars disagree as to the ultimate authenticity of this third volume of the Pali Canon.

The Theravadins adopted the more visionary and psychological teachings found in the Abhidhamma. They continued to preserve the Vinaya and Sutta Pitaka through the oral tradition. In this way they established themselves as more authentic to the Buddha's direct teachings. Theravadins continue to consider themselves as part of the "Hinayana" or original branch of Buddhism.

Modern Theravadin Buddhism is the least culturally and philosophically influenced of modern-day Buddhism. There are significant differences to the Buddha's original teachings incorporated in Theravada that can be traced back to the Third Council and reliance on the Abhidhamma.

I am not implying that Theravadin Buddhism is not a legitimate and well-established Buddhist religion, or that any of the other later developed Buddhist religions are not legitimate or well-established. It is vitally important to recognize the how, what, when, and where the adaptations and accommodations to the Buddha's original teachings developed. This is the only way to continue the preservation of the Buddha's original teachings. This is the only way to continue to provide a clear distinction between what the Buddha taught and what has developed in the intervening years.

This also is when the split between the "Hinayana" and the "Mahayana" schools became firmly established. There would be no historical reference to Hinayana or Mahayana until the beginning of the common era.

Hinayana is sometimes translated to mean "lesser vehicle" as opposed to the Mahayana branch of Buddhism, which is translated to "greater vehicle." The inference being that the Hinayana branch is a "lesser" or incomplete teaching.

Although often used to denigrate the earliest form of Buddhism, this is an incorrect interpretation of the two "vehicles." The original meaning of Hinayana related to geography. Hinayana describes a "lower vehicle" or "southern vehicle" to account for the geographic spread of Theravadin Buddhism. Theravadin Buddhism spread south through southern India to Southeast Asia and Sri Lanka.

Mahayana or "greater vehicle" describes how this branch of Buddhism spread. Mahayana Buddhism spread from India north through Nepal hence the definition as the "upper vehicle" or "northern vehicle." Mahayana Buddhism then spread to China, Japan, and

Korea approximately around the beginning of the Common Era.

There is more on the split between the Hinayana and Mahayana forms of Buddhism and the impact of the Abhidhamma further on.

Subsequent Buddhist Councils

There would be additional Buddhist Councils following the Third Council. By now the original sangha had mostly lost identity. In the first century BCE two competing sects held councils at approximately the same time. The Theravadins convened their council amid much political upheaval. They continued the oral tradition of recitation and verification. The Pali Canon was recorded in written form for the first time, including the Abhidhamma.

A competing council organized by the Sarvastivadins was used to introduce additional teachings. These teachings have further influenced modern Buddhism such as the Bodhisattva ideal, environmental emptiness, cosmic interdependence, and many of the later sutta's.

A fifth Theravadin Buddhist Council was held in 1871 in Burma. This five-month council was used primarily to recite the (now) three books of the Canon to continue to check for authenticity to the original Canon and the later addition of the Abhidhamma.

In 1954, in Rangoon, an international Theravadin council was convened that lasted two years. Again the entire Canon was recited and verified, and all three books were carved into marble slabs.

Despite the addition of the Abhidhamma to the Pali Canon, the oral tradition of recitation and verification has preserved the original teachings of an awakened human being to this day. The preserved sutta's continue the lineage of the Dhamma first established by the Buddha.

Evolution of Buddhist Practice

The Abhidhamma is an intricately detailed theoretical and conceptual account of ordinary phenomena. The Abhidhamma is, in essence, an adaptation and nullification of Dependent Origination. Dependent Origination (or Dependent Co-Arising) is a simple and direct teaching on confusion, delusion, and all manner of suffering arising from ignorance of Four Noble Truths. With this third book the foundation was in place for the term Dependent Origination to be used to describe creation of all phenomena. This has directly diminished the Four Noble Truths as the primary teaching and path taught by the Buddha.

The mythology used to establish the Abhidhamma as a teaching of the Buddha's can be traced back to the Mahasanghikas and the establishment of a supernatural Buddha. It is told that the origin of the Abhidhamma occurred when the Buddha, in the seventh year after his awakening, left the physical world for the realm of the devas. There for the next three months he taught what would become this third book of the Canon.

Establishing a supernatural Buddha is necessary to allow for the mystical and magical adaptations that have taken place. The Abhidhamma is obviously inconsistent with the original first two books of the Pali Canon.

The Abhidhamma became an (unintended) link between Theravada and the developing Mahasanghika influenced Mahayana schools. The Abhidhamma is an essential influence in many of the modern Theravadin and Sarvastivadin influenced Mahayana schools. This has further obscured what the Buddha taught as preserved in the first two books or the Canon.

In a little over a century between the second and third Councils, the license taken by the Mahasanghikas and, to a lesser degree, the Theravadins, had significantly altered the Buddha's original teachings. Since then, the Buddha's teachings have become obscured and are often diminished in importance, or completely dismissed.

This has led modern Buddhism to be a thicket of competing views and bewildering contradictions. These bewildering contradictions have themselves become a part of Buddhist lore and presented as

84

"interwoven threads of all dharma's." Authority is given by claiming they all present the same basic philosophy and all lead to the same conclusion.

This rationalization has only served to further mystify Buddhism and create a hierarchy within modern Buddhism. Modern Buddhism places emphasis on special empowerments, conceptual higher realms of consciousness, meditation-only schools, and on "gaining merit" through rituals and practices never intended by the Buddha.

As has been shown all modern adaptations can be traced to the Second Buddhist council and the desire for a significantly different "dharma" not founded in what the Buddha taught.

The first Mahayana texts, or sutra's, appeared around the first century CE. This is also the time when a magical and mystical idea of receiving the dhamma through a mind-to-mind transmission developed. The idea of mind-to-mind transmission may have developed to account for the split in the continuity of the Dhamma as well as mixing teachings between the different schools. A supernatural Buddha is obviously necessary to establishing a mind-only Dharma transmission and a mind-only meditation method and lineage.

With the introduction of spontaneously appearing sutra's the intent and purpose and path of the Buddha's teaching has been altered and the alterations and accommodations to the original Dhamma have become further obscured.

Some of the most influential sutra's in Mahayana Buddhism directly contradict the Buddha's teachings as preserved in the Sutta Pitaka. The Heart Sutra which appears around 600 CE (some date it as early as 200 CE, or 800 to 1400 years after the Buddha's passing) is taught by a Hindu god, Avalokitesvara, to Sariputta, one of the senior monks of the original sangha.

Avalokitesvara teaches the "Dharma" using emptiness as the theme in a way that contradicts the Buddha's meaning of emptiness - to empty oneself of ignorance of Four Noble Truths.

The Heart Sutra dismisses the Four Noble Truths stating "there is only emptiness and there is no path." The Heart Sutra states that it alone is the ultimate truth of emptiness and non-attachment. This is also a text that the Bodhisattva ideal is presented as the highest path in Buddhism. The Bodhisattva ideal also diminishes the Four Noble Truths. The Fourth Noble Truth is the truth of the Eightfold Path as the Arahant path the Buddha taught.

Throughout the Sutta's the Buddha describes himself prior to his awakening as "an unawakened Bodhisatta." (Sanskrit: Bodhisattva) The Nagara Sutta included further on is but one example. He did this to describe himself as a being of great compassion who still required the development of understanding the conditions that bind human beings to ignorance in order to fully awaken.

There is also an adaptation in the Heart Sutra of the Five Clinging-Aggregates describing them as merely empty phenomena to be summarily dismissed. This is an extreme view that lacks the context of the Buddha's use of the Five Clinging-Aggregates. The Five Clinging-Aggregates describe the real and human experience of personal disappointment and suffering. Dismissing the Five Clinging-Aggregates by stating that they are "empty" of any significance dismisses the primary usefulness of understanding them in the context of the Buddha's Dhamma.

The Heart Sutra teaches emptiness as a to-be-realized all-pervasive experience of "reality." Experiencing a conceptual environment of "emptiness" is the goal presented rather than to develop the Eightfold Path to "empty" oneself from all self-referential views rooted in ignorance of Four Noble Truths.

The direct dismissal of The Four Noble Truths is another example of using a conceptual application of emptiness to directly dismiss what an awakened human being spent the last forty-five years of his life teaching.

The Heart Sutra continues ignorance by dismissing fundamental and essential teachings of the Buddha.

The Phena and Kaccayanagotta Sutta's, included in this book explains the Buddha's meaning of emptiness in the proper context.

The Diamond Sutra follows a similar theme as the Heart Sutra. This sutra appears around 500 CE. The Diamond Sutra expands the theme of emptiness and continues to elevate the Bodhisattva path as a superior path. The Diamond Sutra further alters Dependent Origination using it as a vague creation myth. This sutra is an excellent example of the adaptation and accommodation of the teachings preserved in the Sutta's having a loose resemblance to themes the Buddha taught but adapted to fit the purpose of the Bodhisattva ideal and a conceptual meaning of emptiness.

The most significant difference between the Buddha's direct teachings and the Mahayana doctrine is presented in the Lotus Sutra. In the Lotus Sutra the Bodhisattva path is presented again as a more advanced path and the Arahant path, the Eightfold Path, as an inferior path to awakening.

The Lotus Sutra has been continually adapted to accommodate the many different modern Buddhist religions that use this sutra as the foundation for their particular dharma. The Lotus Sutra is a foundational text of the Chan, Zen, Soen, and Tentai, Nichiren, PureLand, and is even referenced in the Tibetan Buddhist Religions.

There are many actors in the Lotus Sutra that are similar to actors in the Sutta Pitaka. It is commonly agreed that the Lotus Sutra was first developed around the beginning of the Common Era and added to over the next few hundred years. Along with the Heart Sutra and Diamond Sutra, much of Mahayana Buddhism rests on these three sutra's.

This is a very brief description of these sutra's. I have included sources in the source notes below for further study, if desired. I include this here to again clearly show the contradictions in the path the Buddha taught in both purpose and practice and what has developed since the first adaptations to the Buddha's Dhamma were made at the Second Buddhist Council.

There is nothing unreasonable in what has developed in Buddhism over the past two-thousand six-hundred years. It is what we all do as human beings. We are always in a struggle to adapt what human life presents in a way that hopefully brings more comfort and agreement with how we want to live our lives. It is the nature of conditioned views to continue conditioned views. This was the motivation to seek a more visionary and mystical "dharma" that motivated the Mahasanghikas. Confusion and disappointment continues as the result of ignorance of Four Noble Truths.

An understanding of The Four Noble Truths clearly explains how and why this occurs. The First Noble Truth states that dukkha occurs as a direct result of ignorance of the origination of all manner of confusion and deluded thinking. The Second Noble Truth states that craving for and clinging to any object, event, view, or idea rooted in this initial ignorance of Four Noble Truths continues dukkha.

It is craving for something other than what the Buddha taught that has led to adapted "dharmas." It is clinging to an adapted dharma that continues adapted dharmas. The Eightfold Path develops both recognition and cessation of craving and clinging to contradictory views.

The Buddha presented the Dhamma in the form of Four Noble Truths to be understood and acted upon. He taught that to gain understanding one would take refuge in the Buddha, the Dhamma, and the Sangha. It is within true refuge that understanding arises.

Refuge is a place of safety and comfort. In taking refuge one takes comfort and direction in the understanding that a human being developed profound understanding and awakened. This human being left his teachings, the Dhamma, so others could do the same. A well-focused sangha provides the environment and supportive community to develop the Buddha's Dhamma. Taking refuge is entirely practical and not conceptual or an empty ritual.

The Ratana Sutta, the sutta on the Triple Refuge, is included in the last section of this book.

The "transmission" of the dhamma occurs when a mind that has encountered The Four Noble Truths integrates the path leading to the cessation of dukkha. This is an authentic lineage of transmission that can be traced directly to the Buddha.

It is the preserved teachings in the Sutta Pitaka that establishes a lineage to the Buddha.

This is what is referred to when the Buddha "Set The Wheel of Truth in Motion" at his first discourse on The Four Noble Truths. The preserved Dhamma originating in the Buddha is the means of true Dhamma transmission.

Associating with the wise, the practicing Sangha, supports the understanding and integration of The Four Noble Truths.

The Buddha consistently taught the necessity for each individual interested in his Dhamma to actually develop a well-focused understanding of what he taught and what he did not teach. He used the word "ehipassiko" which means "come and see for yourself" to emphasize this critical point.

The following reference to the Kalama Sutta is to reinforce the wisdom in developing the Buddha's teachings as preserved in the Sutta Pitaka.

In the Kalama Sutta the Buddha is teaching the Kalama's how to choose a useful and effective Dhamma. The Kalama's were confused as to who and what to follow due to the many "spiritual" teachers that visited them on the popular trade route that passed through their area.

The Buddha told them "do not go by reports, or legends, or traditions, or scripture, or conjecture, or inference, or analogies, or common agreement, or unexamined loyalty. When you know from your own experience that the qualities taught are skillful, shameless, unambiguous, and direct, these teachings should be developed. When these teachings are praised by the wise they should be developed. When these teachings lead to unbinding and calm they should be developed."

The Kalama Sutta is a perfect example of how the preservation of the Pali Canon continues to provide clear direction for developing the Buddha's teachings and avoid the confusion that follows from ignoring the original Sutta's.

It should be noted that many modern teachers alter and accommodate this simple and direct sutta, much like Tissa did during the Third Council, in order to claim that the Buddha is actually teaching to alter and accommodate his teachings to fit a desired view of what Dhamma practice should be.

It is not necessary to affiliate with any established "lineage" or modern Buddhist religion in order to develop the Buddha's Dhamma. True Dhamma lineage is established and continued through the Buddha's Dhamma and not through any individual or cultural adaptations to the Dhamma.

The Buddha presented a complete and accessible Dhamma that anyone can develop and awaken - develop full human maturity - in this lifetime.

As shown earlier, modern Mahayana doctrine originated from the Mahasanghikas sect. All modern Buddhist religions have interesting and colorful histories too elaborate to explore further here. All were influenced by the culture and philosophy in which their particular form of Buddhism developed.

Each Mahayana school has their own historical patriarchs and lineages contributing their own influence and view. All later-developed Buddhist schools have proven highly effective in establishing religions based on their own views of what Buddhist practice should be. All deserve respect, as does the Buddha's direct teachings as preserved in the Sutta Pitaka.

There is no record of the Buddha ever asking his followers to take the Vow of The Bodhisattva or follow the Bodhisattva path. In fact, the words of the Buddha near the time of his passing were: "With firm resolve, guard your own mind! Who so untiringly pursues the Dhamma and the Discipline (The Sutta's and The

Vinaya) shall go beyond the round of births and make an end of suffering. Decay is relentless. Strive diligently for your own salvation!" (Maha-Parinibbana Sutta)

The Buddha is placing utmost importance in individual responsibility for one's own salvation. An awakened being would have true compassion AND the wisdom necessary to effectively assist others in their awakening.

Nowhere in the Pali Canon is it found that the Buddha initiated a separate salvific path for Bodhisattva's to pursue. The Buddha was consistent throughout his teaching career by teaching individual responsibility to develop an Eightfold Path leading to awakening, or Arahantship.

No individual can impose awakening on another no matter how sincere the vow to do so. One can develop the Buddha's Dhamma and then be a living example to others. This is the example given to us by the Buddha.

As the Buddha did after his awakening, it was understood that those awakened would help others to awaken by teaching and exemplifying the same Four Noble Truths.

Some of the Mahayana schools place an emphasis on esoteric, mystical or hidden teachings. Some emphasize teachings that require certain empowerments often attached to specific times of the year. This is contrary to the Buddha's words in the Maha-parinibbana Sutta: "my teachings are not like that of a teacher with a closed fist who keeps something back. I have taught you everything you need to develop your own awakening." He further stated "my teachings are the same (in practice) for monks and lay people."

Many Mahayana schools place significance on deity worship and ritual over understanding and integrating The Four Noble Truths.

Some schools emphasize their own type of meditation or intricate visualizations without any mindful intention of developing tranquility leading to insight.

Other schools place an emphasis on koan or hwadu practice as a way of creating great mental absorption without directly developing tranquility and insight. There is no mention of "just sitting," or wall gazing, or koan or hwadu study in the Sutta's. These widespread methods came into use well after the passing of the Buddha, most in the past five hundred years.

Insight Meditation is a very popular modern Buddhist religion that developed in the past one hundred and fifty years. It began as the Vipassana movement in Burma by a monk, U Narada, intending to develop a meditation-only practice. U Narada's inspiration came from an adapted version of the Satipatthana Sutta from the Abhidhamma. It dismisses much of what the Buddha taught as a path to awakening in favor of a highly adapted form of intense analytical "labeling meditation."

Some modern schools reject meditation entirely in favor of mantra recitation and visualizations. Pure Land Buddhists rely on the Lotus sutra as their foundation. The Bodhisattva ideal, savior visualizations, and chanting replace the Eightfold Path. It is taught that if properly followed, Amitabha Buddha will provide rebirth in the Pure Land of everlasting paradise. Pure Land Buddhism is one of the most popular forms of Buddhism in the world today. (Pure Land Buddhism is much deeper than this brief explanation provided here.)

There is no mention of this type of worship or salvation in the Sutta's. The Buddha never presented himself as a god with the powers of a savior-god. The Buddha taught that each individual determines their own fate through wisdom, virtue, and concentration developed through the Eightfold Path.

Again, this is in no way meant to disparage or diminish the teachings of other schools of Buddhism. My only intent here is to point out the significant differences in the Buddha's direct teaching and later developments influenced by individual desire and cultural influences.

The general explanation given for many of these differences has the Buddha presenting these "advanced" teachings to deities on a non-physical plane to be brought into the human realm hundreds, sometimes many hundreds of years after the Buddha's death when people were advanced enough to understand them.

The inference here is that those alive at the time of the Buddha were not able to grasp these "advanced" teachings. Of course it is impossible to prove that this did not in fact happen, but it is not in keeping with what is presented in the Pali Canon.

The inference is an insult to the Buddha implying that he wasted the time he spent teaching those that were not capable of grasping an "advanced" dharma. The inference is rooted in ignorance.

The Buddha's very first teaching developed awakening in Kondanna. Hearing the words of the Buddha Kondanna declared "All conditioned things that arise are subject to cessation." The Buddha replied "You are now Anna-Kondanna, the one who understands." Many thousands awakened during the Buddha's teaching career.

Nothing has proven to be more effective in developing the Buddha's stated purpose for teaching the Dhamma: To develop a profound understanding of confusion, deluded thinking, and ongoing disappointment and to experience the cessation of all craving and clinging arising from ignorance of Four Noble Truths.

The adaptations and accommodations to the Buddha's Dhamma do not make any of these other forms of Buddhism less legitimate practices. Millions of practitioners are engaged and committed to these other forms of Buddhist practice.

It is important to understand that there are differences, sometimes vitally important differences. What the Buddha taught and what has developed from the original teachings are significantly different in content, path, purpose, and practice.

The Buddha predicted the altering and diminishing in importance of his teachings near the end of his life: "The end of my dispensation will come not from direct oppression, but from confused dhamma." (Digha Nikaya 16)

The Buddha was the most influential and radical thinker of his time, and ours, too. His entire teaching went against the accepted religious and spiritual practices of his time. His teachings are still radical today and contrary to many modern Buddhist religions that continue to claim a lineage to the historical Buddha. This should not come as a surprise or even be a cause for controversy or animosity. It is what has occurred.

The Buddha was not interested in starting yet another religion so his teachings need not threaten any religion. The Buddha was not a "Buddhist" continuing to cling to views. The Buddha was an awakened human being whose intention was to show other human beings how to free themselves from confusion, deluded thinking, and resulting dukkha.

The Buddha never shied away from pointing out the differences between his teachings and the accepted practices of his time.

That contradictions and often antagonistic "Dhammas/Dharmas" that have developed since the Buddha's passing is to be expected. It is most skillful to see these differences in the context of Four Noble Truths. There is Dukkha - even in modern Buddhism, as modern Buddhism is part of human life.

Craving and clinging continue to impact the Buddha's teachings. It is in keeping with the Buddha's Dhamma to not view the modern situation as either "right" or "wrong" but rather as what is skillful or unskillful.

It is most skillful to view all things, including the many variations and contradictions within modern Buddhism, in the context of Four Noble Truths. By using the framework and guidance established by the Buddha in his very first discourse these contradictions can be recognized and abandoned, or developed wholeheartedly, depending on each individual.

Understanding the differences and contradictions within modern Buddhism then allows for a clear and mindful choice as to what will constitute an individual Dhamma or Dharma practice.

It is important to note that continual and skillful Right Effort for over two thousand six hundred years has resulted in an accurate and complete record of the teachings of the Buddha. Even so, the Sutta's are not meant to be a course of only intellectual scriptural study. The teachings of the Buddha are to be experienced by each individual and usefulness and effectiveness assessed based on unfolding understanding.

A good teacher of the dhamma will understand that all that they can do is point to the Four Noble Truths, as the Buddha himself did. Nothing in the dhamma can be imposed or magically transferred from one human being to another.

A person following the original teachings of the Buddha would soon realize that what is most important is not to cling to associations, dogma, ritual, scripture, or hybrid method. The Buddha taught that a deep and experiential understanding of The Four Noble Truths is necessary for cessation of suffering. The Buddha always taught to weigh practice against results, to "come and see for yourself."

If modern Buddhist practice seems confusing or unattainable, consider placing your mindfulness on the Four Noble Truths and follow the path the Buddha presented. The Eightfold Path is the path presented as leading to the cessation of confusion, deluded thinking, and resulting disappointment and suffering. The Buddha repeatedly said "I teach the truth of the arising of dukkha and the cessation of dukkha, nothing more."

As has been seen, it is when something more is desired and incorporated into Dhamma practice that confusion often arises and a direct and immediately accessible path is lost.

[1] https://crossrivermeditation.com/modern-buddhism-a-thicket-of-views/

Sources for this chapter are here:
https://becoming-buddha.com/pali-canon-buddha-taught/

Impermanence
Not-Self
Stress

Anicca, Anatta, Dukkha

Three Marks of Human Experience

Anicca - impermanence, Anatta - not-self, and Dukkha - stress, disappointment, dissatisfaction, are the three linked characteristics of life in the phenomenal world. These are "The Three Marks of Human Experience" or "The Three Marks of Existence."

All life is impermanent and impersonal, prone to disappointment, and lacking a definable permanent "self." All human beings carry these three marks, or inherent characteristics of human experience.

The attempted establishment of a permanent and substantial self is   through craving for, and clinging to, objects, events, views, and ideas. This occurs within an impermanent environment that initiates distraction and the underlying and pervasive unsatisfactory experience of human life.

Life becomes a constant struggle to maintain what is satisfying and avoid anything that would detract from satisfaction. This contradicts the First Noble Truth and ignores, is ignorant of, the pervasive impermanence of life.

The purpose of the Dhamma is to recognize and abandon all craving and resulting clinging arising from a misunderstanding of self. Once recognized, the confusion, deluded thinking, and suffering that follows can be mindfully abandoned.

Rooted in ignorance of Four Noble Truths, craving for and clinging to objects, events, views, and ideas causes the confusion and distraction of Dukkha. Abandoning self-referential craving and clinging brings an end to Dukkha.

"Free of craving and clinging one is not agitated. Un-agitated this one is totally unbound and free of Dukkha, an Arahant, Rightly self-awakened." (Samyutta Nikaya 38.14)

Upon his awakening, the Buddha spent the last forty-five years of his life teaching his Dhamma. He taught his profound understanding of the truth of human life, to bring insight into The Three Marks of Existence and end ignorance, to empty one's self of ignorance, of Four Noble Truths.

Anicca - Impermanence

"Be mindful of impermanence to end conceit. When impermanence is understood it is also understood that none of this is (represents) self. Understanding not-self uproots conceit, uproots I-making. When fully established release is complete." (Anguttara Nikaya 9.1)

Impermanence is an essential concept of the Dhamma. Impermanence describes the environment in which confusion, deluded thinking, and stress arises and is maintained. All things in the phenomenal world are impermanent and all events are uncertain as to occurrence, effect and duration. Even a view of "self" changes from moment to moment.

Impermanence, stress, and the not-self characteristic - the ego-self, are all observable aspects of human existence. What the Buddha discovered upon his awakening, with a quiet and well-concentrated mind, is that all things are conditioned particles of energy that have coalesced into the appearance of form. Out of the formless state we now have form. These discrete forms that we perceive as permanent are seen with Right View as impermanent and absent of any self-inherent nature, including the form perceived as "I."

Quantum Mechanics is now able to show the impact that thought has on energy and that objects have characteristics of both particles and waves. This is known as wave-particle or energy-matter (or formless-form) duality which contradicts the modern Buddhist compulsion to reconcile everything into a non-dual reduction. It is the thoughts of the perceiver that determine what is perceived.

This is what the Buddha taught two thousand six hundred years ago in describing the impact that intentional thoughts and what is held in mind (mindfulness) have on the experience of life as life unfolds.

Also, there are limits to the precision with which quantities can be known. Quantum mechanics would say that inherent instability (impermanence) between particles (form) and waves (formlessness) precludes identifying a root cause, or unifying principle. This is known as the uncertainty principle.

The Buddha teaches that seeking a root cause, or unifying principle, or "ground of being" (such as non-duality or inner Buddha-Nature) is rooted in ignorance of Four Noble Truths. An aspect of impermanence is that due to impermanence all things are discrete and uncertain as to occurrence and duration.

Due to the truth of impermanence and uncertainty, "Awakening" is recognizing and abandoning self-reflective views rooted in ignorance and developing a calm and well-concentrated mind free of the need to continually establish a permanent and substantial "self."

A further explanation of this phenomenon in relation to quantum mechanics is beyond the scope and purpose of this book.

Developing a profound understanding of the Buddha's Dhamma brings the direct understanding of the process of thoughts defining experience. Awakening is understanding how thoughts rooted in ignorance of Four Noble Truths originates confusion, deluded thinking, and ongoing Dukkha.

I am not using quantum mechanics to provide validity to the Buddha's Dhamma. Rather, to show that brilliant minds are just now understanding what the Buddha profoundly understood with no measurements or instruments or modern theories. He understood the arising and passing away of all phenomena and that this ongoing process is entirely impersonal. The Buddha taught that personalizing experience is determined by what is held in mind.

When concentration is developed to support refined mindfulness of the Eightfold Path one's thoughts will continually establish a calm mind. Free of craving and clinging the mind is at peace while impermanent events arise and pass away.

It requires continued, ever-vigilant directed thought to maintain an ego-self in an impermanent environment. Another way of describing this hyper-vigilance is clinging to form. Clinging to form is stress. Clinging to form is dukkha.

The process of confused and conditioned thinking maintaining clinging to self-referential views can be refined and purified. The ongoing process of becoming rooted in ignorant views can be brought to cessation.

Understanding that all things are impermanent, including self-referential thoughts and conditioned views, is the key to understanding how confused and deluded thinking has created individual contributions to stress.

Some physical objects, such as a mountain, or planet, or the universe, maintain a physical form for a longer period of time than a butterfly, an apple, a thought, or a human body. All will decay, change form, and fade from existence. In this way continuity often obscures the recognition of impermanence.

Another way of describing the impermanence of all phenomenal things is that uncertainty is characteristic of all phenomenal things. We can never know what the next moment will bring. Ignorance of uncertainty develops additional clinging and additional stress. Wisdom is knowing, understanding, and accepting impermanence and uncertainty. Wisdom brings a mind of calm and spacious equanimity.

The importance of understanding impermanence cannot be overstated. It was impermanence that the Buddha spoke of in his last teaching: "Impermanent are all conditioned things.

Decay is relentless. Work diligently for your own understanding." (Digha Nikaya 16)

The Buddha understood the impermanence of all things in the phenomenal world. He did not over-emphasize chasing insight into all phenomenal impermanence or create anything special regarding the general impermanence of the world. This only furthers clinging views and is rooted in a doctrine that only furthers conceit.

What I am referring to here is modern applications of mindfulness that would over-emphasize common activities such as washing dishes, eating a grape, exaggerated slow walking, or "breath-work," for example, and call this mindfulness or gaining insight. While it is certainly skillful to be mindful of what is occurring, by over-emphasizing common activities the activity is then often substituted for developing insight into the origination of all stress dependent on ignorance of Four Noble Truths. Eating a grape, etcetera, becomes more significant than whole-hearted engagement with the Dhamma.

It is enough to understand that all conditioned thoughts are themselves impermanent. Once

116

recognized, conditioned thinking can be abandoned. Over-emphasizing mindful focus on the objects that conditioned thoughts are attached to only continues clinging and can only further ignorance.

"Just as in the autumn a farmer, plowing with a large plow, cuts through all the spreading rootlets as he plows; in the same way, my dear friends, the perceiving of impermanence, developed and frequently practiced, removes all sensual passion... removes and abolishes all conceit of "I am." (Samyutta Nikaya 22.102)

Anatta - Not-Self

Anatta is the word the Buddha used to describe what is commonly referred to as "self." The Buddha describes the mental-physical ego-self as "anatta" to show that what is thought of as self, as me or mine, is a deluded view rooted in ignorance of the Four Noble Truths. The views are "wrong views" and do not accurately describe a self. He teaches to recognize the views as wrong views and develop Right View.

When wrong views are used to establish or defend a self, distraction, disappointment, dissatisfaction, and all manner of suffering arises. This pervasive dissatisfaction is known as Dukkha and is described as the First Noble Truth - Dukkha Occurs. These self-referential views rooted in ignorance are Anatta - not-a-self.

Dukkha is explained in detail below.

It is possible to understand and abandon the process of the establishment of "not-self." Awakening is the cessation of clinging to views ignorant of Four

119

Noble Truths.

The Buddha describes awakening in relation to Four Noble Truths simply and directly, without any ambiguity, mysticism, or magical thinking:

"Awakening is understanding stress, abandoning the cause of stress (craving and clinging), experiencing the cessation of stress, and developing the path leading to the cessation of stress." (Samyutta Nikaya 56.11)

It is in the continual attempt to establish and maintain anatta, wrong views of self, within the environment of impermanence, that perpetuates dukkha. Some modern "Buddhist" schools do just this by over-emphasis on conceptual notions of not-self. These are typically referred to as "non-self," "nothingness," and "emptiness."

These are extreme nihilistic views avoided by developing the Middle Way Eightfold Path.

These are views that have more in common to the Vedas. The Vedas are the foundational scripture for modern Hinduism. The Vedas are teachings that Alara Kalama and Udakka Ramaputta taught. The Buddha studied with both teachers and rejected their teachings.

The Buddha does not teach that there is no such thing as a self, only that the views of self are rooted in ignorance - let go of the views.

One example of this is the notion of an inner or obscure Buddha-Nature. It is often taught that a permanent inner Buddha will spontaneously arise following sufficient effort. Another example is an inner "Buddha-Hood" that an ego-personality should aspire to. These confused doctrines assume an inherent, permanent, and substantial "Buddha-self."

An inner Buddha to develop, or as inherent potential, denies Dependent Origination. The Buddha understood that Dukkha arises from ignorance of Four Noble Truths. There is no mention of developing "Buddha-Nature" or aspiring to Buddha-Hood in the Sutta's. The Eightfold Path develops an understanding of ignorance and the framework and guidance to abandon wrong views.

The Buddha describes an awakened, fully mature human being, as "unbound" or "released" from clinging. An awakened human being has developed the Eightfold Path and no longer clings to ignorant views of "self."

Any further establishment of self-identity in any form or in any realm, physical or non-physical, will only lead to more confusion and suffering. Modern Buddhist doctrines of an inherent Buddha-Nature or a "self" achieving Buddha-Hood are creating another conceptual (imaginary) framework to house a self-referential ego-personality. These doctrines are contrary to the Buddha's teachings.

The refined mindfulness developed through the Eightfold Path brings an understanding of all impermanent views and ideas rooted in ignorance. Awakening brings the end of all deluded self-referential views and a mind of lasting peace.

There is nothing that can be shown to have any permanence, including a "Buddha-Nature" or "Buddha-Hood." As will be seen in the Anatta-Lakkhana Sutta the Buddha teaches that any impermanent view should be seen as it truly is: "This is not mine, this is not I, this is not my self."

All self-reflective views are impermanent and established within an impermanent self-reflective ego-personality. There is no teaching of the Buddha's that seeks to reveal a hidden Buddha-Nature or latent

122

Buddha-Hood. Attempting to establish a "saved" self in a future Buddhist "heaven" through special rituals or chants is the same general doctrine of continued "I-making."

Not-Self has also been misinterpreted and misapplied in some modern Buddhist schools to mean that the self is nothing, or a void. This has led some modern schools to create a doctrine of "nothingness" or "emptiness."

This is an extreme view of annihilation that was rejected by the Buddha early in his search for understanding. (This is the basic doctrines of Alara Kalama and Uddeka Ramaputta mentioned earlier.)

The Buddha did not teach that there is no self. He taught that the self is fabricated from ignorance through an observable process. Fabricated, this self is not worth defending or continually re-establishing. Anatta, not-self, refers to a fabricated ego-personality rooted in ignorance.

It is this fabricated ego-personality that is prone to experience endless confusion and suffering. It is this fabricated ego-personality that is abandoned upon awakening.

Not-Self simply means that what is commonly viewed as "self" is impermanent and insubstantial and is rooted in ignorance. Anatta requires a continual process of "I-making," or conceit, to continue.

I point out these contradictions between modern Buddhism and what the Buddha taught to show that these notions only serve to establish a self-referential ego-self in a conceptual realm that is continually subject to further confusion and suffering.

Awakening is not a matter of discovering or realizing an obscured inner Buddha-Nature, or inherent Buddha-Hood. The Buddha never described any inherent Buddha-Nature, Buddha-Hood, or inner "ground of being." If examined mindfully in the context of Four Noble Truths these views are clearly seen as self-referential views.

Awakening, becoming Buddha, is dependent on recognizing and releasing all self-referential views originating in ignorance of Four Noble Truths. There is nothing substantial or worth attaining that originates in ignorance. The confused assumption of anything substantial or worth attaining within Anatta contradicts the most fundamental teachings of the Buddha.

Anatta, the not-self characteristic, is unique to the teachings of the Buddha. Anatta may be the most difficult truth to observe and understand. The Nagara Sutta in the next section describes the Buddha's experience of becoming stuck in the feedback loop of self-referential views.

Conditioned thinking, consciousness rooted in ignorance, is "conditioned" to ignore the confusion that arises from self-referential views. Anatta requires continual ignorance, confusion, and contradiction to continue.

From wrong view (a view ignorant of Four Noble Truths, lacking wisdom) a perception of self arises from contact with the six-sense. "Self" is now the "perceiver," with all perceived phenomenon as outside of self. A "self" is now established in form and continually re-established by a wrong view. Seeking permanence, ignorance of the arising and passing away of all phenomenon is established. (The six-sense base is the five physical senses interpreted and moderated by consciousness.)

125

The mental fabrications that develop within this feedback loop continually maintains the confused view that there must now exist a permanent and substantial "self." The self is now perceived as uniquely established from other observed phenomenon. What is perceived as "outside" of the "perceiver" become objects for desire or aversion.

Self-identities are developed through clinging to what is craved for. All objects, events, views, and ideas are impermanent. Craving and clinging to impermanent phenomena establishes and continues distraction and disappointment - Dukkha. Once established, life becomes an endless experience of satisfying and maintaining what has become from ignorance.

Note that the origination of fabrications is dependent on ignorance. What is perceived as a self is a self-referential ego-personality that has arisen from certain conditions known as the "12 Links of Dependent Origination." (Dependent Origination is explained in the next section.)

This initial fabrication continues ignorance through an observable process. This process results in all manner of confusion, deluded thinking, and ongoing unsatisfactory experiences - in Dukkha. A self-referential ego-personality is the mental-physical form arisen from wrong views and maintained by clinging to wrong views.

Though firmly entrenched in the human psyche, the belief in a self-referential ego-self as a permanent and sustainable individual entity is a wrong view and leads to endless confusion and suffering. This wrong view can only perpetuate wrong view. Ignorance can never lead to wisdom. Only the wisdom gained through an Eightfold Path abolishes ignorance.

All things in the phenomenal world are impermanent and subject to decay. No permanent self can be established in this ever-changing environment. This is the nature of all things, including self-referential views.

A misapplication of Dependent Origination originating Dukkha has led to a subtle but distraction-causing over-emphasis on interdependence and interconnectedness. Due to the nature of how an ego-self arises - dependent on ignorance - all self-referential views share this common ignorance. Ignorance of Four Noble Truths is the common Human Problem.

127

Creating a doctrine of interdependence, interconnectedness, or inter-being is rooted in this same ignorance.

All views are impermanent and insubstantial. All views are lacking any meaningful or significant interdependence, interconnectedness, or inter-being. Creating conceptual doctrines of interconnectedness, interdependence, or inter-being, only fosters clinging and promotes ongoing confusion, delusion, and suffering.

Adapting the Dhamma to fit individual or group views follows the license taken by the Mahasanghikas and many later-developed Buddhist sects.

The Buddha consistently avoided the myriad attempts at establishing anatta in endless conceptual realms. He understood this would prove a distraction to his stated purpose. He consistently stated he taught the Dhamma for developing a profound understanding of Dukkha and the cessation of individual craving and clinging.

"Not-self" refers to an insubstantial and impermanent self-referential ego-personality. Wrong View

mistakes this "self" as a substantial and permanent individual identity.

The Eightfold Path brings understanding of the process of giving birth to an impermanent ego-self rooted in ignorance. Rooted in ignorance only confusion, deluded thinking, and suffering follows.

The Eightfold Path presents a clear and practical path of recognizing and abandoning all self-referential views rooted in ignorance of Four Noble Truths.

The Eightfold Path avoids the distracting and misinformed doctrines of nothingness or emptiness.

The Eightfold Path avoids the distracting and contradictory doctrines of inter-being, interdependence, or interconnectedness.

The suffering caused by ignorance should not be further ignored. Right View shows that creating specialness of impermanent objects, events, views, and ideas due to impermanent phenomenal inter-connection perpetuates ignorance, distraction, and stress.

Ignoring Right View that would bring insight into ignorance is delusion. Anatta, a self-referential ego-personality, insists on ignoring anything that would diminish its hold on delusion.

Any further establishment of anatta in any realm to support any idea or ideal rooted in ignorance will only create further confusion and suffering as it encourages further craving and clinging. This includes the establishment of a "special" or "advanced" type of Buddhist practice.

The Buddha taught a common solution to the common human problem of Dukkha. He taught that anatta is maintained by craving and clinging. This includes craving self-referential views that "cling" the self to forms, feelings, thoughts, and later-developed doctrines.

The Eightfold Path develops useful insight into ignorance and impermanence, uncertainty, and clinging. Insight into how ignorance contributes to the establishment and maintenance of a "self" develops the ability to abandon all wrong or ignorant views of self.

These are not abstract, mystical, magical, or esoteric ideas. Developing and maintaining Right View and Right Intention establishes virtuous thoughts, words, and deeds.

Remaining mindful of Right Speech, Right Action and Right Livelihood develops insight into impermanence and craving for, and clinging to, impermanent objects, events, views, and ideas.

Developing Right Concentration by engaging in Right Effort, Right Mindfulness, and Right Meditation supports the refined mindfulness necessary to recognize the feedback loop that prevents awakening. As the Buddha describes in the Nagara Sutta: "Vision arose, understanding arose, discernment arose, knowledge arose, illuminating insight arose within me with regard to things never known before."

Though insubstantial and ever-changing, an ego-self's sole purpose is to continue to establish it's "self" in every object, event, view, or idea that occurs. Anatta has created endless views of itself that are all subject to impermanence and suffering. It is in this underlying impermanence that the pervasive unsatisfactory experience of dukkha arises and is maintained.

The stress that arises is due to the constant attention required to continue ignorance and avoid reality. The preoccupation with Dukkha creates constant distraction.

131

Insight into this one thing, that all self-referential views arising from ignorance of Four Noble Truths is the cause of stress and discontent, will bring understanding and lasting peace and happiness. Within the framework of The Eightfold Path all self-referential views of self are recognized and abandoned. It is the purpose of the Eightfold Path to recognize all self-referential views and overcome conditioned thinking rooted in ignorance of Four Noble Truths.

Seeking insight into everything and anything that occurs often becomes another distraction. The compulsion to be "mindful" often over-emphasizes holding in mind mundane events. The refined mindfulness developed through the Eightfold Path provides the framework and guidance necessary to avoid the continuing distraction caused by chasing "insight" into every object that arises in the mind.

The Eightfold Path provides the framework to remain focused on gaining insight of the Three Marks of Existence. The Buddha emphasized understanding the impermanence of what is commonly viewed as a self and the self's relationship with the impermanence of the phenomenal world and resulting Dukkha.

"Friends, form (physical objects and the physical body) is like foam. Seeing clearly, form is empty and without substance. Whether past, present or future, internal, external, subtle or obvious, seeing form as it is, like foam on the water, brings wisdom to the well-instructed. Clearly seeing they become disenchanted with form, disenchanted with feeling, disenchanted with perception, disenchanted with fabrications and disenchanted with consciousness. Disenchanted one grows dispassionate. With dispassion comes release from craving and clinging.

"Friends, when a learned follower has heard the truth and understands the truth they will no longer cling to form, or to feeling, or to perceptions, or to fabrications, or to the flow of thoughts. They will see clearly 'this is not me, this is not mine, this is not myself.' They are fully released." (Samyutta Nikaya 22.95)

Form, feelings, perceptions, fabrications, and consciousness are the five factors of The Five Clinging-Aggregates. The Five Clinging-Aggregates are explained further on in the context of Dukkha and in context of emptiness in the chapter on the Phena Sutta.

133

The constantly clinging self-referential views of self as a substantial and sustainable physical entity animated by a likewise self-referential consciousness is initially difficult to understand and abandon. By developing concentration and refined mindfulness through the Eightfold Path this ongoing process can be clearly observed and abandoned.

As all things are impermanent and without any sustainable substance, like foam on the water, it is foolish to cling to anything, including form, feelings, perceptions, fabrications, or any ignorant thought.

Within a well-developed Eightfold Path, as new self-referential views arise they are quickly recognized and abandoned. It is the nature of an ego-personality to be subject to stress and disappointment. It is only this fabricated, impermanent, and insubstantial ego-personality that is to be abandoned. The purpose of skillful insight is to recognize impermanence and all self-referential wrong views. Once recognized these views can be mindfully abandoned.

Ongoing clinging is "I-making," or ongoing conceit. The simplest way to describe the Buddha's teaching on Not-self is this: anything that the ego-self craves for, or clings to, whether objects, people, events, views, or ideas, will create confusion, disappointment, and lasting dissatisfaction - let all craving and clinging views go.

Still another way to see this is by definition and association. The self is defined by clinging/attachments. Association is another word for attachments. Who is associated with and what is associated with defines experience. This does not mean that there should be no associations. It does mean that mindfulness of all associations is paramount and to not try to make what is impermanent permanent. As clinging to an ego-personality ceases, self-identification through associations also ceases.

In establishing an authentic Dhamma practice it is vitally important to be mindful that associations can support or hinder developing understanding within the framework of The Eightfold Path. Common in modern Buddhism is reinforcing self-identification through a "special" lineage or hybridized practice. It is interesting to note that there was no special name or lineage attached to the first Sangha - there was only identification through location. Now there are seemingly endless lineages, religions, sects, and special "orders" all reinforcing their own type of Buddhist practice that continues to foster self-referential views.

It is important to be mindful of associations that increase confusion and suffering through validation of unskillful thoughts and actions. It is the nature of a clinging mind to cling to the views common to associations. The Eightfold Path provides a highly effective framework for choosing associations and continued focus on Dhamma practice.

The Buddha taught a complete and direct path to awakening. His path often becomes confused and ineffective through adapting and accommodating the Dhamma to fit the views of charismatic individuals, cultural influences, and "sangha" or group association.

It is not necessary to associate with any lineage or school to develop the Buddha's Dhamma. What is paramount is to associate with what the Buddha taught.

Once clinging is recognized and abandoned, there will no longer be clinging to objects, people, events, views, or ideas. This brings the ability to be mindfully present in the world and with others with no expectations or insistence that your life, or the people in your life, including yourself, be any different from what is occurring.

All aspects of self are impermanent and any conditioned thought or thought construct that attempts to distract from this truth is also clinging, specifically clinging to views and ideas. Clinging to views and ideas maintains the distraction of stress and ongoing disappointment.

Anatta, not-self, continually seeks to establish itself in impermanent objects, events, views, and ideas. This "self" is established in the phenomenal world. This is why the ego-self is so enamored with the world and continually attempts to associate with "special" or "superior" people, groups, objects, events, views, and ideas. As long as anatta continues this quest, confusion and suffering will prevail. As long as anatta continues this quest, disappointing karma will continue.

Due to unquenched desire for continued existence, an ego-personality creates karma. Karma unfolds moment-by-moment as the distraction of stress and unhappiness. Though physical form will change due to impermanence, karma continues the experience of stress and unhappiness.

137

Karma and Rebirth is explained in detail further on.

This is an important example of impermanence as impermanence relates to Anatta. Continuity obscures impermanence but does not establish permanence. Continuity is reoccurrence due to repeatedly recreating the conditions leading to an experience, in this case continued re-establishment of an ego-self subject to confusion and suffering.

Reoccurring life situations and intellectual or emotional reactions are simply an impermanent, but repetitive, and discursive product of discriminating consciousness, or conditioned mind.

Conditioned thinking and conditioned mind is formed due to ignorance of impermanence, maintained by the distraction of stress, and given validity by a self-referential ego-personality.

Continuity of ignorance caused by clinging conditioned mind is ongoing Dukkha.

The Personal Experience
of Dukkha
Five Clinging-Aggregates

Dukkha is a Pali word. Pali is an ancient language that is very similar to the language spoken by the Buddha. Dukkha means unsatisfactory, uncertain, disappointing, deluded thinking, stressful, confusing, distracting, and all manner of mental and physical stress and suffering. I will use these words interchangeably to signify dukkha.

The Buddha teaches: "Birth is dukkha, aging is dukkha, death is dukkha; sorrow, regret, pain, grief, & despair are dukkha; association with the un-beloved is dukkha; separation from the loved is dukkha; not getting what is desired is dukkha. In short, the Five Clinging-Aggregates are dukkha." (Samyutta Nikaya 56.11)

Here the Buddha is describing the First Noble Truth. As a consequence of having a human life, Dukkha occurs. An awakened mind experiences dukkha impersonally and with dispassion. A mind ignorant of Four Noble Truths self-identifies with stress - clings to stress and joins with stress. This joining with or clinging to stress occurs through Five Clinging-Aggregates.

"And when one has seen the Five Clinging-Aggregates as they really are, the arising and the passing away, understanding the attraction and the distraction, seeing the arising of desire and the continued delusion, and being delivered from the Five Clinging-Aggregates, this one is released from clinging. All defilements are destroyed. What must be done has been done, perfection is attained, the burden has been put down, the highest goal attained. This one is liberated by perfect insight." (Samyutta Nikaya 22.110)

The following two paragraphs relate directly to Dependent Origination, explained in the next section.

"Clinging has craving as its cause. Craving is dependent on feelings, feelings dependent on contact. Contact is dependent on the six-sense base and the six-sense base dependent on the establishment of an ego-personality. The ego-personality is dependent on consciousness, consciousness dependent on fabrications. And what is the root of fabrications and the entire mass of confusion and suffering? Fabrications are dependent on ignorance for it's cause."

False assumptions, acquired views rooted in ignorance, is a simple and useful description of fabrications.

Ending ignorance of confusion, deluded thinking, and resulting unsatisfactory experiences - Dukkha - is the purpose of the Fourth Noble Truth. The Fourth Noble Truth is the truth of the Eightfold Path developing the cessation of ignorance and the cessation of Dukkha.

"From the cessation of ignorance comes true insight and the cessation of fabrications. From true insight comes cessation of clinging to sensory stimulus, to views and ideas, to rituals and practices, to doctrines of self. This wise one is free of clinging, unbound, at peace. Being at peace they know confusion and stress have ended. The integrated life has been lived. All tasks have been completed. There is nothing further for this world." (Majjhima Nikaya 11)

141

Five Clinging-Aggregates

Form, physical matter - The physical body and the physical domain. Included in the physical body are the senses and conditioned thinking. The physical or phenomenal domain is all that is perceived through contact with the senses. Any physical form is called the form aggregate.

Feeling - Feeling is the experienced reaction to mental or physical stimulus. Any emotional or physical feeling is called the feeling aggregate. In this context any mental disturbance is a feeling.

Perception - Perceptions are views formed by conditioned thoughts. Reaction to perceptions further integrates perception and further conditions thinking. Perceptions bound to a wrong view of self results in a deluded view of reality. Perceptions convey permanent and individuated reality where none exists. Any perception is called the perception aggregate.

Mental Fabrications - Mental fabrications are thought constructs and held views resulting in assumptions rooted in ignorance. Mental fabrications develop from sensory stimulus perceived through wrong view, further conditioning clinging conditioned mind. Mental fabrications incline a mind towards continued wrong views creating unskillful actions. It is unskillful intentional actions originating in deluded thinking that cause karma. Fabrications are a component of consciousness. Any mental fabrication is called the fabrication aggregate.

Consciousness - Ongoing thinking rooted in ignorance of Four Noble Truths. Ongoing thinking rooted in ignorance can only continue ignorance. Consciousness bound to the clinging-aggregates is also impermanent. Consciousness is the active and reactive process of an ego-personality continually establishing itself. Any aspect of consciousness is called the consciousness aggregate.

The Buddha is using the concept of Five Clinging-Aggregates to show the insubstantial and impermanent nature of what is perceived as an individual:

"The five aggregates are anicca, impermanent; whatever is impermanent, that is dukkha, unsatisfactory; whatever is dukkha, that is without self. What is without self, that is not mine, that I am not,

143

that is not my self. Thus should it be seen by perfect wisdom as it really is. Who sees by perfect wisdom as it really is their mind, not grasping, is detached from fabrications; they are liberated." (Samyutta Nikaya 22.48)

When any aggregate binds to any other element through clinging it is called a clinging-aggregate. It is through these aggregates of observable phenomenon that a perception of a self arises. For example: when a physical form binds to a mental fabrication called John it is now a clinging-aggregate. John has a pleasant (or unpleasant) experience. Clinging (or aversion) to the experience arises. Perception evaluates the feeling and further conditions consciousness to crave more (or less) of the experience. Through self-identification with experience self-referential views are formed. John now desires more (or less) of the conditioning experience.

Life becomes an endless experience of sensory input followed by discrimination. For example: "I" want more of this experience, "I" want less of this experience. Each experience is filtered through discriminating and conditioned thought. Each experience provides more validity to the arisen form further conditioning the consciousness of form.

Notice that each of these five factors are impermanent. Through unskillful and deluded intention to establish a self based on these five impermanent factors, a self-referential ego-personality is formed. From a wrong, or ignorant view, an ego-personality is born.

An ego-personality is defended and maintained by clinging to objects, events, views, and ideas. It is an ego-personality, anatta, that is subject to unsatisfactoriness, unhappiness, disappointment, stress and suffering. In this context it can be clearly seen that anatta is the result of fabrications originating in ignorance.

Dependent Origination shows that it is from the condition of craving that the condition of clinging arises. Understanding the Five Clinging-Aggregates as the personal experience of suffering begins to unbind the aggregates. Understanding the Five Clinging-Aggregates brings the refined mindfulness to see the impermanence of each aggregate. Once impermanence is clearly understood, clinging is abandoned.

145

The Eightfold Path provides the framework for developing concentration and mindfulness. Concentration and mindfulness brings insight into the truth of the Five Clinging-Aggregates giving rise to the illusion of a permanent self. Right View reveals the aggregates as impermanent manifestations of mental and physical phenomenon given substance by conditioned thinking.

It is what is perceived as an individual self, as a mental/physical personality, that has arisen from a mind conditioned by ignorance. Individuality or an individual personality should be understood as a combination, or aggregation, of phenomena. The desire for the establishment of an individual and permanent form is the cause of suffering. This is craving for (self-referential) existence - or craving for becoming.

All conditioned thoughts and fabrications arise from this initial craving. The concept of a substantial and eternal self endowed with a soul arises from craving for existence. Acquiring a view of a soul brings a conditioned belief of eternity to the temporary phenomenon of an ego-personality, or not-self,

146

continuing delusion and suffering. This is an extreme view as is the view that there is no-self.

Developing the Eightfold Path shows that what is perceived as "self" is continually impermanent and continually in the process of becoming. This is useful insight.

Becoming is explained in detail further on.

The skillful view here is to not get too analytical as analysis does not develop insight. It is enough to recognize that by phenomenal contact with five physical senses interpreted by "wrong" or conditioned thinking reaction occurs and Dukkha arises. The Five Clinging-Aggregates describe the personal experience of Dukkha.

Reaction to sensory stimulus seems to give an experience validity. The experience is only "validated" within ignorant views associated with the impermanence of Five Clinging-Aggregates. Initial reaction to the implications of the truth of the Five Clinging-Aggregates can be disconcerting at first. Conditioned mind will reject any thought that self is without any permanent substance.

147

Understanding the Five Clinging-Aggregates does not limit or annihilate anything of actual substance. Understanding the Five Clinging-Aggregates shines the light of wisdom on the darkness of ignorance. Understanding frees one from a limited and ignorant view of self that is bound to an impermanent and insubstantial "heap" of phenomenal elements.

Some references to The Five Clinging-Aggregates call these The Five Khanda's. Khanda's is a Pali word that loosely translates to "heap" or "pile."

The insistence on maintaining the delusion that an individual self is anything more than these Five Clinging-Aggregates continues to give rise to dukkha. It is the constant preoccupation with the distraction of self-identifying with dukkha that obscures impermanence and obscures wisdom.

The Four Noble Truths explains the truth of stress, its origins, and the path leading to the cessation of stress. The Five Clinging-Aggregates explains the ongoing personal experience that leads to the belief in an individual self subject to suffering. Anicca, Anatta, and Dukkha, describe the environment that the

148

appearance of self, and The Four Noble Truths are interrelated aspects.

Abandoning craving for self-referential existence and clinging to form is awakening. The distraction of the preoccupation with dukkha is lifted and awakened Right View arises.

The Five Clinging-Aggregates refer to the appearance of a "self" that craves for existence and clings to what seems to establish "self-existence." This process originates and perpetuates delusion, confusion, and ongoing unsatisfactoriness.

The teaching of the Five Clinging-Aggregates is a simple and practical explanation of the personalization of impersonal phenomena. The Five Clinging-Aggregates do not describe an established self in an absolute sense. The Five Clinging-Aggregates describe, in a relative sense, in the context of The Four Noble Truths, and relative to worldly phenomena, the process of the personal manifestation of dukkha.

Once it is clearly seen that these five aggregates are insubstantial and dependent on ignorance to maintain, and prone to constant unsatisfactory experiences, self-referential thoughts and fabrications will be abandoned.

The Five Clinging-Aggregates explains that from ignorance a confused and deluded view is formed. This ignorant view obscures reality and creates distraction. This results in the combining of five disparate parts, or aggregates, to objectify and provide the personal experience of continued confusion, deluded thinking, and ongoing suffering.

This is a key concept of the Dhamma. If this is unclear at this point, remember that the Eightfold Path develops the wisdom and understanding to see this reality clearly.

From the point of view of an ego-personality this often sounds like nonsense. Resistance to seeing clearly, to useful insight, is rooted in wrong view. An aspect of ignorance is the ego-personality's inclination to ignore anything that would challenge ignorance.

When faced with truths that would bring wisdom to the ignorance that the ego-self is dependent on for continuance, questions such as "what am I" and "what happens to me" arise. (when I awaken, when I die, etc.) These questions seek answers that would continue to establish the Five Clinging-Aggregates through speculative assumptions.

These are inappropriate questions as they are rooted in ignorance of Four Noble Truths. Continued ignorance cannot abolish ignorance. Insisting on answers to questions rooted in ignorance continues ignorance. Clinging to views that have arisen from ignorance will only further ignorance and continue confusion and suffering.

As shown in the Panha Sutta from the introduction, the Buddha consistently refused to answer self-referential questions, often replying "I teach suffering and the cessation of suffering. I teach The Four Noble Truths, nothing more."

The Buddha was cautious in discussing and giving validity to any mental fabrications that would likely generate more confusion and stress.

The wanderer Vacchagotta had many questions about the nature of the cosmos, eternity, infinitude, the self and the soul, existence after death, and others. After he put these questions to the Buddha, the Buddha responded: "You are confused (by your own questions). The phenomenon (Dependent Origination)

151

you question is hard to understand and realize. This phenomenon is tranquil and subtle and beyond discriminating thought. Realization only comes to the awakened." (Majjhima Nikaya 72)

The purpose of the Buddha's Dhamma is not to provide answers to every speculative mystical or existential question a clinging mind desperate for continued establishment develops. The purpose of the Buddha's Dhamma is to understand and abandon suffering born of self-referential views arising from ignorance of Four Noble Truths.

The Five Clinging-Aggregates are taught to develop the understanding of confusion, deluded thinking, and ongoing disappointment. Understanding the Five Clinging-Aggregates begins to diminish attachment to ignorant views allowing for wisdom and Right View to arise.

Anicca, impermanence, shows that what is perceived of as a substantial and eternal self is impermanent, insubstantial, and unsustainable. Being impermanent, the ego-self is subject to stress and unhappiness due to craving and clinging to views of a permanent, substantial, and sustainable self.

It is ignorance that brings suffering. It is the belief in an individual soul or permanent ego-personality that provides the vehicle for the establishment and continuation of suffering. It is the constant preoccupation and distraction of dukkha that obscures the path to liberation and freedom.

One cannot know what is not known until what is believed to be true is recognized and abandoned. Insisting on maintaining the delusion of an individual self is a wrong view that is blocking Right View.

Understanding the Five Clinging-Aggregates does not answer the question of "what am I?" Understanding the Five Clinging-Aggregates brings wisdom to the personal experience of suffering.

"When ignorance is abandoned and true knowledge has arisen one no longer clings to sensual pleasures. One no longer clings to views, or to rules and observances, or to a doctrine of self. When one does not cling, one is not agitated. When one is not agitated, one attains Nibbana (awakening). Wisdom arises and (giving) birth (to further ignorance) is left behind. The life of virtue, mindful concentration and wisdom has been lived. The righteous Eightfold Path has been developed. There will be no more becoming to any state of being." (Majjhima Nikaya 11)

The Buddha's teachings are not to be only studied intellectually. The Buddha's teachings are to be understood through wisdom born of the experience of integrating these teachings as the framework for life experience.

Observe the Five Clinging-Aggregates and how they give rise to a belief in self. Notice that nothing (agitating) arises without clinging, craving or desire. Notice the unskillful intention to acquire or to become. Notice how the belief in the self continues the discursive cycle of craving, acquisition, disappointment, and more craving.

This is also a practical lesson in Dependent Origination. The root craving for existence gives rise to a self that clings. The clinging-self is dependent on clinging for existence, and on continued craving to maintain existence. Clinging to the notion of a permanent individual self lessens and eventually ceases by developing understanding through The Eightfold Path.

The Eightfold Path is the practical and direct way of understanding The Four Noble Truths and the belief in a self within the environment of Anicca. Wisdom and understanding arise and the idea of a permanent sustainable self is abandoned. There is no more becoming a self subject to confusion and suffering as there is nothing for desire to arise from. The veil of dukkha is lifted. When seen clearly through a well-concentrated mind supporting refined mindfulness, it is clear that awakening is an ongoing process of developing wisdom.

"Magandiya, when you hear the true Dhamma, you will practice the Dhamma correctly. When you practice the Dhamma correctly, you will know and see for yourself: 'This is where confusion and suffering ceases without trace. With the cessation of clinging comes the cessation of becoming. With the cessation of becoming comes the cessation of birth. With the cessation of birth then (reaction to) aging & death, sorrow, regret, pain, distress, & despair all cease. Such is the cessation of this entire mass of suffering and stress. When released from clinging the mind is without feature or surface, limitless, outside of time and space, freed from the six-sense base." (Majjhima Nikaya 11)

Being mindful of the Right Intention to recognize and abandon craving and clinging begins to unbind the Five Clinging-Aggregates. This establishes the refined mindfulness necessary to see the individual components for what they are and to (eventually) abandon the need to continue the ego-self through continued clinging and maintaining.

Dukkha is an ongoing experience of the interaction with an impermanent environment and fixed views rooted in ignorance. This is an important point to be developed. Once the understanding that it is a (wrong) view of self that is the cause of confusion, stress and ongoing delusion, these views can be mindfully abandoned.

"There are these three forms of stress, my friend: the stress of pain, the stress of fabrication, the stress of change. These are the three forms of stress." (Samyutta Nikaya 38.14)

It is the self-referential ego-personality, what is shown to be anatta, not-a-self, that experiences the three forms of stress. To re-state the Four Noble Truths in this context, there is an underlying and pervasive unsatisfactoriness to life that the ego-self experiences but often ignores. The experiencer is also joined (clinging to) to the experience and the environment that the experience arises. Continued clinging to a wrong view of self continues dukkha.

It is due to the effects of stress that make understanding stress paramount in the Buddha's teaching. It is preoccupation with stress, with Dukkha, that prevents awakening. It is the preoccupation with the need to continually establish and defend an impermanent, ever-changing, ego-personality that continues confusion and stress.

Jambukhadika the wanderer asks the Buddha: "What is the path, what is the practice for the full comprehension of these three forms of stressfulness?"

"Precisely this Noble Eightfold Path, my friend - right view, right intention, right speech, right action, right livelihood, right effort, right mindfulness, right meditation. This is the path, this is the practice for the full comprehension of these three forms of stressfulness." (Samyutta Nikaya 38.14)

157

In describing the refined mindfulness of an awakened mind the Buddha stated "Dukkha is understood" and "Free of craving and clinging one is not agitated. Un-agitated this one is totally unbound and free of Dukkha, an Arahant." (Majjhima Nikaya 11)

The Eightfold Path develops understanding and release from dukkha.

As concentration increases through Shamatha-Vipassana meditation the process of establishing and maintaining an ego-self is mindfully observed. Once this process is recognized, with Right Intention, and the other mutually supportive factors of the Eightfold Path, the continual establishment and defense of an ego-self is finally abandoned.

The process of recognizing and abandoning confused and deluded thinking is addressed throughout this book and in the Satipatthana Sutta in the section on Meditation and Mindfulness.

Impermanence, stress, and the ego-self are all observable facts of human existence. It requires continued, ever-vigilant directed thought to maintain the ego-self in an impermanent environment. Another way of saying this is clinging to form. Clinging to form is stress. Clinging to form is dukkha. This confused and conditioned thinking can be refined and purified and bring relief from craving and clinging.

The cause of the unsatisfactory nature of life is rooted in the deluded belief in a fixed and permanent mental-physical self, the self-referential ego-self. Craving for the establishment of a self and clinging to the perception of an established self establishes the unsatisfactory nature of life.

The human form is a discrete component of the physical universe that has arisen to interact with the physical world and is dependent on the same causes and conditions of all phenomena for its existence. This mental-physical ego-self, subject to the same truth as all physical phenomena, arises from the formless, becomes form, and will again enter the formless state.

The wisdom of the Dhamma shows the foolishness to cling a self-identity to a form that is impermanent and insubstantial, and prone to confusion and stress.

This mental-physical form, rooted in ignorance, acquires the characteristics that craving directs it

159

towards through seeking sensory satisfaction. Clinging establishes and maintains this form by holding on to constant sensory fulfillment.

The Buddha's Dhamma brings insight into this process. Complete development of the Eightfold Path brings release from the process of continual selfing, or "I-making."

The Five Clinging Aggregates are addressed in slightly different contexts further on.

Siddartha Awakens

There is a common misunderstanding of the meaning of awakening, of becoming Buddha. Modern Buddhism has many competing and contradictory themes. The Buddha was direct and clear: Empty of ignorance. He described emptiness of ignorance as unbound or released from clinging to views rooted in ignorance. He described the quality of an awakened mind as calm.

A prevalent misconception is that awakening is establishing a self in an interdependent, interconnected, environment that is empty of any recognized separateness or discreteness - a nothingness soup of "inter-being" where all apparent duality is reconciled in non-duality.

This is a teaching proclaimed in the Veda's and made popular with the modern Advaita movement. This non-dual philosophy has more in common with modern Hinduism than the teachings of the Buddha. These are doctrines taught by Alara Kalama and Uddaka Ramaputta mentioned in the introduction. These vague non-dual doctrines were rejected by the Buddha prior to his awakening as not leading to the understanding he sought.

Other variations on the emptiness or nothingness theme is the belief in an inner Buddha-nature, or inherent Buddhahood. As will be seen, these are simply more strategies for establishing a permanent and individual self in the same non-dual soup.

A significant modern Buddhist religion's doctrine holds that awakening is achieving an ultimate reward of abiding in an ever-lasting "Buddhist" heaven. This heaven is presided over by a supreme Buddha-god who grants perennial bliss, provided a few requirements are fulfilled while alive.

These and many other variations are all well established and completely legitimate Buddhist religions. They are not what the Buddha taught as awakening.

The Buddha taught that awakening is recognizing and abandoning ignorance of Four Noble Truths - emptying oneself of ignorance.

As shown in the previous chapter on the Three Marks of Existence, it is a misunderstanding of the interplay between the impermanent characteristic of all phenomena and a misunderstanding of what constitutes a "self," - the not-self characteristic - that results in ongoing confusion, deluded thinking, and stress/suffering - Dukkha.

Throughout his teaching career the Buddha continually emphasized the purpose of his Dhamma: "I teach the arising of stress/suffering - Dukkha - and the cessation of stress/suffering, nothing more." (Samyutta Nikaya 22.86 and many other sutta's)

In describing fully developed Right View the Buddha states: Right View profoundly understands stress, Right View (has developed the) abandoning of individual contributions to stress (craving and clinging rooted in ignorance of Four Noble Truths), Right View (has developed) the cessation of stress, Right View is developed through the Eightfold Path.

An accurate description of an awakened human being is full maturity. A fully mature human being has developed the profound understanding of stress and suffering. They have developed the Eightfold Path and ended all individual contributions to suffering in themselves and the world. Full human maturity is a

163

fully developed dispassionate Right View of the arising and passing away of all phenomena.

This is what is described in the following chapter's account of the Buddha describing his own awakening: "I followed this (Eightfold) path. Following it, I came to direct knowledge of (the stress of) aging & death, direct knowledge of the origination of (the stress of) aging & death, direct knowledge of the cessation of (the stress of) aging & death, direct knowledge of the path leading to the cessation of (the stress of) aging & death.

Another explanation of awakening as "emptying oneself of clinging" to ignorance of Four Noble Truths is in the chapter on the Kaccayanagotta Sutta further on.

Nagara Sutta

Samyutta Nikaya 12.65

The Buddha Describes His Awakening

The Nagara Sutta is remarkable in its practical simplicity in describing Dependent Origination. In this sutta the Buddha describes his awakening. He shows how ignorance of Four Noble Truths and The Three Marks of Existence "originates" the process that disappointment, unsatisfactoriness, distraction, and suffering - in a word Dukkha - is "dependent" on.

The Three Marks of Existence, explained earlier, are Anicca, impermanence; Anatta - wrong or deluded views of self; and Dukkha - resulting suffering from this initial ignorance. Dukkha is explained in this context below.

In the Nagara Sutta the Buddha describes his own personal struggle with ignorance when he was an unawakened Bodhisatta. (Sanskrit: Bodhisattva, used here interchangeably) Through understanding the process of suffering arising in ignorance he directly abandoned the wrong   views that would have otherwise continued his ignorance.

The Bodhisattva vow, the customary path of awakening in all modern Mahayana schools of Buddhism is a vow to seek awakening for the sake of all sentient beings. Often included in the vow is to intentionally delay awakening until all beings are awakened.

At first the Bodhisattva path looks like a self-less, highly compassionate, and reasonable "goal." When looked at in the context of Dependent Origination and the Four Noble Truths, the Bodhisattva vow is seen as taking on the role and self-identity of savior and establishes the Buddha's teachings as a salvific religion.

The suffering in the world is not due to the lack of a sufficient number of Bodhisattva's in the world. Dependent Origination shows that it is ignorance of Four Noble Truths that leads to all manner of confusion, deluded thinking, and ongoing Dukkha.

In a somewhat subtle way, taking on the altruistic vow to save all sentient beings creates another self-referential identity as savior. The Buddha never presented himself as a savior or his Dhamma as a salvific religion. The Bodhisattva role is a highly compassionate state but a preliminary state to awakening.

If saving all sentient beings was a reasonable and complete path to awakening there would be no need for an Eightfold Path. Individual development of understanding as described in the Nagara Sutta would be unnecessary.

The Buddha taught for forty-five years presenting many thousands of suttas. There is no mention of substituting a "Bodhisattva path" for the Eightfold Path. If the Bodhisattva Path developed awakening the Buddha would have simply taught to develop great compassion. With unsurpassed wisdom he understood that compassion alone, no matter how great, would still leave one an "unawakened Bodhisattva."

The Buddha taught an Eightfold Path that directly develops individual awakening. Individuals could "save" themselves through direct engagement with this path.

The last words of the Buddha, spoken shortly before he passed, points directly to the Eightfold Path: "Let the Dhamma be your master. Impermanence and

167

decay are relentless, strive diligently for your own salvation."

In order to awaken and have a truly useful impact on others the Eightfold Path is to be developed. The Eightfold Path directly ends conceit and brings profound wisdom to compassion. The development of wisdom ended the Buddha's ignorance. He Became Buddha through developing understanding of the arising and passing away of all conditioned things.

I must mention that I have no disrespect for the Bodhisattva ideal or for those that follow the Mahayana paths. The ideal and path are contradictions to the Buddha's direct teachings that have arisen since his passing. In order to understand what the Buddha actually taught, the many contradictions in modern Buddhism must be clearly seen.

From this understanding any adaptations, accommodations, and alterations to the Buddha's teachings can be developed from wisdom while preserving an awakened human being's Dhamma.

The Buddha felt it was quite important to repeatedly refer to himself as an "unawakened Bodhisatta." He did this to show that a Bodhisatta is a highly compassionate human being lacking understanding of Four Noble Truths.

The Buddha had great compassion prior to his awakening. As seen in this sutta he was lacking understanding of Four Noble Truths. Joined with worldly conditions he suffered from confusion, deluded thinking, and ongoing disappointing experiences. He did not understand the originating conditions that Dukkha depends on.

If the Buddha had decided to delay his awakening until all others somehow became awakened, he would have spent eternity in this unsuccessful search. If the Buddha intended to be a savior of all sentient beings, he would have embraced the salvific dharmas of Alara Kalama or Uddaka Ramaputta.

There would be no Dhamma. There would be no Eightfold Path.

Another salvation myth is that when the Buddha awakened, all beings awakened. This is dismisses the very foundation of the Buddha's Dhamma and his entire teaching career. It is interesting and significant that a modern school of Buddhism insists that this is the truth. The implication here is that ignorance of Four Noble Truths is irrelevant. Ignoring ignorance never develops wisdom.

Siddhartha's awakening did not end other human beings individual ignorance of Four Noble Truths. Understanding Four Noble Truths brought him the wisdom and understanding to express his compassion in a truly effective way. He spent the last years of his life teaching a Dhamma so that all individuals could end their own ignorance, one discrete mind at a time.

The Buddha often used the word "ehipassiko." Ehipassiko means "come and see for yourself." The Buddha's Dhamma is to be developed individually and experienced personally. Developing the Buddha's Dhamma is not dependent on other human beings awakening.

The Buddha's awakening and teaching career shows that the most compassionate act anyone can undertake is to develop his Dhamma and awaken.

The Bodhisattva vow alters the Dhamma in a way that the Buddha avoided for his entire Forty-Five year teaching career.

He taught that ending ignorance of Four Truths through an Eightfold Path will bring individual awakening for anyone who engaged with his Dhamma. It is through the Eightfold Path that one becomes "Rightly Self-Awakened" as the Buddha became Rightly Self-Awakened.

The Buddha's boundless compassion informed by true insight and profound wisdom is exemplified by his ongoing efforts at teaching thousands of others in his lifetime. He taught how to develop understanding of Four Noble Truths and develop awakened Right View.

Everything the Buddha taught for the Forty-Five years of his teaching career was taught in the context of The Four Noble Truths.

All manner of human suffering is dependent on and originates in ignorance of Four Noble Truths. Developing profound knowledge of these Four Truths brings liberation. Awakening is not dependent on anything other than direct engagement with the Eightfold Path and direct experience of the cessation of ignorance rooted in wrong views.

In the Majjhima Nikaya (19) the Buddha describes the quality of his mind as an "unawakened Bodhisatta":

"Monks, prior to my awakening, when I was an unawakened Bodhisatta, I thought I could continue to divide my thinking. I continued thinking intended on sensuality, ill-will and harmfulness. I also continued thinking intended on renunciation, good-will and harmlessness."

Notice here the Buddha is describing precisely what happens when a goal other than developing the Eightfold Path and ending conditioned thinking rooted in ignorance. Intention can be both harmful and altruistic simultaneously. This occurs continually in a mind that is ignorant of these Four Truths. This continually distracting "feedback loop" is explained below.

The Buddha continues: "As I remained mindful and well-concentrated, thinking with the intention of clinging arose in me. I now recognized that thinking with the intention of clinging has arisen in me. Thinking with the intention of clinging brings suffering for me and others. This (conditioned) thinking can only lead to more ignorance and does not develop unbinding (from clinging to wrong views).

"As I noticed that wrong intention develops more suffering, wrong intention subsided. Subsequently, when wrong intention arose in me, I simply abandoned it."

When I first read the Nagara sutta many years ago, it was the guidance I needed to look closely at my recently taken Bodhisattva vows in a Tibetan Buddhist tradition. I finally understood the confusing uneasiness I had over these vows.

I realized that the path the Buddha taught was not founded in a Bodhisattva ideal but in ending ignorance of Four Noble Truths. I realized the Buddha was not a savior-god. I realized that I was not directed to aspire to be a savior, either.

I realized that it was ignorance of Four Noble Truths as described in the Paticca-Samuppada-Vibhanga Sutta that originated my confusion, deluded thinking, and ongoing unsatisfactory experiences.

The Paticca-Samuppada-Vibhanga Sutta is the sutta on Dependent Origination presented in the next chapter.

This single realization changed the entire focus of my Dhamma practice - and my life. I ended my clinging self-identification to the Bodhisattva vow. I began wholehearted engagement with the Eightfold Path.

In the Nagara Sutta the "world" is metaphor for the ongoing struggle with Dukkha for everyone in the world. Dukkha is described by the Buddha as "Now this monks, is the Noble Truth of dukkha: Birth is dukkha, aging is dukkha, death is dukkha; sorrow, regret, pain, grief, & despair are dukkha; association with the unbeloved is dukkha; separation from the loved is dukkha; not getting what is wanted is dukkha. In short, the five clinging-aggregates are dukkha." (Samyutta Nikaya 56.11 and many other suttas)

The Nagara Sutta

The Buddha was at Savatthi at Jeta's Grove, Anathapindika's monastery. There he addressed those gathered:

"Friends, before my awakening, when I was only an unawakened Bodhisatta, (Sanskrit: Bodhisattva) I came to the realization of the difficulties of the world. The world is born, it ages, it dies, it falls away and returns, but there is no understanding of ending the stress and suffering of aging and death. When will the world understand the cessation of the stress and suffering from aging and death?

"Then I had the thought: What initiates aging and death? What is the requisite condition that aging and death are dependent on for arising?

"From my appropriate mindfulness came a breakthrough of understanding: From birth as the requisite condition comes aging and death.

175

"Then I had the thought: What initiates birth? What is the requisite condition that birth is dependent on for arising?

"From my appropriate mindfulness came a breakthrough of understanding: From becoming (ignorant) as the requisite condition comes birth.

In most translations "becoming ignorant" is written only as becoming, leaving out the word ignorant. This alone has led to much confusion. In the Paticca-Samuppada-Vibhanga sutta it is ignorance as the initiating condition that begins the process that becomes "birth, sickness, aging, death and the entire mass of suffering."

"Then I had the thought: What initiates name-&-form? What is the requisite condition that name-&-form is dependent on for arising?

Name-and-form (Pali: nama-rupa) means self-identification through clinging to forms and self-referential views.

"From my appropriate mindfulness came a breakthrough of understanding: From consciousness as the requisite condition comes name-&-form.

In the Paticca-Samuppada-Vibhanga Sutta the Buddha shows that it is ignorance of Four Noble Truths as the condition that mental fabrications are dependent on. Consciousness is dependent on mental fabrications. Consciousness in this context is ordinary ongoing thinking arising from ignorance. What arises from ignorance can only further ignorance.

"Then I had the thought: What initiates consciousness? What is the requisite condition that consciousness is dependent on for arising?

"From my appropriate mindfulness came a breakthrough of understanding: From name-&-form as the requisite condition comes consciousness.

What the Buddha is beginning to describe here is the feedback loop caused by self-referential views then relying on these views, rooted in ignorance, to describe self-referential "reality." This much like "I think; therefore I am" the famous quote from Rene Descartes who hoped to find an irrefutable statement. His reasoning was that he could not refute his own existence and so it must be that his (self-referential) thoughts prove that he existed.

Lacking understanding, the resulting reality described ignores (continued ignorance) any thought, word,

177

or idea that arises that would challenge views now conditioned by ongoing ignorance. Once established, a framework for recognizing this feedback loop is now necessary in order to recognize and abandon these wrong views.

When the Dhamma is developed it is clearly understood that what constitutes a "self" is always in a constant state of becoming. Consciousness rooted in ignorance can only continue this feedback loop, furthering ignorance. The world becomes the mirror feeding back wrong views. As the Buddha's path is developed consciousness is framed by the Eightfold Path. Views rooted in ignorance are recognized and abandoned. becoming awakened, Becoming Buddha, is now possible.

The difficulty that many have with seeing this clearly is that a mind rooted in ignorance insists on ignoring anything that challenges ignorance. This is the essence of continued "I-making." Understanding this is the essence of the Buddha's Dhamma.

"Then I had the thought: This consciousness turns back at name-&-form and goes no farther. It is to this extent that there is birth, aging, death, falling away and returning. This is where ignorance is established.

178

Name-&-form (self-referential views) is the requisite condition that brings consciousness and consciousness is the requisite condition that brings name-&-form.

The Buddha here is clearly stating that it is self-referential views that establishes and continues I-making. Continued I-making continues Dukkha. This directly relates to his use of the word Anatta to mean "Not-self" - self-referential views rooted in ignorance are not-a-self. The Eightfold Path is developed to recognize and abandon ignorant views and the entire mass of stress that follows.

"Then I had the thought: The six-sense base (five physical senses and consciousness) is dependent on the condition of name-&-form, dependent on self-referential views. This is the origination of the entire mass of suffering!

The Buddha is stating that seeing all objects, events, views, and ideas from the perspective of "me" or "I" is being stuck in the feedback loop of self-referential views interpreted by consciousness rooted in ignorance. Wrong view is personalizing impermanent objects, events, views, and ideas.

Joining with impermanent phenomena creates the distraction of Dukkha. Life is then an ongoing struggle to possess what is desired and avoid what is disappointing and unsatisfactory. Identifying with - joining with - Dukkha develops from craving and clinging. Craving and clinging occurs due to ignorance of Four Noble Truths:

"Vision arose, understanding arose, discernment arose, knowledge arose, illuminating insight arose within me with regard to things never known before.

"The I had the thought: What is the condition that the cessation of the stress of aging and death is dependent on?

"From my appropriate mindfulness came a breakthrough of understanding: From the cessation of birth (of ignorance) as the requisite condition comes the cessation of the stress of aging and death.

"From my appropriate mindfulness came a breakthrough of understanding: From the cessation of consciousness (thinking rooted in ignorance) as the requisite condition comes the cessation of name-&-form.

"From my appropriate mindfulness came a breakthrough of understanding: From the cessation of name-&-form as the requisite condition comes the cessation of consciousness.

Notice the reference here and below to what the Buddha awakened to - Dependent Origination."

I have attained this path to awakening:

- From the cessation of name-&-form comes the cessation of consciousness.

- From the cessation of consciousness comes the cessation of name-&-form.

- From the cessation of name-&-form comes the cessation of the six sense base.

- From the cessation of the six sense base comes the cessation of contact.

- From the cessation of contact comes the cessation of feeling.

- From the cessation of feeling comes the cessation of craving.

- From the cessation of craving comes the cessation of clinging/maintenance.

- From the cessation of clinging/maintenance comes the cessation of becoming.

181

- From the cessation of becoming (ignorant) comes the cessation of birth (of ignorance).

- From the cessation of birth, then aging & death, sorrow, regret, pain, distress, & despair all cease.

"This is the cessation of the entire mass of stress.

"Vision arose, understanding arose, discernment arose, knowledge arose, illuminating insight arose within me with regard to things never known before.

The confusion that often arises in modern Buddhism is taking these teachings out of the context of Dependent Origination and The Four Noble Truths.

Each of these statements when seen in the proper context shows that ignorance of Four Noble Truths originates the process of becoming stuck in a feedback loop of wrong views, a thicket of views.

When wisdom and understanding is developed through the Eightfold Path then "giving birth" to further views rooted in ignorance ceases. The conditions that the stress of aging and death, of sorrow, regret, pain, distress, & despair are dependent on are gone.

"In this way I saw a timeless path to be traveled by Rightly Self-awakened Ones. And what is this timeless path traveled by Rightly Self-awakened Ones?*

"Just this Noble Eightfold Path:

1. Right View.

2. Right Intention.

3. Right Speech.

4. Right Action

5. Right Livelihood

6. Right Effort

7. Right Mindfulness

8. Right Meditation

"This is the timeless path traveled by Rightly Self-awakened One. I followed this path.

"Following it, I came to direct knowledge of (the stress of) aging & death.

"Following it, I came to direct knowledge of the origination of (the stress of) aging & death.

"Following it, I came to direct knowledge of the cessation of (the stress of) aging & death.

"Following it, I came to direct knowledge of the path leading to the cessation of (the stress of) aging & death.

"Following it, I came to direct knowledge of birth, of becoming, of clinging, of craving, of feeling, of contact, of the six sense media, of name-&-form, of consciousness.

"Following it, I came to direct knowledge of the origination of consciousness.Following it, I came to direct knowledge of the cessation of consciousness.

"Following it, I came to direct knowledge of the (Eightfold) Path leading to the cessation of consciousness.

"Following it, I came to direct knowledge of fabrications.

"Following it, I came to direct knowledge of the origination of fabrications.

"Following it, I came to direct knowledge of the cessation of fabrications.

"Following it, I came to direct knowledge of the Eightfold Path leading to the cessation of fabrications.

"Knowing the Eightfold Path directly, I have revealed it to monks, nuns, male lay followers & female lay followers. I teach an Eightfold Path so that this path becomes powerful, rich, detailed, well-populated, wide-spread, and proclaimed by all wise beings."

End of Sutta

The Buddha taught the Eightfold Path to overcome the common human problem of self-referential views keeping one stuck in the feedback loop of conditioned thinking - thinking conditioned by ignorance of Four Noble Truths.

*The Buddha's statement "In this way I saw a timeless path to be traveled by the Rightly Self-awakened One. And what is this timeless path traveled by the Rightly Self-awakened One" is often translated as 'In the same way I saw an ancient path, an ancient road, traveled by the Rightly Self-awakened Ones of former times. And what is that ancient path, that ancient road, traveled by the Rightly Self-awakened Ones of former times?

I have made these corrections as this presentation does not contradict the Buddha's statement here and many other suttas that state "This is the cessation of the entire mass of stress. Vision arose, understanding arose, discernment arose, knowledge arose, illuminating insight arose within me with regard to things never known before."

The Buddha is not teaching a way of immortality or of annihilation, both extreme views. He is teaching how to end, in this present life, the stress of reacting to ordinary and inherently human events and to cease creating the karmic entanglements that give birth to further ignorance for now and for all time.

Dependent Origination, Paticca-Samuppada-Vibhanga Sutta

Samyutta Nikaya 12.2

From ignorance of Four Noble Truths

all manner of suffering arises

As has been shown in the Nagara Sutta, the Buddha "awakened" to the profound understanding that the common human problem of the underlying unsatisfactory nature of life is rooted in ignorance. In the ancient language of the Pali Canon this unsatisfactory experience is known as Dukkha. The origination of Dukkha is explained in the Buddha's teaching of Dependent Origination. Dependent Origination shows that it is ignorance of Four Noble Truths, through twelve observable causative links, that all manner of confusion, delusion, and suffering, in a word, Dukkha, arises.

Dependent Origination is the Buddha's teaching on how personal phenomena arises within the environment of anicca, impermanence. The entirety of the Dhamma is to bring understanding of Four Noble Truths. It is within the context of Four Noble Truths that understanding of Dependent Origination develops. Understanding Dependent Origination brings awareness of the relationship between the Five Clinging-Aggregates and the impermanent phenomenal world.

The Four Noble Truths is explained further on.

The Five Clinging-Aggregates are physical and mental factors that through individual intentional clinging a personality is formed. This self-created ego-personality perceives that it is a permanent, substantial, and sustainable self. Once formed the ego-self tenaciously insists on establishing it's "self" in every object, event, view, and idea that occurs.

Dependent Origination directly shows the 12 causative links that determine the experiences of a self-referential ego-personality. In the Paticca-Samuppada-Vibhanga Sutta the Buddha presents the 12 causative links of Dependent Origination. Each of these 12 links are required, or "dependent" on the prior condition in order to give rise to a "self" that will experience dukkha. Rooted in ignorance, (of Four Noble Truths) it is through a continued confused and deluded "wrong view" that "anatta" continues to establish itself in every object, event, view, or idea that occurs. This is known as continued "I-making," or simply, conceit.

The importance of these teachings is to understand that the origination of all clinging views of an ego-self are rooted in ignorance. Once understood, craving and clinging can be abandoned and the 12 causative links in the chain of dependencies unbound. The process of ongoing confusion and stress comes to an end.

Once Dependent Origination is clearly understood, seeking understanding through magical, mystical or esoteric teachings will be seen as distraction and continued I-making.

Once Dependent Origination is clearly understood, the futility of rituals, precepts, and practices rooted in ignorance are abandoned.

Attempts to attract the attention of gods and devas, or to establish the self in a "higher" or more pleasant realm, will be seen as rooted in ignorance and abandoned.

The Buddha awakened to the profound understanding that from ignorance, through twelve observable causative conditions, the ongoing process of stress and suffering is formed. He summarized this understanding when he presented his first teaching.

The Buddha's first discourse was the foundational teachings of The Four Noble Truths. The Four Noble Truths summarize the entire Dhamma.

The First Noble Truth describes the condition caused by ignorance, the noble truth of dukkha (unsatisfactoriness, stress, unhappiness, disenchantment).

The Second Noble Truth describes the truth of individual craving and clinging as the origination of a personal experience of dukkha.

The Third Noble Truth states that cessation of individual contributions to dukkha is possible.

The Fourth Noble Truth is the truth of the Eightfold Path leading to the cessation of dukkha.

It is the development of The Eightfold Path that unbinds clinging to ignorant views, ends dukkha, and brings awakening.

Nibbana (Sanskrit: Nirvana) is a Pali word, that describes the awakened mind state. Nibbana means extinguished or unbound. Cessation of dukkha is the extinguishing of all wrong views that initiate craving, and the unbinding of all clinging attachments.

As seen in the previous section The Buddha taught three linked characteristics of life in the phenomenal world, or "Three Marks of Existence. These three characteristics are Anicca, Anatta, and Dukkha - impermanence, not-self, and stress.

All things in the phenomenal world are subject to impermanence, including what appears as self. All things in the phenomenal world arise and fade away WITHIN the phenomenal world. Nothing is permanent and nothing arises of its own accord.

The Buddha avoided any attempt to define a self in any manner. He simply and directly taught that wrong views rooted in ignorance that establishes a self were "Anatta," Not-Self. The Buddha left unanswered any questions that would seek to make permanent and

191

substantial that which is inherently impermanent and insubstantial.

As shown earlier in the Panha Sutta, (from the Introduction) the Buddha never addressed questions directly that would not lead to ending craving and clinging and cessation of dukkha. Answering questions about the nature of self originating from a deluded belief (in self) would only reinforce delusion and lead to more delusion, confusion suffering. These questions were consistently left unanswered as they were improper questions rooted in ignorance.

The Buddha described these questions as arising from "Inappropriate views not fit for attention. These views will continue to generate confusion and suffering."

The Buddha teaches what is fit for attention while maintaining the context of The Four Noble Truths:

- Understanding Stress.

- Understanding the Origination of Stress.

- Understanding the Cessation of Stress.

192

- Understanding the path leading to the cessation of Stress.

"As one attends appropriately in this way, three fetters are abandoned: identity-view, doubt, and grasping at precepts and practices." (Majjhima Nikaya 1)

Grasping at precepts and practices refers to assuming an inherent "ground of being." From this assumed fabrication preserving the self through engaging in ritualistic or ideological practices becomes reasonable.

If engaging or following popular doctrines, teachers, or rituals develops further self-grasping, it should be recognized as deluded and abandoned.

The continued preoccupation with defining and maintaining a self creates ongoing confusion and suffering. Understanding views rooted in ignorance brings liberation.

As one develops an understanding of the Dhamma, it is important to always be mindful of the context and intent of the teachings of the Buddha. The Buddha consistently emphasized to be mindful of what he taught and why: "I teach the origination of Dukkha and the path leading to the cessation of Dukkha, nothing more."

The Buddha avoided any issues that would prove to be a distraction to his stated purpose. In fact, The Buddha could have nearly as accurately stated "I teach the origination of distraction and the cessation of distraction." It is the ongoing preoccupation with Dukkha that distracts from life as life occurs. It is the self-referential preoccupation with stress and unhappiness that distracts from a life of lasting peace and happiness. It is the distraction of dukkha that prevents awakening.

Life in the phenomenal world is often experienced as both arbitrary and personal and predetermined and unavoidable.

Dependent Origination explains the process of the formation of an ego-personality, a "self," and the personalization of impersonal worldly events.

Holding the view that discrete impersonal objects, events, views, and ideas are occurring to "you" or for your benefit or detriment is personalization of impersonal worldly events. This is "I-making."

Recognizing and abandoning the ongoing process of I-making brings the refined mindfulness of an awakened human being.

An awakened human being experiences life fully present with life as life occurs without the confining craving and clinging conditioned mind that clouds perception and maintains confusion and unsatisfactoriness.

Understanding the process of "I-making" develops the heightened wisdom, heightened virtue, and heightened concentration necessary to refine thinking and reverse the formation of the ego-personality.

Dependent Origination is the Buddha's teaching on how (apparently) personal phenomena arises within the impersonal environment of impermanence.

The purpose of the Dhamma is to end ignorance through developing profound understanding of The Four Noble Truths. It is within the context of Four Noble Truths that understanding Dependent Origination develops.

Understanding Dependent Origination brings awareness of the relationship between the Five Clinging-Aggregates and the phenomenal world. The

Five Clinging-Aggregates are physical and mental factors that cling together to form a personality identified as self - an ego-personality. Dependent Origination explains the 12 causative links that determine the experiences of the ego-personality.

The Five Clinging-Aggregates are the personal experience of confusion, deluded thinking, and ongoing disappointment.

In the Paticca-Samuppada-Vibhanga Sutta the Buddha presents the 12 causative links of Dependent Origination. Each of these 12 links are required to cause the "self" to experience Dukkha.

The Paticca-Samuppada-Vibhanga Sutta

Notice the direct teaching here on how confusion, deluded thinking, and ongoing disappointment - Dukkha - originates in ignorance. From this initial ignorance - of Four Noble Truths - the feedback loop of self-referential views maintained by confused thinking continues. Also notice there is nothing in this sutta that could be seen as a creation myth or to suggest a doctrine of interdependence, inter-connectedness, or inter-being.

It is from a misunderstanding, misapplication, or complete dismissal of this fundamental sutta that resulted in contradictory and confusing alterations and adaptations to the Buddha's Dhamma.

The Buddha was at Savatthi, at Jeta's Grove, Anathapindika's monastery. There he addressed those assembled: "Friends, I will describe in detail Dependent Origination. Listen carefully. And what is Dependent Origination?

- From ignorance as a requisite condition come fabrications.

- From fabrications as a requisite condition comes consciousness.

- From consciousness as a requisite condition comes name-and-form.

- From name-and-form as a requisite condition comes the six sense-base.

- From the six sense-base as a requisite condition comes contact.

- From contact as a requisite condition comes feeling.

- From feeling as a requisite condition comes craving.

- From craving as a requisite condition comes clinging and maintaining.

- From clinging and maintaining as a requisite condition comes becoming.

- From becoming as a requisite condition comes birth.

- From birth as a requisite condition comes aging, sickness, death, sorrow, lamentation, pain, distress and despair."

Then the Buddha describes in slightly more detail, and in reverse order, each of the 12 links:

"Now what is aging and death? Aging is decrepitude, brokenness, graying, decline, weakening of faculties. Death is the passing away of the Five Clinging-Aggregates, the ending of time, the interruption in the life faculties.

"Now what is Birth? Birth is the descent, the coming forth, the coming to be. Birth is the appearance of the six sense-bases and the Five Clinging-Aggregates.

"Now what is becoming? Becoming is sensual becoming, form becoming and formless becoming."

This is explaining that the belief in a self is reinforced by sensory contact and is proliferated by believing in an individual sustainable personality being born, i.e.: becoming a permanent form. This belief is rooted in ignorance of the Four Noble Truths.

The Buddha is explaining becoming the personal experience of suffering - Five Clinging-Aggregates.

Becoming is further explained in the next chapter.

It is also ignorance of The Four Noble Truths to hold the belief that an ego-personality becomes formless at death but survives physical death as the same personality, either in an eternal formless state or being reborn as the same "soul."

Becoming, birth, sickness, old age, death and non-becoming is the environment of Dukkha caused by ignorance. The links of clinging, craving, feeling, contact, the six sense-base, name-and-form, consciousness and fabrications are all part of the process of a self arising from ignorance. This process is maintained by continued ignorance, furthering karma.

The Buddha then describes how clinging to the notion of self maintains this feedback loop of the six-sense base establishing a self and maintaining the cycle of birth, death and rebirth.

"And what is clinging and maintaining? There are four types of clinging: Clinging to sensory stimulus, clinging to views (conditioned thinking), clinging to precepts and practices, and clinging to a doctrine of self."

The Buddha is cautioning against developing or maintaining practices that are given validity simply from the "positive" feeling developed or the "positive" or commonly accepted views reinforced. Engaging in rituals or practices that continue a doctrine of self in any realm, physical or otherwise are to be recognized as rooted in ignorance and abandoned.

The Buddha here has taken a methodical route from the ultimate result of ignorance, suffering, back to the Second Noble Truth or the origination of individual contributions to Dukkha - craving and clinging. Along the way he describes what is clung to: a self that is dependent on continued craving and continued clinging to sensory stimulus to be maintained.

Profound understanding of any one of these links begins to unravel the entire causative chain. For example, a profound understanding that phenomena contacting senses develops feelings, and that feeling develops craving (for more self-affirming contact with worldly phenomena) brings dispassion for constant sensory stimulation.

This develops the understanding that contact framed by ignorance via sensory stimulus is the direct result of the belief in an ego-self, (name & form) and not an inevitable life experience.

Seeing this process clearly de-personalizes the life experience. From this understanding, life experience no longer will define and maintain an ego-personality.

The implications of this realization can be unsettling at first if one is engaging the Dhamma to "fix" a flawed self. There is nothing substantial to fix, or to actualize. What is impermanent and insubstantial is to be seen as such and simply abandoned.

Remember that what is abandoned when this process of I-making is interrupted is only a fabricated ego-

201

personality that is stuck in confusion and unsatisfactory experiences. Once understood the release from the burden of an ego-personality brings the continual experience of lasting peace and happiness.

It is also important to remember that the teachings on Dependent Origination are given to develop understanding of Four Noble Truths. Dependent Origination explains the process of how all personal phenomena arises so that understanding of the distraction of dukkha is understood. Dependent Origination teaches Right View while pointing out that holding wrong (ignorant) views is the cause of all confusion and suffering.

The establishment of anatta, an ego-personality, within an environment of anicca, resulting in the unsatisfactoriness and confusion of dukkha, is not an arbitrary or chaotic development from which there is no liberation.

There is no substantive difference between impermanence, individual confusion, and resulting individual suffering.

The Four Noble Truths are universal truths applicable to all human experience.

Understanding Dependent Origination within the context of The Four Noble Truths is the key to unbinding from the endless karmic entanglements caused by the desire to maintain an ego-self.

The Buddha describes how craving arises from feeling, and how feeling is caused by contact:

"And what is craving?

"There are six classes of craving: Craving for forms.

- Craving for sounds.

- Craving for smells.

- Craving for tastes.

- Craving for physical sensations.

- Craving for ideas.

    "And what is feeling?

    "Feeling has six classes as well:

- Feeling arising from eye-contact.

- Feeling arising from ear-contact.

- Feeling arising from nose-contact.

- Feeling arising from taste-contact.

- Feeling arising from body-contact.

- Feeling arising from intellect-contact.

  "This is called feeling.

  "And what is contact?

- Phenomena contacting the eye.

- Phenomena contacting the ear.

- Phenomena contacting the nose.

- Phenomena contacting the tongue.

- Phenomena contacting the body.

- Phenomena contacting the intellect.

  "This is contact with the six sense-base.

  "And what is name and form? Feeling.

- Perception.

- Intention.

- Attention (all mental aspects)

- Contact.

"Discriminating self-referential consciousness is name. The elements of water, fire, earth and wind, that which makes up physical forms is called form.

"Name-and-form is discriminating consciousness bound to or clinging to physical form.

"And what is consciousness?

"There are six classes of consciousness:

- Eye-consciousness.

- Ear-consciousness.

- Nose-consciousness.

- Tongue-consciousness.

- Body-consciousness.

- Intellect-consciousness.

Through the six-sense base contact with the world is made and mental fabrications, including objectifying a self-referential ego-self, is formed.

205

"And what are fabrications?

"There are three fabrications:

- Bodily fabrications.

- Verbal fabrications.

- Mental fabrications.

All three fabrications are caused by a wrong view of self. Fabrications result in a personality bound to physical form that is perceived as "I" or "me".

The Buddha describes ignorance:

"And what is ignorance?

- Ignorance is not knowing stress.

- Not knowing the origination of stress.

- Not knowing the cessation of stress.

- Not knowing the (Eightfold) path leading to the cessation of stress.

"This is called ignorance.

All confusion, deluded thinking, and ongoing disappointment and suffering - Dukkha - arise from ignorance of Four Noble Truths.

The Buddha relates Dependent Origination back to his first teaching, on Four Noble Truths, and teaches that from ignorance of Four Noble Truths comes all confusion and suffering.

Gaining understanding of The Four Noble Truths is wisdom. Wisdom brings an end to ignorance and an end to the distraction, confusion and suffering caused by ignorance. Wisdom brings an end to the delusion of an permanent, substantial, and sustainable self.

When all ignorance is abandoned awakening arises.

The Buddha continues:

"Now from the remainder-less fading & cessation of ignorance comes the cessation of fabrications.

"From the cessation of fabrications comes the cessation of consciousness.

"From the cessation of consciousness comes the cessation of name-and-form.

"From the cessation of name-and-form comes the cessation of the six sense-base.

"From the cessation of the six sense-base comes the cessation of contact.

"From the cessation of contact comes the cessation of feeling.

"From the cessation of feeling comes the cessation of craving.

"From the cessation of craving comes the cessation of clinging and maintaining.

"From the cessation of clinging and maintaining comes the cessation of becoming.

"From the cessation of becoming comes the cessation of birth.

"From the cessation of birth comes the cessation of sickness, aging, death, sorrow, pain, distress, despair and confusion. Wisdom brings the cessation to the entire mass of stress and suffering.

End of Sutta

The Eightfold Path is a path that develops heightened wisdom, heightened virtue and heightened concentration. All three qualities of mind are requisite conditions to end ignorance. Developing these three qualities through the guidance and framework of the Eightfold Path creates the conditions for the cessation of ignorance.

Dependent Origination describes the ongoing process rooted in ignorance that fabricates an ego-personality and how an ego-personality, how anatta, is maintained by craving and clinging. This is perhaps the most significant difference between the Buddha's teachings and religious and philosophical systems, including most later-developed Buddhist schools.

A modern example of this is the misunderstanding and misapplication of Dependent Origination used to develop a doctrine of interdependence, interconnectedness, and inter-being between individual and insubstantial ego-personality's. These modern doctrines only encourage and maintain craving and clinging.

All human beings are "connected" through the common problem of delusion and suffering. This is described as The First Noble Truth. On an elemental level all things in the universe share common characteristics.

All things are impermanent, insubstantial, and unsustainable - including whatever may be interconnected. Creating something more of this simple fact such as doctrines of universal interdependence, interconnectedness, and inter-being leads to contradictory and confusing doctrines that perpetuates clinging and furthers "I-making."

Notice that there is no actual beginning in time or birth of a "soul" or any individual entity. Dependent Origination is not a creation myth. The process of becoming an ego-self begins in ignorance, produces delusion and suffering, and (the process) can be brought to cessation through wisdom and understanding.

The single issue is ignorance. What occurred prior to ignorance is speculative distraction. What might occur post ignorance is speculative distraction. This type of speculative distraction arises from "Inappropriate views not fit for attention. These views will continue to generate confusion and suffering."

Much of the mystical aspects and contradictions of modern Buddhism developed to provide establishment for this type of speculation and resulting distraction.

Wrong views are formed and deluded beliefs created to provide substance to what is inherently insubstantial. Having arisen from ignorance, only continued ignorance can sustain ignorance and perpetuate Dukkha.

Dependent Origination shows that from a wrong or ignorant view the manifestation of an ego-personality is fabricated. Fabricated, the process of continued fabrication can be brought to an end.

It is within an impermanent environment that a sense-based and sensory-sustained consciousness arises. Here stress arises as consciousness continually struggles to maintain a permanent and substantial view of self. It requires constant vigilance and continual fabrication to maintain the establishment of an ego-self. It is the stress of maintaining wrong views that distracts from recognizing the mirage-like nature of these views.

Through understanding Dependent Origination it is seen that clinging to a view of self occurs. Keeping

211

this self comfortable, safe, engaged, and continually established then becomes the sole purpose for existence.

Maintaining wrong views is continual distraction. Maintaining wrong views is continual dukkha.

From clinging and maintaining as a requisite condition comes becoming (ignorant).

From the cessation of clinging and maintaining comes the cessation of becoming (ignorant).

The Eightfold Path provides the framework and Right View for observing and interrupting Dependent Origination. In order to see this process clearly any notion of "I" or "me" of being the ignorant individual that begins Dependent Origination must be abandoned.

This is another convenient form of self-establishment, of "I-making."

Here is a seeming paradox: The ongoing ignorance of an ego-self must be recognized and abandoned through the development of wisdom. It is also wrong view to conclude that it is an ego-self that is gaining wisdom. There is nothing substantial or sustainable to gain wisdom. The views of an ego-self are rooted in ignorance.

Ignorance or the products of ignorance can never give rise to wisdom, to understanding.

Awakening occurs when ignorance of Four Noble Truths is supplanted by the profound knowledge of origination of Dukkha and the experience of cessation of Five Clinging-Aggregates.

The developed skills of concentration and mindfulness and the ongoing direction and guidance of the Eightfold Path diminishes "I-making" or conceit. It is from this perspective that Dependent Origination can be usefully and effectively understood.

The Buddha was asked on one occasion "is the one who acts the same one who experiences the result of an act?" (Notice the self-identification in the question)

The Buddha responds "To say the one who acts is the one who experiences is one extreme. To say the one who acts is someone other than the one who experiences is the other extreme." (This is the belief in outside forces such as creation, reward, or punishment bringing individual experiences.)

The Buddha continues: "I teach the Dhamma from the middle, a middle way. I avoid those extreme views and teach that (individual) ignorance brings all manner of delusion and suffering. Whoever declares that pleasure and pain are self made, whoever declares that pleasure and pain are other made, are deluded. All experiences are dependent on contact and contact is (initially) dependent on ignorance." (Samyutta Nikaya 22.46)

This brings up another contradictory teaching of later-developed Buddhist schools that misunderstand or misapply Dependent Origination. The ego-self, anatta, has no "inherent nature." There is no Buddhahood or Buddha-Nature for the ego-self to aspire to. This doctrine creates confusion and further establishment of the ego-self. If there is an inner Buddhahood or Buddha-Nature how could it succumb to utter ignorance? These are simply deluded doctrines rooted in ignorance.

It is the ego-self that has no substantial nature. Developing understanding of what is perceived to be an ego-self is paramount so that all attempts at continuing to establish anatta - Five Clinging-Aggregates - are abandoned.

There is nothing in the Buddha's teachings that support the notion of an inner Buddha-Nature or doctrinal "inter-being." Once awakened, a human being is free of craving, clinging, delusion and ongoing suffering. This includes clinging the ego-self to an imaginary idea of an inner, obscure, Buddha-Nature.

All human beings have the potential to awaken, to develop full human maturity. This does not imply an inherent Buddha-Nature. It does show that awakening is possible to anyone who can recognize and abandon all self-referential views including that establish an inherent Buddha-Nature or Buddhahood.

This is what the Buddha taught. Being free of all clinging views is lasting peace and contentment. This is enough!

To reiterate, I am not disparaging later-developed teachings. I am providing clarity as to what the Buddha taught and in the context that he presented his Dhamma.

In the Simsapa Sutta the Buddha explains the refined purpose of the Dhamma: "And what have I taught? 'I teach the nature of dukkha (stress). I teach the origination of dukkha (craving and clinging originate dukkha). I teach that cessation of dukkha is possible. I teach that The Eightfold Path is the path leading to the cessation of dukkha: This is what I have taught. " (Samyutta Nikaya 56.31)

The Buddha describes the insubstantiality of the mental/physical form in the Dhammapada, v.46 as "Having known this body likened unto foam and understanding thoroughly its nature is mirage-like"

Any establishment of a self in any inner or exterior realm including clinging to the notion of an inner Buddha-Nature or Buddhahood is clinging to a mirage.

Dependent Origination shows that continued confusion and suffering is dependent on continued ignorance. Dukkha originates in a series of 12 "dependencies" rooted in ignorance. Developing wisdom and understanding through the Eightfold Path brings an end to ignorance. This is how one Becomes Buddha.

Shamatha-Vipassana meditation is very effective in interrupting the compulsion to continually maintain ignorance and the establishment of an ego-personality.

Mindfulness of the breath settles the mind and develops deep and skillful concentration. As distraction lessens and non-distraction develops it becomes possible to observe Dependent Origination as it occurs.

Useful insight is insight into the formation of self-referential, impermanent, ego-self-sustaining views arising from ignorance.

Aversion to the Dhamma often arises as the Dhamma points directly to seeing clearly the insubstantial nature of self. All manner of adaptations and accommodations have been made to the Buddha's original teachings to avoid this aversion. These general hindrances are included in the chapter on Hindrances. Hindrances arise from the ego-personality's need to continually establish and maintain its existence in every object, event, view, and idea that occurs.

Hindrances are also an important aspect of the Satipatthana Sutta, the sutta on the Four Foundations of Mindfulness presented further on. The Buddha recognized the tendency of an ignorant mind to develop strategies to avoid his Dhamma and substitute anything that allows for continuation of ignorant wrong views.

Ignoring hindrances to the Buddha's Dhamma continues ignorance. The refined mindfulness taught by the Buddha brings recognition of all hindrances. The refined mindfulness taught by the Buddha brings recognition of the confusion, deluded thinking, and ongoing suffering that originates in, and is dependent on, ignorance.

Becoming Explained

The Loka, Bhava, and Mula Suttas

There is much confusion as to the meaning of "becoming." Due to this confusion great license is taken in interpreting what is meant by becoming as taught by the Buddha. This confusion and the following misapplication of the Dhamma can be avoided by simply looking at the Buddha's own words from the following three sutta's.

Depending on the context, becoming can refer to immediately giving birth to another moment rooted in ignorance. This can only continue confusion, deluded thinking, and suffering - continued becoming a "self" prone to suffering.

In the context of remaining ignorant and future becoming, becoming refers to the becoming that would cause a future birth, lacking present self-identification, but continuing the experience of suffering rooted in ignorance. Continuing the impersonal experience of suffering does not establish a "permanent self." Continuity obscures impermanence but does not negate impermanence.

In the overall context of impermanence and the arising and passing away of all phenomena, becoming and non-becoming refers to the arising - becoming - and the passing away - non-becoming - of self-identifying with stress.

Consciousness rooted in ignorance and influenced by the five physical senses can only reinforce deluded wrong views. The Eightfold Path is developed to interrupt the ongoing process of becoming.

Rooted in ignorance one can only become increasingly ignorant.

By developing the Eightfold Path the Dhamma practitioner becomes awakened.

By developing the Eightfold Path the Dhamma practitioner Becomes Buddha.

It is for this reason that the Buddha taught an Eightfold Path.

Consciousness rooted in ignorance "conditions" thinking in such a way that continually either ignores or clings to suffering as described in the Loka Sutta: "The world is aflame. Rooted in ignorance the world is afflicted by sensory contact and perceives suffering as 'self.' Rooted in ignorance, it misunderstands 'self' and becomes anything other than 'self.'

221

Loka Sutta

Samyutta Nikaya 12.44

The newly awakened Siddartha, now Buddha, was enjoying the peace of release. Established in concentration he observed the world around him. He noticed human beings aflame with the fires born of the defilements of passion, aversion, and deluded consciousness.

Realizing the significance of what he was seeing he thought:

"The world is aflame. Rooted in ignorance the world is afflicted by sensory contact and perceives suffering as 'self.' Rooted in ignorance, it misunderstands 'self' and becomes anything other than 'self.'

Reaction to suffering - any unsatisfactory experience - personalizes what is inherently impersonal. As the self-identification is to what has already occurred, self-

223

identification is to a fabrication that is not what is present. Lacking understanding of the impermanence of all things - the arising and the passing away - what is being held in mind, what one is mindful of, is of a fabricated representation of "self" already "passed away."

"Becoming anything other than self, the world clings to becoming, is afflicted by becoming, and yet delights in that very becoming. Where there is delight there is fear. Where there is fear there is stress.

Craving for anything other than what is occurring creates a self-referential view clinging to what is desired rather than understanding the impersonal arising and passing away of ordinary occurrences. This is the onset of deluded thinking.

Fear arises from clinging to what is delightful and fearing the loss of what is delightful. Consequently, self-identifying with disappointment then leads to the fear that unpleasant experiences won't end, or may re-occur. Craving/aversion then becomes ongoing distraction from the constant reestablishment of a fabricated self. This is the onset of confusion.

"The life integrated with the Eightfold Path is lived for the abandoning of becoming. Those that say that escape from becoming is by becoming are never released from becoming, I declare. Those that say that escape from becoming is by non-becoming are never released from becoming, I declare.

Believing that the escape from becoming is by (further) becoming is the underlying motivation to establish an inner Buddha-Nature or Buddhahood - exchanging a permanent view of an inferior self for a permanent view of a superior self.

Any attempt at establishing a self rooted in ignorance through transference (or transformation) is further becoming of an ignorant self.

The desire for escaping becoming by non-becoming is the same as the belief in the conceptual applications of emptiness or nothingness common in some forms of modern Buddhism.

Believing that the escape from becoming is by becoming or by non-becoming is also the feedback loop the Buddha describes in the Nagara Sutta - self-referential views feeding back on ongoing thinking rooted in ignorance.

"Stress (Dukkha) arises in dependence on becoming 'self.' With the ending of clinging to 'self' and maintaining 'self,' no stress will arise.

"Look at the world: Human beings afflicted with ignorance crave for and cling to becoming. All forms of becoming, anywhere, in any way, are impermanent, stressful, always subject to change.

"Knowing this - the arising and the passing away - from Right View craving for becoming and non-becoming is abandoned.

The arising and the passing away refers to all phenomena. All phenomena are impermanent including the phenomenon of "self." As the Buddha teaches in the Anatta-Lakkhana Sutta further on: "Now what is impermanent, what is painful since subject to change, is not fit to be regarded as: 'This is mine, this is I, this is my self'?"

"From the abandonment of craving for becoming and non-becoming comes unbinding. For those unbound from lack of clinging and maintaining there is no further becoming. They have conquered ignorance, completed the task, and have gone beyond becoming (a self rooted in ignorance)."

End of Sutta

Once self-referential views are recognized and abandoned, there can be no initiating reaction rooted in ignorance that becomes a fabricated self. Once self-referential views are recognized and abandoned whatever arises and passes away is experienced impersonally with mindful presence of what is occurring but with dispassion - without the fires of passion.

Bhava Sutta

Anguttara Nikaya 3.76

Even during the Buddha's time there was confusion regarding the meaning of becoming. Here, Ananda, the Buddha's cousin and chief attendant asks for clarity:

On one occasion Ananda went to the Buddha, bowed, and sat to one side. He was unsure of the meaning of becoming and so asked the Buddha, "Becoming, becoming, to what extent is there becoming?"

"Ananda, if there were no karma ripening within the feeling-property, would the feeling-property be noticed?"

Karma is the present unfolding of past intentional actions moderated by the present quality of mindfulness. The "feeling-property," "form-property," and the "formless-property" relates to the Five Clinging-Aggregates. The

229

form/formless-property also relates to the arising and passing away of stress. Karma and rebirth is explained in detail further on.

"No, wise teacher."

"In this way karma is the field, consciousness the seed, and craving the moisture. The consciousness of human beings rooted in ignorance and bound by craving is established in wrong view. Established in wrong view, renewed becoming is produced.

"If there is no karma ripening in the form-property, would the form-property be noticed?"

This one sentence contains the implication of the entire Dhamma. With no karma left to "ripen" there are no self-referential views clinging to form. With no self-referential views remaining - no self-identity clinging to impermanent phenomena - the form-property now is simply a reference point for life mindfully and dispassionately unfolding.

"No, wise teacher."

"In this way karma is the field, consciousness the seed, and craving the moisture. The consciousness of human beings rooted in ignorance and bound by craving is established in wrong view. Established in wrong view, renewed becoming is produced.

"If there is no karma ripening in the formless-property, would the formless-property be noticed?"

"No, wise teacher."

"In this way karma is the field, consciousness the seed, and craving the moisture. The consciousness of human beings rooted in ignorance and bound by craving is established in wrong view. Established in wrong view (ignorance), renewed becoming is produced."

With past intentional actions (karma) providing the environment for ongoing thinking (consciousness) rooted in ignorance of Four Noble Truths and sustained - given sustenance - by craving, one can only "become" continually subject to confusion, deluded thinking, and ongoing disappointing and unsatisfactory experiences - dukkha.

End of Sutta

This sutta also points to what for many is another confusing aspect of the Dhamma: Is it not craving/desire to desire awakening? This is simply a wrong view giving rise to another extreme view. The brilliance of the Buddha is his realization that in order to overcome the common human problem of conditioned thinking - ongoing "consciousness" rooted in ignorance of Four Noble Truths - there would need to be a way - a "path" - that would provide the framework to recognize conditioned thinking *within* conditioned thinking.

The only way to recognize and abandon deluded thinking is to have a framework that supports recognition. The Eightfold Path is the framework for recognizing and abandoning deluded thinking.

Right Intention, the second factor of the Eightfold Path, is holding the intention - being mindful of the intention - to recognize and abandon craving and clinging rooted in ignorance. Right Intention can be seen as desire but it is certainly skillful desire as intention determines the direction and ultimate conclusion of one's Dhamma practice.

This is the purpose of the entire Middle Way Eightfold Path. The refined mindfulness of the Eightfold Path, mindfully framed by Right View and given direction by Right Intention. Right Speech, Right Action, and Right Livelihood provide the focused perspective for recognizing craving and clinging. The concentration developed through Right Effort, Right Mindfulness, and Right Meditation - Shamatha-Vipassana meditation - brings the ability to recognize the feedback loop of self-referential views.

Wholehearted engagement with the Eightfold Path inclines the mind towards becoming awakened, towards Becoming Buddha.

The problem of becoming awakened while continuing to be affected by conditioned mind is resolved by developing the framework of the Eightfold Path for one's Dhamma practice, and one's life. This is illustrated in the Mula Sutta in the following chapter.

Mula Sutta

Anguttara Nikaya 10.58

In this sutta the Buddha asks the assembled monks a rhetorical question:

"Monks, if those of other sects ask you 'In what are all phenomena rooted? How do they come into play? What is their origination? What is their establishment? What is their authority? What is their governing principle? What is their surpassing state? What is their heartwood? Where do they gain footing? What is their cessation?

"On being asked this you should reply:

- All phenomena are rooted in desire.

- All phenomena come into play through attention.

- All phenomena have contact as their origination.

- All phenomena have feeling as their establishment.

- All phenomena have directed thought for their foundation.

- All phenomena have mindfulness as their governing principle.

- All phenomena have discernment as their defining state.

- All phenomena have release as their heartwood.

- All phenomena gain footing in impermanence.

- All phenomena have unbinding as their cessation.

"On being asked this is how you should reply."

End of Sutta

"All phenomena rooted in desire" refers to the Five Clinging-Aggregates, the personal experience of dukkha. Dukkha is established and maintained through attention, contact, feeling, and directed thought. These first five statements relate to the First and Second Noble Truth.

The two statements "All phenomena have mindfulness as their governing principle" and "All phenomena have discernment as their defining state" refers to the potential of each moment.

If what is being held in mind is rooted in ignorance, ignorance will govern the moment. From ignorance one can only become increasingly ignorant. If discernment is rooted in ignorance, ignorance will define a state of mind continually prone to becoming ignorant.

These two statements also point to the possibility of the cessation of dukkha - the Third Noble Truth - cessation of Dukkha is possible. Mindfulness framed by the Eightfold Path will govern the moment and incline the mind towards release. Wise discernment developed through the Eightfold Path will define a spacious and supple mind able to fully awaken.

The final three lines describe how the "heartwood" of the Eightfold Path interrupts conditioned thinking rooted in ignorance and thriving on desire. Once interrupted, the Eightfold Path leads to complete release from clinging to ignorance. The last three statements refer to the Fourth Noble Truth.

This process begins within conditioned, clinging mind - Five Clinging-Aggregates. Through the Eightfold Path refined mindfulness and wise discernment develop. Right View brings the ability to recognize and abandon all self-referential views that would otherwise keep one stuck in the feedback loop the Buddha describes in the Nagara Sutta.

"Becoming" points to the potential inherent in each moment. Each moment holds the potential to continue ignorance and ignore Four Noble Truths and become continually subject to confusion, deluded thinking, and ongoing stress. Each moment also holds the potential to develop the Eightfold Path and become awakened, Become Buddha.

Five Clinging-Aggregates, The Personal Experience of Stress

The Five Clinging-Aggregates are:

- Form.

- Feelings.

- Perceptions.

- Mental Fabrications.

- Consciousness.

Consciousness in this context is ongoing thinking rooted in ignorance of Four Noble Truths. The Five Clinging-Aggregates become the personal experience of confusion, deluded thinking, and ongoing stress due to ignorance of Four Noble Truths.

Most modern forms of Buddhism dismiss the primary importance of understanding Five Clinging-Aggregates. This is due to the difficulty of understanding the Aggregates without the context of Dependent Origination and Four Noble Truths.

A mind rooted in ignorance insists on ignoring anything that would challenge ignorance.

The difficulty in understanding the aggregates is due to the self-referential nature of confused and deluded thinking as described by the Buddha in the Nagara Sutta, and elsewhere. When seen in the proper context, understanding Five Clinging-Aggregates as the personal experience of Dukkha brings release from clinging to ignorant views.

The Five Clinging-Aggregates are a recurring theme as it is skillful to develop understanding of the aggregates in different, but similar contexts.

In the Arahant Sutta the Buddha describes gaining awakening - Arahantship - by understanding the aggregates as they really are.

In the Phena Sutta the Buddha teaches that the aggregates are "empty" of any substantiality and are merely impermanent phenomena arising and passing away.

Arahant Sutta
Putting Down The Burden

Samyutta Nikaya 22.110

The Arahant Sutta is a succinct teaching where the Buddha describes awakening, full human maturity, that is remarkable in its simplicity, straightforwardness, and primary importance:

The Arahant Sutta

"When one has seen the Five Clinging-Aggregates as they really are, the arising and the passing away, understanding the attraction and the danger, the distraction, seeing the arising of desire and the continued delusion, and being delivered from the Five Clinging-Aggregates, this one is released from clinging. All defilements   are destroyed, what must be done has been done, perfection is attained, the burden has been put down, the highest goal attained. This one is liberated by perfect insight."

End of Sutta

Seeing the "Five Clinging-Aggregates as they really are" is understanding Anatta, not-self, a self-referential ego-personality, in relation to Anicca and Dukkha and in the context of Dependent Origination and Four Noble Truths. It is from a wrong understanding of self clinging to the impermanent environment of human life that all stress and suffering arises.

There is much confusion arising from the concept of not-self. The Buddha never taught nothingness or emptiness as a conceptual environment that is empty yet somehow contains a "self." This singular contradiction allows for the dismissal of "seeing the Five Clinging-Aggregates as they really are."

Lacking this understanding there is no possibility to be "liberated by perfect insight." The

244

opportunity to achieve Arahantship - awakening - is lost and other "paths" substituted for the Eightfold Path.

The Buddha taught that what is commonly believed to be a substantial and permanently identifiable-as-me self is born of ignorance and sustained by continued ignorance. He taught that what is perceived of a self is not a self and all deluded views that sustain this belief must be let go of if one is to develop awakening, develop full human maturity.

What is often overlooked is the Buddha continually points to a "one that awakens" as he does repeatedly in this single paragraph. What is this "one that is released from clinging?"

An understanding of the true nature of self arises once all concepts of self that have formed from ignorance of The Four Noble Truths are recognized and put aside.

The perfect example of "one that awakened" is the Buddha. Through Right Understanding he awakened and he continued as the Buddha, providing a way of awakening that has survived 2,600 years.

Upon awakening he did not "become" anything tainted by ignorance. He Became Buddha.

An awakened mind is attainable by anyone who hears and develops the dhamma. Awakening occurs when ignorance is replaced by wisdom.

A deluded mind is only capable of creating more delusion until the skillful direction of the Eightfold Path is engaged with. Conditioned wrong views can be released. Releasing wrong views is creating spaciousness in a mind once confined by continued clinging.

Clinging one self-referential thought immediately to the next clinging self-referential thought is interrupted. As delusional concepts are interrupted, the opportunity for useful insight arises. The Buddha taught an Eightfold Path for developing perfect insight and a calm and liberated mind.

Upon his awakening the Buddha considered if teaching his understanding would be effective. His concern was how to overcome the common and pervasive problem of human conditioned thinking. How could he explain the problem of continual clinging to deluded views?

He taught an Eightfold Path to provide a framework to interrupt conditioned thinking.

He taught an Eightfold Path to develop useful insight into the nature of suffering.

He taught an Eightfold Path to develop recognition and renunciation of craving and clinging.

He taught an Eightfold Path to interrupt and abandon the ongoing process of maintaining the confusion, deluded thinking, and ongoing Dukkha experienced as Five Clinging-Aggregates.

From great compassion informed by profound wisdom, the Buddha taught an Eightfold Path so that others could achieve what he had achieved - Become Buddha.

Phena Sutta
Emptiness of Five Clinging-Aggregates

Samyutta Nikaya 22.95

The Phena Sutta is another sutta on emptiness as the Buddha uses the term. In this sutta he teaches the emptiness of Five Clinging Aggregates. He teaches the emptiness of creating self-identities by clinging to fleeting objects, events, views and ideas. The Buddha teaches the emptiness of perceptions rooted in ignorance - like foam on the river or a drop of water.

He teaches the emptiness of magical teachings. He teaches the ignorance necessary to follow mirages - the futility of following "dharmas" lacking the true heartwood of his Dhamma.

This sutta follows from what the Buddha awakened to. The Buddha awakened to Dependent Origination. Dependent Origination shows that from ignorance of Four Noble Truths, through twelve observable causative links, all manner of confusion, deluded thinking, and ongoing disappointing and unsatisfactory experiences follow.

To restate from the introduction to this section:

The Five Clinging-Aggregates are:

- Form.

- Feelings.

- Perceptions.

- Mental Fabrications.

- Consciousness.

Consciousness in this context is ongoing thinking rooted in ignorance of Four Noble Truths. The Five Clinging-Aggregates become the personal experience of confusion, deluded thinking, and ongoing stress due to ignorance of Four Noble Truths.

The Five Clinging-Aggregates are "empty" of wisdom and understanding.

The Buddha's entire teaching is always in the context of Four Noble Truths. The Eightfold Path is the path the Buddha taught to recognize and abandon all self-referential views arising from ignorance - to become empty of ignorance of Four Noble Truths.

The reference to "appropriately or clearly examining" or "clearly seeing" impermanent phenomena arising and passing is observing life unfolding from the refined mindfulness of the framework and guidance of the Eightfold Path.

The concentration developed through Shamatha-Vipassana meditation is the foundation for appropriately examining. The refined mindfulness framed by the Eightfold Path is the quality of mind necessary to appropriately examine.

The Phena Sutta

The Buddha was staying with the Avojjhans on the banks of the Ganges River. He addressed those assembled:

"Friends, suppose that a large glob of foam were floating down the river, and a person with good eyesight saw it and clearly examined it. To them it would appear empty, void, without any substance. For what substance could there be in glob of foam?

"In the same way, any practitioner well-versed in the Dhamma observes and appropriately examines any form that is past, future, or present, any form that is internal or external, obvious or subtle, common or extraordinary, near or far.

"To those well-versed in the Dhamma it would appear empty, void, without any substance. For what substance could there be in form that is constantly changing?

This is in reference to the "form" aggregate. "Constantly changing" is a reference to the impermanence of all forms.

"Now suppose that in the rainy season it is raining fat heavy drops and a water bubble appears and disappears on the water. A person with good eyesight sees this and clearly examines it. The water bubble would appear empty, void, and without substance. For what substance could there be in a water bubble?

"In the same way any practitioner well-versed in the Dhamma observes and appropriately examines any feeling that is past, future, or present, any feeling that is internal or external, obvious or subtle, common or extraordinary, near or far.

"To those well-versed in the Dhamma it would appear empty, void, without substance. For what substance could there be in feelings that are constantly changing?

This is in reference to the "feeling" aggregate.

"Now suppose during the hot season a mirage was shimmering. A person with good eyesight sees it and clearly examines it. The mirage would appear empty, void, and without substance. For what substance could there be in a mirage that is constantly changing?

"In the same way any practitioner well-versed in the Dhamma observes and appropriately examines any perception that is past, future, or present, any perception that is internal or external, obvious or subtle, common or extraordinary, near or far.

"To those well versed in the Dhamma it would appear empty, void, without substance. For what substance could there be in perceptions that are constantly changing?

253

This is in reference to the "perception" aggregate.

"Now suppose that a person with good eyesight is seeking heartwood? In seeking heartwood they went to a forest with a sharp ax. There they find a large banana tree. They cut it at the root and remove the top. They peel away the outer skin and fail to find even sapwood, to say nothing of finding heartwood.

"Having good eyesight they clearly examine the banana tree. The tree would appear empty, void, without substance. With regard to heartwood for what substance (heartwood) could there be in a banana tree?

"In the same way any practitioner well-versed in the Dhamma observes and appropriately examines any fabrications that are past, future, or present, any feeling that is internal or external, obvious or subtle, common or extraordinary, near or far.

"To those well-versed in the Dhamma fabrications would appear empty, void, without substance. For what substance could there be in fabrications that are constantly changing?

This is in reference to the "fabrication" aggregate.

"Now suppose a magician were to display a magic trick and a person with good eyesight clearly sees the trick. The trick would appear empty, void, without substance. For what substance could there be in a magic trick?

"In the same way any practitioner well-versed in the Dhamma observes and appropriately examines any consciousness that is past, future, or present, any consciousness that is internal or external, obvious or subtle, common or extraordinary, near or far.

"To those well-versed in the Dhamma any consciousness (ongoing thinking rooted in ignorance) would appear empty, void, without substance. For what substance could there be in consciousness (that is impermanent and rooted in ignorance of Four Noble Truths)?

This is in reference to the "consciousness" aggregate.

"Seeing these Five Aggregates clearly, the well instructed follower of the dhamma grows disenchanted with form, they grow disenchanted with feelings, disenchanted with perception, disenchanted with fabrications, and disenchanted with thinking rooted in ignorance.

"They grow disenchanted with The Five Clinging-Aggregates.

"Disenchanted they grow dispassionate. Through dispassion they are released. With release there is the knowledge that they are released (from clinging to ignorant views).

"They know that birth is ended, the fully integrated life has been lived, and the path complete. They know here will be no more moments rooted in ignorance. *The Buddha concludes this sutta with verse:*

Form is like a glob of foam;

Feeling, a bubble;

Perception, a mirage;

Fabrications, a banana tree;

Consciousness, a magician's trick;

When you observe them

and appropriately examine them

It is clear they are empty, void,

and without substance.

To anyone who sees them clearly

they are empty of ignorance.

Beginning with the body

when seen with profound discernment

as taught by the Buddha

Form is rejected, cast aside.

When bereft of wrong views,

The emptiness of form

is seen clearly like a magic trick,

an idiot's babbling.

No substance is found here.

A well-informed Dhamma practitioner,

their persistence aroused,

Should continually view the aggregates

mindful and alert.

They should discard greed, aversion,

and deluded thinking,

and make themselves their own refuge.

They should take to the dhamma as if

their head was on fire

In hopes of gaining nibbana.

End of Sutta

Mindfully observing and appropriately examining clinging to ignorant views allows one to continually view the aggregates clearly and to take true refuge in a mind that is now Becoming Buddha.

The Buddha's First Three Discourses

The Buddha presented these first three discourses within the first two months of his awakening. These first three discourses contain the contextual foundation for the Buddha's Dhamma. There is a significant relationship to these three discourses, Dependent Origination, Five Clinging-Aggregates, and the Three Marks of Existence.

The Buddha's very first teaching - The Dhammacakkappavattana Sutta - is the foundational teaching that the Buddha's entire teaching career rests on. As such, it refers to the direct result of ignorance - Dukkha - and all Three Marks of Existence. It is also a direct teaching on impermanence and the potential within impermanence to develop the Dhamma and "Rightly Self-Awaken," to Become Buddha.

The Anatta-Lakkhana Sutta explains how a wrong view of self arises and how the interrelationship between this wrong view of self within an ever-changing environment results in ongoing suffering.

The Adittapariyaya Sutta - The Fire Discourse - using a group of fire worshippers as metaphor - explains how the "fires" of passion give rise to ongoing disappointment.

Four Noble Truths
Dhammacakkappavattana Sutta

Samyutta Nikaya 56.11

The First Noble Truth states that human life is characterized by stress and suffering - Dukkha occurs. Many, lacking understanding of the purpose of the Buddha's teachings, consider the initial focus on suffering to infer that the Buddha taught a pessimistic or even nihilistic Dhamma.

Unlike the foolish notion that one should only "focus on the positive," the Buddha was being realistic in focusing the mind (refined mindfulness) on the true nature of life in an ever-changing world.

Due to ignorance of Four Noble Truths, Dukkha occurs. To repeat a theme - everything the Buddha taught during his forty-   five year teaching career was taught in this context. The Buddha taught Four Noble Truths to recognize and abandon individual contributions suffering. Developing Right View is developing a realistic view that "positive" thinking hopes to ignore.

For a few weeks after the Buddha awakened he considered if it was possible to teach what he now understood to others. As described in the Nagara Sutta, he knew the difficulty of becoming stuck in the feedback loop of self-referential views and thinking rooted in ignorance.

How could he teach reality to confused and deluded minds?

How could he describe suffering being dependent on and originating in ignorance?

Was there a way, a path, that could lead individuals from ignorance to wisdom?

He decided to present the truth of his understanding as Four Noble Truths that would first describe the result of ignorance. As a consequence of having a human life, Dukkha occurs.

He would teach that craving originates an unsatisfactory life experience and clinging continues Dukkha - the Second Noble Truth.

Notice the relation the Second Noble Truth has to Dependent Origination and craving and clinging/maintaining as the requisite for becoming. Clinging/maintaining is required to continue the process of becoming a self prone to confusion, deluded thinking, and ongoing disappointment.

The Third Noble Truth he would teach that it is possible to end ignorance of these truths and so end craving, clinging, and the resulting unsatisfactory life experience.

The Fourth and final truth he would teach is the truth of the path that develops profound wisdom and unwavering concentration. A non-distracted supports refined mindfulness framed by the Eightfold Path. Refined mindfulness supports the wisdom necessary to overcome conditioned thinking and end ignorance.

The path the Buddha taught is the Eightfold Path. He taught the Eightfold Path to pierce the veil of ignorance and to overcome the common human problem of conditioned thinking.

The Dhammacakkappavattana Sutta

Setting the Wheel of Truth in Motion

The Buddha's First Discourse

The Buddha was staying at Varanasi. There he addressed the group of five friends from his travels, all seeking understanding:

"There are these two extremes that are not to be indulged in by one who has gone forth seeking understanding. Which two? That extreme that is devoted to sensual pleasure with reference to sensual objects. This extreme is base, vulgar, common, ignoble, unprofitable.

"Also, the extreme that is devoted to self-affliction and self-denial. This extreme is painful, ignoble, unprofitable. Avoiding both of these extremes, the middle way is realized by the Tathagata, a rightly self-awakened one, that produces vision and knowledge and develops a calm mind.

'This middle way develops direct knowledge and to self-awakening. This middle way develops unbinding.

"And what is the middle way that produces vision, produces knowledge, and develops a calm mind, a path to direct knowledge, to self-awakening, to Unbinding?

"Precisely this Noble Eightfold Path: Right View, Right Intention, Right Speech, Right Action, Right Livelihood, Right Effort, Right Mindfulness, Right Meditation.

"This is the middle way that produces vision, produces knowledge, and develops a calm mind. A path to direct knowledge, to self-awakening, to Unbinding.

"Now this, friends, is the noble truth of stress: Birth is stressful, aging is stressful, death is stressful; sorrow, regret, pain, distress, and despair are stressful; association with the undesired is stressful, separation from what is desired is stressful, not getting what is wanted is stressful.

265

"In short, the Five Clinging-Aggregates are stressful.

"And this, friends, is the noble truth of the origination of stress: the craving that makes for further becoming, craving accompanied by passion and delight, clinging now here and now there, i.e., craving for sensual pleasure, craving for becoming, craving for non-becoming.

"And this, friends, is the noble truth of the cessation of stress: the remainderless fading and cessation, renunciation, relinquishment, release, and letting go of that very craving.

"And this, friends, is the noble truth of the way of practice leading to the cessation of stress: precisely this Noble Eightfold Path: Right View, Right Resolve, Right Speech, Right Action, Right Livelihood, Right Effort, Right Mindfulness, Right Meditation.

"Vision arose, insight arose, discernment arose, knowledge arose, illumination arose within me with regard to things never heard before: 'This is the noble truth of stress.'

"Vision arose, insight arose, discernment arose, knowledge arose, illumination arose within me with regard to things never heard before: 'This noble truth of stress is to be comprehended.'

"Vision arose, insight arose, discernment arose, knowledge arose, illumination arose within me with regard to things never heard before: This noble truth of stress has been comprehended.'

The Eightfold Path can be seen as a way of developing the skills of concentration and refined mindfulness in a supportive framework so that certain tasks can be accomplished.

Fully comprehending stress is the tasked associated with the First Noble Truth.

"Vision arose, insight arose, discernment arose, knowledge arose, illumination arose within me with regard to things never heard before: 'This is the noble truth of the origination of stress' 'This noble truth of the origination of stress is to be abandoned' 'This noble truth of the origination of stress has been abandoned.'

Recognizing and abandoning craving and clinging is the task associated with The Second Noble Truth.

"Vision arose, insight arose, discernment arose, knowledge arose, illumination arose within me with

267

regard to things never heard before: 'This is the noble truth of the cessation of stress'... 'This noble truth of the cessation of stress is to be directly experienced'... 'This noble truth of the cessation of stress has been directly experienced.'

Developing the direct experience of the cessation of stress is the task associated with The Third Noble Truth.

"Vision arose, insight arose, discernment arose, knowledge arose, illumination arose within me with regard to things never heard before: 'This is the noble truth of the way of practice leading to the cessation of stress'... 'This noble truth of the way of practice leading to the cessation of stress is to be developed'... 'This noble truth of the way of practice leading to the cessation of stress has been developed.'

Developing fully the Eightfold Path is the task associated to The Fourth Noble Truth.

"And, friends, as long as my knowledge and vision concerning these Four Noble Truths as they have come to be was not pure, I did not claim to have rightly self-awakened. But as soon as my knowledge and vision concerning these Four Noble Truths as they have come to be was truly pure, then I did claim to have rightly self-wakened unexcelled in world. Knowledge and vision arose in me: 'Unprovoked is my release. This is the last birth. There is now no further becoming.'"

With ignorance abandoned there is nothing that could give birth to another moment rooted in ignorance resulting in Dukkha. Becoming Rightly Self-Awakened is developed through knowledge of Four Noble Truths.

This is what the Buddha said. Gratified, the group of five friends delighted at his words. And while this explanation was being given, there arose to Kondanna the understanding: "All conditioned things that arise are subject to cessation."

Then the Buddha exclaimed: "So you really know, Kondanna? So you really know! You are now Anna-Kondanna, the one who understands."

End of Sutta

Upon hearing these words Kondanna understood the self-identification caused by joining with Dukkha through conditioned thinking. He realized the ultimate freedom that comes from recognizing the impermanence and lack of substantiality of all conditioned views.

Developing an understanding of Four Noble Truths and integrating the Eightfold Path as the framework for one's life is presented in the next section.

The practical application of Four Noble Truths is explained in the following section.

The following sutta explains the personalization of Dukkha and the fabrication of self-referential views. This next sutta clearly shows the futility of clinging to impermanent objects, events, views, and ideas.

Anatta-Lakkhana Sutta

Samyutta Nikaya 22.59

Not-Self

Five Clinging-Aggregates

The Buddha's Second Discourse

On one occasion the Buddha was staying at Benares, in the Deer Park at Isipatana. There he addressed the group of five (now) Bhikkhus:

"Bhikkhus, form is not-self. Were form self, then this form would not lead to suffering, and one could have it be any form desired, and stress free. Since form is not-self it leads to suffering and none can have it be any form desired and stress free.

"Bhikkhus, feeling   is not-self, as perceptions

are not-self. Fabrications are not-self. Consciousness is not-self. If these aggregates were self they would not lead to suffering and one could direct these aggregates as one wished. Since these are not-self they can only lead to suffering and no one can have these (aggregates) be as they wish.

"Bhikkhus, how do you perceive this: is form permanent or impermanent?" The five relied "Impermanent, venerable Sir."

"Now is what is impermanent painful or pleasant?"

"Painful, venerable Sir."

"Now is what is impermanent, what is painful since subject to change, is this fit to be regarded as: 'This is mine, this is I, this is my self?'

"No, venerable sir."

"Is feeling permanent or impermanent? Is perception permanent or impermanent? Are fabrications permanent or impermanent? Is consciousness permanent or impermanent?"

"All are impermanent, venerable sir."

"Now is what is impermanent, what is painful since subject to change, is this fit to be regarded as: 'This is mine, this is I, this is my self'"?

"No, venerable sir."

"So, bhikkhus any kind of form whatever,

whether past, future or presently arisen,

whether gross or subtle,

whether in oneself or external,

whether inferior or superior,

whether far or near,

must, with right understanding how it actually is, be regarded as: 'This is not mine, this is not I, this is not myself.'

"And so it follows that any kind of feeling whatever, any kind of perception, any kind of determination, any kind of consciousness whatever, whether past, future or presently arisen, whether gross or subtle, whether in oneself or external, whether inferior or superior, whether far or near must, with right understanding how it actually is, be regarded as:

'This is not mine, this is not I, this is not myself.'

273

"Bhikkhus, when a noble follower who has heard the truth sees in this way,

- They find estrangement in form,

- They find estrangement in feeling,

- They find estrangement in perception,

- They find estrangement in determinations,

- They find estrangement in consciousness.

"When they find estrangement, passion fades out. With the fading of passion, they are liberated. When liberated, there is knowledge that they are liberated. They understand: 'Birth is exhausted, the integrated life has been lived out, what can be done is done, of this there is no more beyond."

Now during this discourse the hearts and minds of the bhikkhus were liberated from craving, aversion, and deluded thinking.

End of Sutta

In most translations the phrase 'integrated life' is referred to as 'holy life.' The Buddha did not intend to start a new religion. He taught an Eightfold Path to be integrated in one's life in order to Become Buddha.

As a result of whole-hearted engagement with the Eightfold Path disenchantment with the ego-self, with Anatta, with the Five Clinging-Aggregates is developed. From disenchantment with the Five Clinging-Aggregates comes the cessation of the compulsive need to continually establish an ego-personality.

Once disenchantment is established the process of unbinding begins. The cessation of delusion, confusion, and continued unsatisfactoriness is now possible.

The simplest way to describe the Buddha's teaching on Not-self is this: anything that the ego-self clings to, whether objects, people, events, views, or ideas, or craving through the pursuit of happiness through acquisition of objects, people, events, views, or ideas, will create confusion, disenchantment and lasting unhappiness.

The futility of creating self-identity by clinging to impermanent objects, events, views, and ideas becomes apparent. Following this initial Right View the Right Intention is generated to recognize and abandon craving and clinging rooted in ignorance.

Still another way to see this is by definition and association. The self is defined by attachments. Association is another word for attachments. Who is associated with and what is associated with defines the experience of "self." This does not mean that there should be no associations. It does show the importance of being mindful of all associations and to not attempt to make what is impermanent permanent.

Do associations support developing understanding within the framework of The Eightfold Path? Do associations confusion and suffering through validation of unskillful actions?

The Eightfold Path provides a highly effective framework for guiding associations and focus for practice. As clinging to an ego-personality ceases, self-identification through associations also ceases.

It is within Dhamma practice - when developing the Eightfold Path - that wise associations are most important.

Once clinging is recognized and abandoned, one no longer clings to others. This brings the ability to be

276

mindfully present in the world and with others with no expectations or insistence that life, or the people in our lives, including ourselves, be any different from what is occurring.

All aspects of self are impermanent and any conditioned thought or thought construct that attempts to distract from this truth is also clinging, specifically clinging to views and ideas. Clinging to views and ideas maintains the distraction of stress and generates karma.

Anatta, not-self, continually seeks to establish itself in impermanent objects, events, views, and ideas. This is the purpose of the phenomenal world and why the ego-self is so enamored with the world. As long as anatta continues this quest, confusion and suffering will prevail. As long as anatta continues this quest, karma will continue.

Due to unquenched desire for existence, the ego-personality creates karma. Karma unfolds moment-by-moment as the distraction of stress and unhappiness. Though physical form will change according to impermanence, karma continues the experience of stress and unhappiness.

This is an important example of impermanence as impermanence relates to anatta. Continuity is not permanence although continuity obscures impermanence and the not-self characteristic. Continuity is reoccurrence due to repeatedly recreating the conditions leading to an experience. Continued re-establishment of an ego-self obscures impermanence resulting in a wrong view of a permanently sustainable self.

Reoccurring life situations and intellectual or emotional reactions are simply an impermanent, but repetitive, and discursive, product of discriminating consciousness, or conditioned mind. Conditioned thinking and conditioned mind is formed due to ignorance of impermanence, maintained by the distraction of stress, and given validity by an ego-personality.

Continuity caused by clinging conditioned mind is ongoing Dukkha.

Once the pain associated with clinging to impermanent objects, events, views, and ideas is recognized and abandoned further becoming rooted in ignorance comes to cessation.

What is perceived as a permanent self is, in reality, in a constant process of becoming. Each moment holds the potential for future becoming. A mind rooted in ignorance can only become further ignorant. A mind framed by the Eightfold Path has the potential to become awakened, to Become Buddha.

Adittapariyaya Sutta

Samyutta Nikaya 35.28

The Fire Discourse - Clinging to Passion

The Buddha's Third Discourse

The Buddha presented his first two discourses to the ascetics he had previously befriended. The first discourse on The Four Noble Truths explained the cause of delusion in the world and the path to understanding. The second discourse explained how the perception of individuality arises and what forms the belief in "self."

About one month after the Buddha's first two discourses, he presented The Fire Discourse to approximately 1,000 followers. Upon hearing this short discourse, most of those in attendance awakened.

At that time in northern India and southern Nepal there were various cults who engaged in ritualistic worship, sacrifice, and mystical practices. One of these cults was a popular fire cult, devoted to rituals using fire. The Buddha used the fire-worshippers as metaphor to show how individual personalities "worship" what self-referential views formed by contact with the senses.

The Fire Discourse presented below is a brief but insightful look at how the six-sense base reinforces the belief in "self." The six-sense base is the five physical senses and consciousness. Consciousness in this context is ongoing thinking rooted in ignorance of Four Noble Truths.

The Fire Discourse

The Buddha was staying in Gaya, at Gaya Head, with 1,000 monks. There he addressed the monks:

"Monks, the All is aflame.

What All is aflame?

The eye is aflame.

Forms are aflame.

Consciousness at the eye is aflame.

Contact at the eye is aflame.

And whatever there is that arises in dependence on contact at the eye - experienced as pleasure, pain or neither-pleasure-nor-pain - that too is aflame.

Aflame with what?

Aflame with the fire of passion, the fire of aversion, the fire of delusion.

Aflame, I tell you, with birth, aging & death, with sorrows, regrets, pains, distresses, and despairs. *(Aflame with Dukkha!)*

The ear is aflame. Sounds are aflame...

The nose is aflame. Aromas are aflame...

The tongue is aflame...

Flavors are aflame...

The body is aflame...

Tactile sensations are aflame...

The intellect is aflame...

Ideas are aflame...

283

Consciousness at the intellect is aflame...

Contact at the intellect is aflame...

"And whatever there is that arises in dependence on contact at the intellect - experienced as pleasure, pain or neither-pleasure-nor-pain - that too is aflame.

"Aflame with what?

Aflame with the fire of passion, the fire of aversion, the fire of delusion.

Aflame, I say, with birth, aging & death, with sorrows, regrets, pains, distresses, and despairs.

"Seeing clearly, the well-instructed disciple of the noble ones grows disenchanted with the eye,

They grow disenchanted with forms,

They grow disenchanted with consciousness at the eye,

They grow disenchanted with contact at the eye.

And whatever there is that arises in dependence on contact at the eye, experienced as pleasure, pain or neither-pleasure-nor-pain: With that, too, they grow disenchanted.

They grow disenchanted with the ear...

They grow disenchanted with the nose...

They grow disenchanted with the tongue...

They grow disenchanted with the body...

They grow disenchanted with the intellect...

They grow disenchanted with ideas...

They grow disenchanted with consciousness at the intellect...

They grow disenchanted with contact at the intellect.

"And whatever there is that arises in dependence on contact at the intellect, experienced as pleasure, pain, or neither-pleasure-nor-pain, They grow disenchanted with that too.

Disenchanted, they become dispassionate.

Through dispassion, they are fully released.

With full release, there is the knowledge, 'Fully released.'

They discern that 'Birth is ended, the integrated life fulfilled, the task done. There is nothing further for this world.'

That is what the Blessed One said. Gratified, the monks delighted at his words. And while this explanation was being given, the hearts of the 1,000 monks, through no clinging (not being sustained), were fully released from fermentation and effluents.

As stated earlier, in most translations the phrase 'integrated life' is referred to as 'holy life.' The Buddha did not intend to start a new religion. He taught an Eightfold Path to be integrated in one's life in order to Become Buddha.

End of Sutta

As described in Dependent Origination the Buddha is teaching how thinking rooted in ignorance of Four Noble Truths interprets contact with the senses and self-referential views. Feeling becomes inflamed with desire continuing the process of further becoming rooted in ignorance.

286

The components that make up the self are "inflamed" by the passions that arise from desire and aversion. This passion drives the worship (attachment) of sensory fulfillment and reinforces dukkha (suffering).

It is the preoccupation with dukkha that perpetuates delusion. The lesson to the 1,000 followers is how delusion and a wrong view of self arises and is maintained. The Buddha taught that reacting to phenomenon contacting the senses creates an identity that is attached to those sensations.

The last section of this book contains a chapter on practicing restraint at the point of contact with the six-sense base - at the point of "I-Making."

The Eightfold Path is the framework for mindful recognition of the origination of dukkha and for abandoning its causes.

Awakening occurs as understanding develops through The Eightfold Path. Through The Eightfold Path understanding of the nature of reality arises and disenchantment with the six-sense base develops. Disenchanted with constant sensory fulfillment, the mind quiets and wisdom arises.

The becoming of an ego-self experienced through Five Clinging-Aggregates is maintained by discursive thinking fueled by desire. Developing Right View brings renunciation. The strong attachment to wrong views of self manifests as hindrances to practice.

The Buddha's teachings on hindrances is in the next section.

Doubt rooted in self-referential views and the constant need for sensory input is to be recognized and abandoned.

Doubt rooted in self-referential views manifests as resistance to accept anything that would diminish or negate the image of self. This is Anatta's insistence on ignoring anything that would challenge recognizing ignorance of Four Noble Truths.

A defining characteristic of a mind stuck in wrong view is restlessness, always seeking sensory stimulation. The Eightfold Path, including Shamatha-Vipassana meditation, is the path of direct experience that ends doubt and brings insight to sense contact.

The Eightfold Path develops a tranquil mind with the ability to see passions as they arise. With a tranquil mind, useful insight, and Right Intention develop. Further becoming rooted in ignorance is interrupted and becoming awakened begins.

Becoming Buddha Wisdom, Virtue, Concentration

Becoming Buddha is the skillful application of meditation and mindfulness developing profound Right View and emptiness of ignorance of Four Noble Truths.

The path Siddhartha Gotama taught for others to also become Buddha - become awakened - is a path characterized by developing profound wisdom resting on pure virtue and gentle concentration.

The defining quality of mind of an awakened, fully mature human being is tranquility. Tranquility is a quality of mind of unwavering calm and peace - fully and dispassionately mindful of life as life occurs.

Refined   mindfulness is the skill

that is supported by the gentle concentration developed in Right Meditation - Shamatha-Vipassana meditation. Mindfulness means to hold in mind or to recollect. As has been shown it is what is held in mind that will determine experience. It is the mind-less-ness caused by the distraction of dukkha that is to be overcome to break free of clinging, craving, aversion, and all deluded thinking.

Holding in mind self-referential views rooted in ignorance of Four Noble Truths will only continue confusion, deluded thinking, and ongoing unsatisfactory experiences.

Thoughts preoccupied with clinging, craving and aversion will lead to more confusion and stress. Thoughts well-concentrated on mindfulness of the Dhamma will bring lasting peace and happiness.

Distracted thoughts focused on fleeting desires, achievements, and acquisitions can only lead to more confusion and stress.

Thoughts and actions that create additional self-identities can only lead to more confusion and stress. This includes altruistic self-identities.

Thoughts that establish and reinforce a self-referential ego-personality in any manner, in any mind state, in any inner or outer "realm," can only lead to more distraction, confusion and stress.

Holding in mind the skillful qualities of the Eightfold Path provides the framework for recognizing ignorance and developing the profound wisdom of ongoing Right View.

Mindfulness in the context of Four Noble Truths is to hold in mind the principles of the Eightfold Path.

The Eightfold Path develops understanding that will end the confusion and suffering born of ignorance of Four Noble Truths.

It is not skillful to equate the mindfulness of the Dhamma with modern applications of mindfulness. The generally stated purpose of modern mindfulness techniques is to manage mental and physical pain, and stress. Mindfulness techniques when applied in this context are often successful in achieving this purpose.

There is no need to abandon any mindfulness technique for specific health issues as long as they do not reinforce an ego-personality. This often occurs when modern "mindfulness" practices are

293

incorporated as a part of Dhamma practice. This will always distract from the simple and direct applications of mindfulness taught by the Buddha.

Throughout the Buddha's teaching career he emphasized developing two very specific applications of mindfulness. Both applications of mindfulness are taught in the Satipatthana Sutta further on in this section.

Mindfulness in the context of Four Noble Truths is the quality of mind that brings insight to the Buddha's teaching. Mindfulness is the foundation of the teachings of the Buddha. Mindfulness applied within the context of The Four Noble Truths will develop an awakened mind, a mind of pure equanimity.

The refined mindfulness of the Dhamma is to develop understanding of Four Noble Truths. Profound understanding of Four Noble Truths abandons ignorance. Becoming empty of ignorance is the quality of mind necessary to Become Buddha.

As shown in the Buddha's description of his own awakening in the Nagara Sutta, becoming stuck in the feedback loop of self-referential views feeding back on ongoing thinking rooted in ignorance - conditioned thinking - that continues suffering.

Conditioned thinking requires a framework or path to recognize and abandon discursive thinking. Interrupting conditioned thinking is the purpose of the Eightfold Path.

Without the singular guidance and framework of the Eightfold Path wrong views are continually biased towards maintaining ignorance of Four Noble Truths. This has been shown in the many adaptations and accommodations that have become a part of modern Buddhism. Diminishing or dismissing the Eightfold Path continues ignorance.

Any minimizing or dismissal of Four Noble Truths only substitutes conditioned ignorant thinking for the wisdom and guidance of the Buddha's Dhamma. Any minimizing or dismissal of Four Noble Truths continues ignorance and negates the opportunity to Become Buddha.

The following chapter in this section shows the Four Noble Truths as the practical foundation and defining purpose of the Buddha's forty-five year teaching career. The Eightfold Path is described in

295

detail and in the Buddha's own words in this chapter. One application of mindfulness taught by the Buddha is to be mindful of each factor of the Eightfold Path and is described here.

As stated, the Buddha placed an emphasis on mindfulness in two very specific applications.

One application of mindfulness is during Shamatha-Vipassana Meditation. In the Satipatthana Sutta teaches the Four Foundations of Mindfulness. The Four Foundations of Mindfulness are taught to describe the dispassionate mindfulness of what occurs during meditation. The concentration developed supports mindfulness of the arising and passing away of internal and external phenomena.

As shown further on in this section, Shamatha-Vipassana meditation is the only meditation method taught by the Buddha. The Buddha did not teach meditation for having experiences during meditation - mystical or otherwise, grand or mundane.

The Buddha taught meditation for developing the concentration necessary to support the refined mindfulness of the Eightfold Path.

The two mutually supportive skills of unwavering concentration and refined mindfulness - knowing what is most skillful to hold in mind - provide the qualities of mind necessary to gain insight into the Three Marks of Existence and recognize and abandon all ignorant views.

This is what is meant as "living the holy life" or a life well-framed and well-integrated with the Eightfold Path.

Holding in mind the Eightfold Path develops the framework of the Eightfold Path as the foundation for life. As the path becomes integrated, moment-by-moment life becomes an expression of profound wisdom, pure virtue, and unwavering concentration.

The two applications of mindfulness are presented in the context intended by the Buddha. The purpose of meditation in deepening Samadhi, the quality of a non-distracted mind, is to support refined mindfulness.

The two cornerstones of the Buddha's Dhamma are profound concentration and refined mindfulness.

As will be seen in the chapter on Samadhi and the Jhanas, the Buddha taught meditation for developing unwavering concentration.

Concentration supports the refined mindfulness necessary to develop and integrate the Eightfold Path.

The Jhanas - levels of meditative absorption - describes the direct experience of the development of four levels of meditative absorption. These are levels of meditative absorption that anyone who engages wholeheartedly with Shamatha-Vipassana meditation within the framework of the Eightfold Path will develop.

There is nothing extraordinary to these levels of meditative absorption. Developed within the framework of the Eightfold Path they support the extraordinary experience of Becoming Buddha.

The Yuganaddha Sutta shows the importance of a meditation practice that combines concentration with the intention of gaining insight.

A well-concentrated mind supports the refined mindfulness of the Eightfold Path.

The Eightfold Path provides the framework for useful insight into the Three Marks Of Existence.

Useful insight into the Three Marks Of Existence develops the cessation of ignorance.

It is the concentration developed in Shamatha-Vipassana meditation that supports mindfulness of all eight factors of the Eightfold Path. A well-concentrated mind interrupts the feedback loop described in the Nagara Sutta. A well-concentrated mind interrupts ongoing ignorance of Four Noble Truths.

The chapter is on the Vitakkasanthana Sutta. This sutta describes the quality of a well-concentrated mind framed by the refined mindfulness of the Eightfold Path as one who 'thinks what they want whenever they want and does not think what is unskillful.' This is the essence of profound concentration and refined mindfulness.

The chapter on Karma and Rebirth brings clarity to a commonly misunderstood and often dismissed key teaching of the Buddha. As will be seen, karma is the present unfolding of past intentional acts modified by the present level of concentration and mindfulness.

This directly leads to rebirth, or more accurately, what one is becoming.

What is held in mind will determine what is given birth to in the next moment. What is held in mind, if rooted in ignorance, can only lead to additional becoming rooted in ignorance. As the framework of the Eightfold is developed and held in mind, becoming awakened becomes the direction and purpose of life.

The final chapter in this section describes five common hindrances to awakening taught by the Buddha. Recognizing these hindrances dispassionately as they arise and returning mindfulness to the Eightfold Path will ensure continued progress towards Becoming Buddha.

Many people come to a meditation or mindfulness practice believing that a meditation or mindfulness technique alone will be sufficient to relieve the causes of all discontent and stress. It is true that any technique that brings a measure of calm will have positive physical and mental benefits.

Meditation alone without the supportive guidance of the Eightfold Path will often reinforce

300

conditioned thinking and provide an "acceptable distraction" from developing useful insight and ending ignorance.

The purpose and intent of the Buddha's Dhamma is not for stress reduction, although as progress is made, stress is naturally reduced. The purpose and intent of the Dhamma is become empty of ignorance. In order to develop useful insight and the ending of stress and unhappiness, meditation and mindfulness must be developed within the broader framework of The Eightfold Path.

In the Appamada Sutta, Samyutta Nikaya 3.17, King Pasenadi asked the Buddha:

"Is there one quality that develops understanding (of The Four Noble Truths) both now in this life and for all time?" The Buddha responded: There is one quality that develops understanding in this life and for all time. That quality is mindfulness."

The Buddha then offered this verse:

"For one who desires long life, health, nibbana The wise praise mindfulness of the Eightfold Path.

When mindful and wise You develop understanding now and for all time.

By breaking through to your own understanding You are called awakened."

As mindfulness of The Four Noble Truths develops, excited, agitated, and confused mind states will be recognized as a distraction from mindfulness. As Dhamma practice deepens all impermanent distractions will be recognized and abandoned. With wholehearted practice of mindfulness as the Buddha taught mindfulness, all causes of confusion and unhappiness will abandoned. Lasting peace and contentment will be experienced as the abiding quality of a well-concentrated mind.

The last words of the Buddha, spoken moments before his death:

"Impermanence is relentless, decay inevitable. Work diligently for your own salvation. **Mindful** you should dwell, clearly comprehending. This I exhort you."

Four Noble Truths In Practice

Buddha means "awakened." Awakening means to develop full maturity. Maturity has the qualities of mind of knowledge, understanding, and wisdom. Patience, calm, and true compassion are characteristics of a fully mature human being.

The Buddha's quest for awakening led him to develop profound understanding of the origination of suffering. The Pali term for suffering is "Dukkha." Dukkha means disappointment, unsatisfactoriness, and all manner of physical and mental pain. Confusion and deluded thinking are aspects of Dukkha caused by ongoing preoccupation with Dukkha.

Upon his awakening the Buddha understood that Dukkha originated in and is dependent on ignorance. This is known as Dependent Origination.

Dependent Origination shows that it

is ignorance of Four Noble Truths that results in Dukkha. Also known as the "12 Links of Dependent Origination" it is through twelve observable causative links, that all manner of confusion, delusion, and suffering originates.

The section on the Buddha's Awakening explains Dependent Origination in detail.

The Buddha taught Four Noble Truths to develop understanding of the common human problem of Dukkha - of stress. Included in the Four Noble Truths is a clear explanation of individual contributions to stress - craving and clinging. The Fourth Noble Truth is the truth of the path developing awakened understanding and cessation of craving and clinging.

The defining aspect of a mind rooted in ignorance is the tenacious desire to ignore anything that would challenge ignorance. The Eightfold Path provides the guidance and framework necessary to overcome deluded thinking resulting from ignorance.

The Eightfold Path provides the foundation for understanding the three common and prevalent aspects of human experience - The Three Marks Of Existence.

The Three Marks of Existence are explained in a previous section.

The purpose of Four Noble Truths relates directly to Dependent Origination. The purpose of Four Noble Truths is to understand the nature of stress and suffering and to end individual contributions to confusion, deluded thinking, and ongoing disappointment.

The distraction of the preoccupation with Dukkha obscures ignorance and continues conditioned thinking. The concentration developed in Shamatha-Vipassana meditation supports the refined mindfulness necessary to hold in mind the Eightfold Path. Fully integrating the Eightfold Path as the framework for experiencing life as life unfolds develops awakening.

Profound understanding is developed through individual experiential understanding of Four Noble Truths.

The Buddha describes awakening in the context of Four Noble Truths and the Eightfold Path as completing four tasks:

- Awakened Right View understands Stress.

- Awakened Right View understands the origination of Stress.

- Awakened Right View understands the cessation of Stress.

- Awakened Right View understands the Eightfold Path developing the cessation of Stress.

First Noble Truth

The Truth of Stress and Unhappiness

Stress occurs impersonally to all. As a consequence of birth all human beings are subject to physical phenomena that is stressful. No person, regardless of social position, associations, intellect, religious or spiritual understanding, or "grace," can avoid stress.

All human beings are subject to sickness, aging and death. Along the way everyone will face loss, some minor, some quite devastating. According to personal circumstances everyone acquires views of how to live life. Choices are made about who and what to associate with. We all form views of what we would like to achieve and an endless list of likes and dislikes.

These acquired views and resulting choices form self-referential identities. Self-referential identities are formed in this manner from craving for specific experiences. Once formed, one clings an identity to these experiences. Views rooted in ignorance are the

307

foundation for defining "self" from fleeting experiences.

All of these experiences and the resulting discriminating thoughts contribute in a cumulative manner to stress. We all know that every experience is subject to change. Impermanence and uncertainty are a part of life. Underlying this knowing is a subtle tension.

We know that certain activities may bring disappointment or discontent. We may not feel secure financially and fear of personal physical loss will be present. Whatever our position in life might be, we create attachments to our lives being a certain way. These are different for everyone but the result is the same. These attachments form a self-referential identity, or ego-personality.

Stress - disappointment - arises in our lives the instant we want the people and events of our lives to be different from what is occurring. Due to the impermanence of all things, wanting the people and events of our lives to remain as they are also brings stress. This desire for difference includes ourselves and our view of ourselves.

This is a meaning of 'becoming other than self ' referenced from the Loka Sutta in a previous section.

Craving or desiring more of an experience is stressful. Craving or desiring less of an experience - aversion - is stressful. Constantly seeking something new - an object, event, view, or idea - is stressful. Fear of change is stressful. Fear that something undesired won't change is stressful. Boredom, the need for constant distraction, is stressful. This list is endless.

All thoughts rooted in ignorance produce stress and distract from life as life is occurring.

This is clinging or joining, an ego-self to objects, events, views, and ideas. Clinging to views describes and defines (and severely limits) what is commonly and wrongly viewed as a person - as me or mine.

Position, power, wealth, or intellect can insulate one temporarily from stress. Continued ignorance, the right religion, philosophy, or spiritual discipline can insulate one temporarily from stress. Stress continues, but is often ignored. This is a form of mindlessness about stress.

Continuously seeking what brings pleasure and attempting to avoid that which is unpleasant, is to be constantly grasping after the impermanent and transitory.

Continuously grasping after satiating an insatiable ego-personality through achievements and acquisitions, including intellectual or 'spiritual' achievements, is to be constantly grasping after the impermanent and transitory.

Inherent in life there will be difficulties, disappointments and unhappiness. All things in life change and all human beings are prone to sickness, aging and death. Events will arise and pass away that will bring great pleasure and great disappointment.

It is within this impermanent environment that stress arises. It is also within this impermanent environment that stress and discontent can be understood. Once understood, craving and clinging can be abandoned.

A life of freedom and true happiness is possible for anyone. All that is required to gain freedom from stress is to understand and integrate Four Noble Truths, beginning with the truth of stress.

Ignorance is insisting that the personality viewed as I or me is permanent and well-established.

Ignorance is continually reacting to life based on what makes an ego-personality satisfied. This is simply 'feeding the ego.' Attempts at satisfying what cannot be satisfied is foolish and a constant distraction that only continues ignorance.

*Engaging in practices that ignore ignorance only contributes to **becoming** continually ignorant.*

Ending ignorance and developing wisdom is gaining an understanding of the interaction of impermanence, stress, and a self-referential ego-personality.

Wisdom is recognizing wrong views and unskillful attachments to objects, events, views, and ideas that have arisen from ignorance.

Wisdom is making mindful choices and conclusions based on the true nature of existence.

Wisdom is the understanding developed through the Eightfold Path.

The task associated with the First Noble Truth is to understand stress - Dukkha - on a deep experiential level:

• Birth is stressful. As a consequence of having a human life, there will be stress.

311

- Aging is stressful. As a consequence of having a human life aging will occur and contribute to stress.

- Sickness is stressful. As a consequence of having a human life sickness will occur and contribute to stress.

- Death is stressful. As a consequence of having a human life death will occur. Clinging to form and being enamored with Dukkha and contribute to stress.

- Not getting what is desired is stressful. Disappointment is an inevitable aspect of impermanence and uncertainty.

- Receiving what is undesired is stressful. Disappointment is an inevitable aspect of impermanence and uncertainty.

- The Five Clinging-Aggregates are stressful. Clinging self-referential views to physical form, feelings, perceptions, mental fabrications, or thinking rooted in ignorance is the personal experience of stress.

Second Noble Truth

The Truth of the Origination of Stress

The problem of conditioned thinking maintaining ignorance is complex. The originating cause is simple:

Clinging, craving, desire and aversion originate stress. Wanting the people and events of life to be different from they are, including one's self, is craving or desire. Wanting the people and events of life to remain as they are, including one's self, is clinging. Clinging arises from ignorance and defines the experience of self through continued clinging. Clinging binds wrong views of self to ignorance - what is held in mind determines experience.

Wrong views condition thinking creating the "conditions" underlying the experience of self. Another term for conditioned thinking is "confirmation bias." Confirmation bias means that one becomes biased to view experience in a way that confirms the established (conditioned) view. Once   fabricated, views of self

313

are clung to and determine the life experience.

The Eightfold Path develops the recognition of clinging to wrong views conditioned by ignorance. Through developing Right View clinging to a self that is prone to confusion and suffering can be seen clearly and mindfully abandoned.

Letting go of clinging does not mean that you won't have physical and emotional needs met. Letting go of clinging means letting of your need to have an insatiable ego-personality's needs met.

Letting go of clinging means letting go of the mental preoccupation arising from the attachments to the people and events of your life, including yourself, to be different from what is occurring. Desiring permanence where only impermanence is possible is thinking rooted in ignorance. Letting go of clinging is letting go of all views arising from ignorance.

As clinging to wrong views diminishes, an understanding of the difference between acceptance and approval develops. A clinging conditioned mind must approve or disapprove of an event prior to accepting the event. This is a subtle form of attachment or clinging a self-referential view to an event.

This is due to the self-referential nature of conditioned thinking. Anatta is a "self" defined by wrong views of self rooted in ignorance. Anatta is compelled to establish itself in all objects, events, views, and ideas. This makes all of life's events personal and self-reflective.

As understanding of the impermanent and impersonal nature of all things develops, craving for and clinging to self-referential views is seen as foolish and unskillful. This includes clinging to impermanent and impersonal thoughts and mental fabrications.

The need to approve or disapprove events is abandoned and acceptance of life as life occurs becomes the foundation of a life of lasting peace and contentment.

Developing the Eightfold Path brings the understanding that there is no permanent self and that all things are in a constant of becoming. As what constitutes a self is always in a state of becoming, nothing can be seen as impacting a "self."

The realization arises that it is only fixed conditioned views of "self" that are affected by the events of life. As these fixed views of self are released a supple and peaceful mind develops free of craving for

315

or clinging to the need for anything to be any different from what is occurring. This is an awakened, fully mature quality of mind.

The task associated with the Second Noble Truth is to recognize and abandon Craving and Clinging.

This task directly relates to Right Intention.

Holding in mind the Right Intention to recognize and abandon craving and clinging is directly supported by being mindful of Right Speech, Right Action, and Right Livelihood.

This provides the perspective to recognize thoughts, words, and deeds that arise from self-referential clinging views.

The concentration factors of the Eightfold Path - Right Effort, Right Mindfulness, and Right Meditation develop the concentration necessary to develop refined mindfulness.

Third Noble Truth

The Truth of the Cessation of Stress

The Third Noble Truth shows that it is possible to undo the process dependent on ignorance resulting in all manner of confusion, deluded thinking, and ongoing disappointing and unsatisfactory experiences.

The Third Noble Truth shows that it is possible to disentangle the Five Clinging-Aggregates and bring to cessation all wrong views rooted in ignorance.

As the Eightfold Path is developed the clinging relationship between the Three Marks of Existence is recognized and the impermanent nature of all things, including self-referential views, is understood.

Once understood, the profound realization develops that "all conditioned things that arise are subject to cessation." Where once only Dukkha occurred, a calm and peaceful mine prevails.

As the Eightfold Path is developed and fully

317

integrated as the framework for experiencing life as life unfolds, the direct experience of the cessation of confusion, deluded thinking, and ongoing disappointment occurs.

The task associated with the Third Noble Truth is to become empty of ignorance. This task relates directly to Right View and Right Effort explained below.

Fourth Noble Truth

The Truth of the Path Leading to the Cessation of Dukkha

As stated earlier, the Buddha taught that awakening means that The Eightfold Path has been developed: "Vision arose, insight arose, discernment arose, knowledge arose, illumination arose within me with regard to things never heard before: 'This is the noble truth of the way of practice leading to the cessation of stress'... 'This noble truth of the way of practice leading to the cessation of stress is to be developed'... 'This noble truth of the way of practice leading to the cessation of stress has been developed.'

The purpose of the Buddha's entire teaching is to develop the Eightfold Path and abandon the origination of Dukkha - Ignorance of Four Noble Truths.

The Buddha taught that by abandoning clinging in all its forms, the skillful means to the cessation of stress can be developed.

The eight factors   of   the   Eightfold   Path

provides a practical framework for mindful living. This refined mindfulness develops the insight, knowledge, wisdom, and ethical behavior necessary to methodically and purposefully recognize and abandon the distraction of stress maintained by clinging to conditioned thinking rooted in ignorance.

The purpose of the Eightfold Path is to recognize, interrupt, and abandon conditioned thinking rooted in ignorance and become awakened- Become Buddha.

It is the ongoing preoccupation with stress that obscures ignorance and continues stress. Once this is fully comprehended the mind awakens. Once the blocks to awakening have been abandoned awakening, becoming Buddha occurs.

The Buddha teaches: "And this, friends, is the noble truth of the way of practice leading to the cessation of dukkha, precisely this Noble Eightfold Path."

The Eightfold Path

Magga-Vibhanga Sutta

Analysis of the Path

Samyutta Nikaya 45.8

I have heard that at one time the Buddha was staying in Savatthi at Jeta's Grove, Anathapindika's monastery.

There he addressed those assembled: "Friends, I will explain the Eightfold Path. Listen & pay close attention.

"Now what is the Noble Eightfold Path?

"Right View, Right Intention, Right Speech, Right Action, Right Livelihood, Right Effort, Right Mindfulness, Right Meditation.

"This is the middle way that produces vision, produces knowledge, and develops a calm mind. A path to direct knowledge, to self-awakening, to Unbinding." From the Dhammacakkappavattana Sutta in the previous section.

"And what is Right View?

"Knowledge with regard to stress, knowledge with regard to the origination of stress, knowledge with regard to the stopping of stress, knowledge with regard to the way of practice leading to the cessation of stress.

"This is called Right View.

"And what is Right Intention?

"Being intent on renunciation and abandoning craving and clinging. Being intent on freedom from ill will. Being intent on harmlessness.

"This is called Right Intention.

"And what is Right Speech?

"Abstaining from lying, abstaining from divisive speech, abstaining from abusive speech, abstaining from idle chatter.

"This is called Right Speech.

"And what is Right Action?

"Abstaining from taking life, abstaining from taking what is not freely given, abstaining from sexual misconduct.

"This is called Right Action.

"And what is Right Livelihood?

"There is the case where a disciple of the noble ones, having abandoned dishonest livelihood, is sustained with right livelihood.

"This is called Right Livelihood.

"And what is Right Effort?

"Right Effort is generating the sincere intention and ongoing persistence for avoiding evil and unskillful qualities that have not yet arisen.

"Right Effort is generating the sincere intention and ongoing persistence for the abandonment of evil and unskillful qualities that have arisen.

"Right Effort is generating the sincere intention and ongoing persistence for development of the arising of skillful qualities that have not yet arisen.

"Right Effort is generating the sincere intention and ongoing persistence for the development, recognition, increase, and maintenance of skillful qualities that have arisen.

"This, friends, is called Right Effort.

"And what is Right Mindfulness?

"Right Mindfulness is remaining focused on the body in and of itself - ardent, aware, and mindful - putting away greed and distress with reference to the world.

"One remains focused on feelings in and of themselves - ardent, aware, and mindful - putting away greed and distress with reference to the world.

"One remains focused on the mind in and of itself - ardent, aware, and mindful - putting away greed and distress with reference to the world.

"One remains focused on mental qualities in and of themselves - ardent, aware, and mindful - putting away greed and distress with reference to the world.

"This, friends, is called right mindfulness.

'Remaining focused on the body in & of itself — ardent, aware, and mindful — putting away greed and distress with reference to the world' refers to being mindful of life as life occurs without the need for any event or person, including one's self, be any different from what is occurring

- *the essence of dispassionate and well-concentrated mindfulness.*

As becoming awakened develops, the ability to separate approval of what is occurring from dispassionate acceptance of what is occurring also develops. Approval joined to acceptance is a self-referential view rooted in ignorance. Dispassionate acceptance of what is occurring is an awakened Right View.

This reference to Right Mindfulness refers to the Four Foundations of Mindfulness as taught in the Satipatthana Sutta presented in the next chapter.

"And what is Right Meditation?

"Right Meditation is being withdrawn from sensuality, withdrawn from unskillful mental qualities. With Right Meditation one enters and remains in the first jhana: delight and pleasure born from withdrawal, accompanied by directed thought and evaluation.

"With the stilling of directed thoughts and evaluations, one enters and remains in the second jhana: delight and pleasure born of concentration, unification of awareness free from directed thought and evaluation, the development of inner poise.

"With the fading of delight, one remains equanimous, mindful, and alert, and senses pleasure with the body. One enters and remains in the third jhana, equanimous & mindful, a pleasant abiding.

"With the abandoning of pleasure and pain one enters and remains in the fourth jhana - purity of equanimity and mindfulness free of the experience of pleasure nor pain.

"This, friends, is called right concentration."

That is what the Blessed One said. Gratified, those gathered delighted at his words.

End Of Sutta

'Free of the experience of pleasure nor pain' is another reference to the Buddha's description of his awakening in the Nagara Sutta. In the Nagara Sutta the Buddha states that Becoming Buddha is 'direct knowledge of the cessation of fabrications.' This is the cessation of the feedback loop of self-referential views rooted in ignorance of Four Noble Truths.

The jhanas - ordinary levels of meditative absorption are often over-emphasized and portrayed as highly advanced states only attainable by the most "advanced' meditators. As described here and in additional detail in the chapter on Samadhi and the Jhanas, these are levels of meditative absorption achieved by anyone whole-heartedly engaged in Shamatha-Vipassana meditation practice.

Right Meditation is practiced within the framework and guidance of the entire Eightfold Path with the "Right" intention to deepen concentration.

In the Majjhima Nikaya, 117, the Buddha teaches mindfulness as mindfulness relates to the Eightfold Path:

• Be mindful to abandon wrong view and enter and remain in Right View.

• Be mindful to abandon wrong intention and enter and remain in Right Intention.

• Be mindful to abandon wrong speech and enter and remain in Right Speech.

• Be mindful to abandon wrong action and enter and remain in Right Action.

• Be mindful to abandon wrong livelihood and enter and remain in Right livelihood.

- Be Mindful to abandon wrong effort and enter and remain in Right Effort.

- Be mindful to abandon wrong mindfulness and enter and remain in Right Mindfulness.

- Be Mindful to abandon wrong meditation and enter and remain in Right Meditation.

The task associated with the Fourth Noble Truth is to engage wholeheartedly with all eight factors of the Eightfold Path and develop awakened, fully mature, Right View. Fully mature Right View brings release from clinging to all self-referential views rooted in ignorance.

Satipatthana Sutta
Four Foundations of Mindfulness

Majjhima Nikaya 10

In the Satipatthana Sutta the Buddha teaches the Four Foundations of Mindfulness as the framework for what occurs during meditation and as a reference for mindfulness in all areas of a Dhamma practitioners moment-by-moment life.

Four Noble Truths is the context for meditation practice. Shamatha-Vipassana meditation is practiced for deepening concentration. It is the concentration developed during meditation that supports the refined mindfulness necessary for integration of the Eightfold Path as the framework for Dhamma Practice.

In the Satipatthana Sutta, the Buddha first teaches the Four Foundations of Mindfulness as instruction for Shamatha-Vipassana meditation.

Much is made of the detailed account of the different breaths and bodily functions to imply that the Buddha is teaching to manufacture the experience of these differences. This contradicts the fundamental teaching to not establish a self in any event or isolated experience. What is described here is a simple dispassionate mindfulness of what is occurring.

The Satipatthana Sutta

On one occasion the Buddha was in Kammasadhamma where he addressed those assembled:

"Friends, there are four frames of reference - four foundations of mindfulness - that are required for the purification of all beings, for the overcoming of sorrow and regret, for the disappearance of pain and distress, for establishing the right method of practice, and for complete unbinding. What are these four?

Being mindful of the breath in the body, determined and alert and abandoning craving and aversion to what is occurring.

330

Being mindful of feelings arising from the six-sense base, determined and alert and abandoning craving and aversion to what is occurring.

Being mindful of thoughts arising from the six-sense base, determined and alert and abandoning craving and aversion to what is occurring.

Being mindful of the present quality of mind, determined and alert and abandoning craving and aversion to what is occurring.

The six-sense base is the five physical senses and conscious thought. It is through the six-sense base that self-referential contact and self-identification (attachment) with phenomena is established. Feelings in this reference is any disturbance in the mind and conscious thought is ongoing thinking that is rooted in ignorance prior to awakening.

Mindfulness Of The Breath In The Body

"And how does one remain mindful of the breath in the body in and of itself?

"Finding a secluded spot - the shade of a tree or an empty hut - sitting erect with legs crossed in front, placing attention on the breath.

"Remaining mindful of the breath - breathe in and breathe out. Mindful of the breath, long or short, breathe in and breathe out. Training yourself to be sensitive to the breath and calming any bodily fabrication. Ever mindful calming the body with each in-breath and each out-breath.

"Remaining mindful of the breath in the body - mindful of the in-breath and the out-breath - the arising and passing away of phenomena with regard to the body.

"In this way one remains mindful internally and externally with regard to the body. With no self-reference, calmly noticing 'there is a body,' remaining independent of, and not clinging to anything in the world.

The first foundation of mindfulness is being mindful of the breath in the body. This is the initial establishment of the breath in Shamatha-Vipassana meditation. Quieting the mind and developing concentration begins by putting aside thoughts as thoughts arise and becoming mindful of the breath.

Concentration is the foundation that supports refined mindfulness.

Being mindful of what is occurring in relation to The Eightfold Path is refined mindfulness.

Being mindful of the breath in the body is the foundation of developing understanding of an ego-personality and its relation to the distraction of stress.

Being mindful of the breath in the body interrupts outer-focused clinging conditioned thinking and begins to quiet the mind with directed inner mindfulness.

Being mindful of the in-breath and the out-breath brings mindfulness to the arising and passing away of all phenomena. Notice that there is no specialness or applied emphasis attached to the normal breath cycle.

What is being described here is simple and direct mindfulness of the breath.

Supported by the concentration developed in Shamatha-Vipassana meditation, the Buddha then teaches how to apply mindfulness outside of formal meditation:

When walking, be mindful of walking.

333

When standing, be mindful of standing.

When sitting, be mindful of sitting.

When lying down, be mindful of lying down.

In any function, be mindful that 'there is a body.'

When going about, looking this way and that, be fully mindful.

When bending or reaching, be fully mindful.

When carrying a bowl or a cloak, be fully mindful.

When eating, drinking, or savoring food, be fully mindful.

When eliminating waste, be fully mindful.

When walking, standing, sitting, sleeping, waking, talking or silent, be fully mindful.

"In this way one remains mindful of the breath in the body - the in-breath and the out-breath.

"In this way one remains mindful of the breath in the body - the arising and the passing away of the body - independent of and not clinging to anything in the world.

"Just as a person with good eyesight, emptying a bag full of mixed grains, would know 'this is wheat, this is rice, these are beans, these are sesame seeds.' In this same way one remains mindful from the soles of the feet to the top of the head, encased in skin, there is hair, nails, teeth, tendons, bones, marrow, organs, feces, phlegm, blood, urine, sweat, fat, tears, saliva, mucous, and fluid in the joints.

"In this way one is mindful of the four elements - the earth element, the water element, the fire element, and the wind element.

The four elements that comprise a human being are impermanent.

"Be mindful of the impermanence of the body to develop dispassion. If left unattended, a corpse decays quickly. It becomes bloated and infested. It is picked at by birds and dogs and other creatures. Eventually, nothing is left but dust.

"Be mindful that 'this very body, too' will die and pass away. This the nature of the world - and unavoidable fate.

"In this way one remains mindful of the breath in the body - the in-breath and the out-breath.

335

"In this way one remains mindful of the arising and the passing away of the body - independent of and not clinging to anything in the world.

"This how one remains mindful of the breath in the body."

Without creating and specialness or over-analysis of normal bodily activities or functions, including the impermanence of the body itself, maintain mindfulness of life as life occurs.

What follows teaches a dispassionate mindfulness of feelings arising and passing away, and thoughts arising and passing away. Finally, one becomes mindful of the arising and passing away of the quality of mind.

Mindfulness of Feelings

"And how does one remain mindful of feelings in and of themselves?

"When feeling pain be mindful that there is pain. When feeling pleasure be mindful that there is pleasure. When feeling neither pleasure nor pain *(ambivalence)* be mindful that there is neither pleasure nor pain.

"When feeling the pain of the body be mindful that there is pain of the body. When feeling pain not of the body *(a disturbance in the mind)* be mindful that there is pain not of the body.

"When feeling pleasure in the body be mindful that there is pleasure in the body. When feeling pleasure not in the body *(an excitement in the mind)* be mindful that there is pleasure not in the body.

"When feeling neither pleasure nor pain in the body be mindful that there is neither pleasure nor pain in the body. When feeling neither pleasure nor pain not in the body be mindful that there is neither pleasure nor pain not in the body.

"In this way one remains mindful of feelings and the arising and the passing away of feelings - independent of and not clinging to anything in the world.

"In this way one remains mindful internally and externally with regard to feelings. This is how one remains mindful of feelings in and of themselves.

337

The second foundation of mindfulness is being mindful of feelings. Mindfulness of feelings becomes possible once the mind has quieted enough to be able to hold in mind the breath in the body for a few moments.

Once a tranquil mind state has been achieved and mindfulness of the breath is maintained, notice any feelings, emotional or physical, that arise. If physical pain arises, let go of any thoughts in reference to the feeling. If an emotion such as frustration, anger, fear, resentment, joy, bliss, etcetera, simply recognize that a feeling has arisen. While maintaining mindfulness of the breath, let go of any thoughts in reference to the feeling.

You may want to begin to blame yourself or others to justify the feeling. Put these thoughts aside. You may be drawn to analyze the feeling in some other way. You may ask yourself where did the feeling come from, what circumstances took place to bring a rise to the feeling? Put these thoughts aside. It is enough to recognize the feeling for what it is while maintaining mindfulness of your breath.

With mindfulness of your breath let go of the feeling. Let go of the judgment attached to the feeling. Judging a feeling creates clinging and develops emotion. An emotion is a reaction to an event, judging an event in some way.

Reaction caused by judgment further intensifies feeling and further conditions conditioned mind.

Notice that there is no instruction by the Buddha to create self-referential attachment by "embracing" pain or to "breathe into the pain." This will only further personalize what is intended to be a dispassionate experience of mindfulness of what is occurring. This will only continue clinging self-referential views.

Notice that this is not instruction to perform an elaborate body scan. This is a subtle way of encouraging further distraction through self-identification with the body. The Buddha's instruction develops a dispassionate awareness of 'remaining mindful of feelings and the arising and the passing away of feelings - independent of and not clinging to anything in the world' including impermanent phenomena arising and passing away within the body.

Notice that it is often a reaction to an external event that was perceived through one or more of the six senses that initiated the feeling. It is at the point of contact with the external experience that a personal, self-referential, attachment is made.

Mindfulness of this process develops useful insight into impermanence.

Mindfulness of this process brings understanding of the subtle but pervasive and continual establishment of a self that is prone to confusion and suffering. This is the ongoing process of "I-making" also known as conceit.

Recognition of the initiation of I-making develops the ability to bring continued I-making to cessation.

Mindfulness is a dispassionate focused awareness on whatever is arising in the present moment without being distracted by judgments or discriminating thoughts. Being mindful of feelings as feelings arise allows the feeling to dissipate and allows a tranquil mind to deepen.

If a physical sensation arises such as pain or discomfort in some area of your body, remain mindful of the sensation of breathing. Note the physical sensation and the immediate self-identification and return your mindfulness to your breath. Again, do not judge the physical sensation in any way. Do not wish that you are not having the experience of discomfort or agitation. Simply note the experience while maintaining mindfulness of your breath.

Being mindful of physical sensations without further judgment often will minimize the sensation. Returning mindfulness to the breath interrupts reaction to physical and emotional feelings.

This is the second foundation of mindfulness: being mindful that through contact with the five physical senses and consciousness, feelings arise. Being mindful of feelings, being ardent and aware of feelings as feelings arise, begins to de-condition conditioned mind by interrupting the discursive and self-perpetuating judgment and analysis of feelings.

Simply and dispassionately be mindful of feelings as feelings arise while maintaining mindfulness of the breath.

Mindfulness of Thoughts

"And how does one remain mindful of thoughts in and of themselves?

"When thoughts are passionate be mindful that thoughts are passionate. When thoughts are dispassionate be mindful that thoughts are dispassionate.

"When there are thoughts of aversion be mindful that there are thoughts of aversion. When thoughts are free of aversion be mindful that thoughts are free of aversion.

341

"When thoughts are deluded be mindful that thoughts are deluded. When thoughts are free of delusion be mindful that thoughts are free of delusion.

How does one know delusion? Thoughts and actions that contradict the Eightfold Path are deluded.

"When the mind is constricted be mindful that the mind is constricted. When thoughts are scattered be mindful that thoughts are scattered. When the mind is spacious be mindful that the mind is spacious.

"When thoughts are common be mindful that thoughts are common. When thoughts are unsurpassed be mindful that thoughts are unsurpassed.

"When the mind is not concentrated be mindful that the mind is not concentrated. When the mind is concentrated be mindful that the mind is concentrated.

"When the mind is not released be mindful that the mind is not released. When the mind is released be mindful that the mind is released.

"In this way one remains mindful internally and externally with regard to thoughts.

The third foundation of mindfulness is being mindful of the thinking process. With dispassionate mindfulness notice how thoughts cling to impermanent qualities of mind. Notice if the present quality of mind is agitated or peaceful. Notice if the present quality mind is constricted or spacious. Dispassionately notice thoughts attached to the quality of mind, often driven by feelings. This begins to develop insight into how thoughts have created confusion and suffering. With insight you can begin to incline your mind towards release from clinging conditioned mind.

Remember that Shamatha-Vipassana meditation is primarily used to develop unwavering concentration. This entire process of noting feelings and thoughts is done with dispassionate mindfulness. Feelings arise that take your attention. Note that a feeling has your attention and return your mindfulness to your breathing. When you find that you are distracted by discriminating thoughts related to the changing quality of your mind simply note the quality of your mind and return your mindfulness to your breath.

The sequence of this sutta is not meant to imply a fixed sequence. In meditation one becomes mindful of the breath. As the mind calms one may become mindful of feelings followed by thoughts driven by feelings or awareness of thoughts may initiate a reaction - a feeling.

Mindfulness during meditation is holding in mind the breath while feelings and thoughts arise and pass away. Being mindful that thoughts are flowing develops your innate ability to control thoughts. Being mindful of thoughts is recognizing that thinking is taking place. Unless concentration is developed, thoughts will "feed" themselves from conditioned thought patterns. This is discursive thinking and is an aspect of clinging mind.

Through refined mindfulness it becomes clear that thoughts are an ongoing evaluation or judgment of feelings and mental states. Much mental energy and distraction is spent on recollecting harsh or extreme judgments. This is a form of unskillful or unrefined mindfulness. This type of unrefined mindfulness can be debilitating. If left unchecked, this can lead to ever intensifying emotions that can result in depression and anxiety, or other mental disease.

Dispassionately remaining ardent and aware of thinking while maintaining mindfulness of the breath in the body will interrupt discursive thinking. This allows the mind to quiet and for concentration to develop. As mindfulness and concentration develops, the afflictions caused by discursive thinking subside and a mind of equanimity, a non-reactive mind, is maintained.

Mindfulness of The Present Quality of Mind

"And how does one remain mindful of the present quality of mind in and of itself? One remains focused on the mind internally or externally on the mind itself. One remains focused on the origination of the mind and the arising and the passing away of with regard to the mind itself. One knows 'there is a mind.' They remain independent of and not clinging to anything in the world. This how one remains mindful of thoughts in and of themselves."

The fourth foundation of mindfulness is being mindful of the present (but impermanent) quality of your mind. Is your present quality of mind inclined towards craving, clinging, and the continuation of stress? Is your present quality of mind inclined towards developing wisdom and release from craving and clinging?

Knowing that 'there is a mind' is mindfulness of the process resulting in the present quality of mind and that one has control over the present quality of mind.

During meditation 'remaining mindful of the present quality of mind' is dispassionate awareness of the process of

345

feelings and thoughts affecting the present quality of mind and noticing the impermanent quality of all mind states - the arising and passing away of qualities of mind.

During meditation 'remaining mindful of the present quality of mind' is dispassionate awareness of the process of feelings and thoughts affecting the present quality of mind while being mindful of the impermanent nature of all mind states. Concentration supports mindfulness and insight of the arising and passing away of qualities of mind. This develops the singular quality of samadhi, non-distraction - remaining at peace with less than peaceful mind-states. This is the quality of a well-concentrated mind during meditation and otherwise.

All mind-states are impermanent. Be at peace with less than peaceful mind-states.

The conclusion of the Satipatthana Sutta expands the Four Foundations of mindfulness from formal Shamatha-Vipassana meditation to apply these 'Four Frames of Reference' first to the Five Hindrances which often arise during meditation.

If one or all of the hindrances arise, simply remain mindful of the particular disturbance and return mindfulness to the breath. When the Hindrances arise outside of meditation a well-concentrated mind will not be further distracted by the particular hindrance but will dispassionately notice the arising and passing away of the hindrance.

Applying the Four Foundations of Mindfulness in reference to the Hindrances, or the Aggregates, or the Six-Sense Base, or the Seven Factors of Awakening, or The Four Noble Truths, should not be taken as direction on what to contemplate during meditation. Rather, it is important to remain mindful of the purpose of meditation is to deepen samadhi - non-distraction.

Notice that the last four themes - the Aggregates, the Six-Sense Base, the Seven Factors of Awakening, and The Four Noble Truths - are preceded by the word 'furthermore' to show that these are themes to be considered outside of formal meditation but supported by the concentration supporting the refined mindfulness developed during meditation.

During meditation, remain mindful when thoughts are directed towards these themes and return mindfulness to the breath.

In this way these important themes become integrated into the overall process of Becoming Buddha without becoming a distraction during formal Shamatha-Vipassana meditation. This avoids the possibility of getting caught in a feedback loop during meditation and directly contributes to the useful and skillful insight that will arise outside of meditation within the framework and guidance of the Eightfold Path.

Mindfulness of the Five Hindrances

Notice the guarantors offered by the Buddha. When one completely abandons a hindrance it will not arise again. Completely abandoning the hindrances is a reasonable goal and skillful reference to progress.

"Remain mindful of the quality of mind in reference to the five hindrances. When sensual desire is present be mindful that sensual desire is present. When sensual desire is not present be mindful that sensual desire is not present. Be mindful of abandoning sensual desire when it arises. Be mindful that when sensual desire has been (*completely*) abandoned, sensual desire will not arise in the future.

"When ill-will is present be mindful that ill-will is present. When ill-will is not present be mindful that ill-will is not present. Be mindful of abandoning ill-will when it arises. Be mindful that when ill-will has been (*completely*) abandoned, ill-will will not arise in the future.

"When laziness and drowsiness is present be mindful that laziness and drowsiness is present. When laziness and drowsiness is not present be mindful that laziness and drowsiness is not present. Be mindful of abandoning laziness and drowsiness when it arises. Be mindful that when laziness and drowsiness has been (*completely*) abandoned, laziness and drowsiness will not arise in the future.

"When restlessness and anxiety is present be mindful that restlessness and anxiety is present. When restlessness and anxiety is not present be mindful that restlessness and anxiety is not present. Be mindful of abandoning restlessness and anxiety when it arises. Be mindful that when restlessness and anxiety has been (*completely*) abandoned, restlessness and anxiety will not arise in the future.

"When doubt and uncertainty is present be mindful that doubt and uncertainty is present. When doubt and uncertainty is not present be mindful that doubt and uncertainty is not present. Be mindful of abandoning doubt and uncertainty when it arises. Be mindful that when doubt and uncertainty has been (*completely*) abandoned, doubt and uncertainty will not arise in the future.

"In this way one remains mindful of the quality of mind and the arising and the passing away of the qualities of mind - independent of and not clinging to anything in the world. This how one remains mindful of the quality of mind in and of itself.

This is a broader type of mindfulness that notices the quality of your mind that has developed from defining yourself through self-referential experiences driven by feelings and conditioned thinking. Notice when your mind seeks further sensual stimulation. Notice when your mind is distracted by ill-will. Notice when your mind is dull or restless or anxious or distracted by uncertainty. Return mindfulness to the breath. This is developing mindfulness of The Five Hindrances. Mindfulness of Hindrances directed by the Right Intention to abandon Hindrances brings release.

Mindfulness of Five Clinging-Aggregates

"Furthermore, one remains mindful of the quality of the mind in reference to The Five Clinging-Aggregates.

Remain mindful of form and the arising and passing away of form.

Remain mindful of feelings and the arising and passing away of feelings.

Remain mindful of perceptions and the arising and the passing away of perceptions.

Remain mindful of consciousness and the arising and passing away of consciousness.

"In this way one remains mindful of The Five Clinging-Aggregates and the arising and the passing away of The Five Clinging-Aggregates - independent of and not clinging to anything in the world. This how one remains mindful of The Five Clinging-Aggregates in and of themselves.

The Buddha is teaching here to be mindful of self-identification to the Five Clinging-Aggregates. He is teaching to be mindful of the impermanence of each of these aggregates - the arising and passing away of each aggregate.

351

This relates to Dependent Origination and supports insight into the process rooted in ignorance that confusion, deluded thinking, and ongoing disappointment is dependent on. Outside of formal meditation a well-concentrated mind will become increasingly less self-identified to these impermanent aggregates and become increasingly awakened.

Mindfulness of the Six-Sense Base

"Furthermore, one remains mindful of the quality of the mind in reference to the six-sense base.

"Remain mindful of the eye-form and the clinging that arises from the eye-form. Be mindful of the arising of clinging to the eye-form. Be mindful that when clinging to the eye-form is *(completely)* abandoned, clinging to the eye-form will not arise in the future.

"Remain mindful of the ear-form and the clinging that arises from the ear-form. Be mindful of the arising of clinging to the ear-form. Be mindful that when clinging to the ear-form is *(completely)* abandoned, clinging to the ear-form will not arise in the future.

"Remain mindful of the nose-form and the clinging that arises from the nose-form. Be mindful of the arising of clinging to the nose-form. Be mindful that when clinging to the nose-form is *(completely)* abandoned, clinging to the nose-form will not arise in the future.

"Remain mindful of the tongue-form and the clinging that arises from the tongue-form. Be mindful of the arising of clinging to the tongue-form. Be mindful that when clinging to the tongue-form is *(completely)* abandoned, clinging to the tongue-form will not arise in the future.

"Remain mindful of the body-form *(touch sense)* and the clinging that arises from the body-form. Be mindful of the arising of clinging to the body-form. Be mindful that when clinging to the body-form is *(completely)* abandoned, clinging to the body-form will not arise in the future.

"In this way one remains mindful of six-sense base and the arising and the passing away of six-sense base - independent of and not clinging to anything in the world. This how one remains mindful of six-sense base in and of themselves.

353

Mindfulness of the various sense-based-consciousness brings a profound understanding of creating self-referential views through sense contact and also directly relates to Dependent origination.

Avoid being distracted by the six-sense base and 'remain mindful of six-sense base and the arising and the passing away of six-sense base - independent of and not clinging to anything in the world.' This includes becoming analytical of what should be dispassionate mindfulness of the six-sense base.

Mindfulness of the Seven Factors of Awakening

"Furthermore, one remains mindful of the quality of the mind in reference to the Seven Factors of Awakening.

"Remain mindful that 'mindfulness is a factor of awakening within me.' If mindfulness as a factor of awakening is not present, be mindful that 'mindfulness as a factor of awakening is not present within me' and be mindful of how mindfulness as a factor of awakening will arise. *(through appropriate mindfulness)*

"Remain mindful of the culmination of the development of mindfulness as a factor of awakening.

"Remain mindful that investigation of the Dhamma is a factor of awakening. If investigation of the Dhamma as a factor of awakening is not present, be mindful that investigation of the Dhamma is not present and be mindful of how investigation of the Dhamma as a factor of awakening will arise. *(through appropriate mindfulness)*

"Remain mindful of the culmination of the development of investigation of the Dhamma as a factor of awakening.

"Remain mindful that persistence is a factor of awakening. If persistence as a factor of awakening is not present, be mindful that persistence is not present and be mindful of how persistence as a factor of awakening will arise. *(through appropriate mindfulness)*

"Remain mindful of the culmination of the development of persistence as a factor of awakening.

"Remain mindful that joyful engagement with the Dhamma is a factor of awakening. If joyful engagement with the Dhamma as a factor of awakening is not present, be mindful that joyful

355

engagement with the Dhamma is not present and be mindful of how joyful engagement with the Dhamma as a factor of awakening will arise. *(through appropriate mindfulness)*

"Remain mindful of the culmination of the development of joyful engagement with the Dhamma as a factor of awakening.

"Remain mindful that serenity is a factor of awakening. If serenity as a factor of awakening is not present, be mindful that serenity is not present and be mindful of how serenity as a factor of awakening will arise. *(through appropriate mindfulness)*

"Remain mindful of the culmination of the development of serenity as a factor of awakening.

"Remain mindful that concentration is a factor of awakening. If concentration as a factor of awakening is not present, be mindful that concentration is not present and be mindful of how concentration as a factor of awakening will arise. *(through appropriate mindfulness)*

"Remain mindful of the culmination of the development of concentration as a factor of awakening.

"Remain mindful that equanimity is a factor of awakening. If equanimity as a factor of awakening is not present, be mindful that equanimity is not present and be mindful of how equanimity as a factor of awakening will arise. *(through appropriate mindfulness)*

"Remain mindful of the culmination of the development of equanimity as a factor of awakening.

"In this way one remains mindful of the Seven Factors of Awakening and the arising and the passing away of the Seven Factors of Awakening - independent of and not clinging to anything in the world. This how one remains mindful of the Seven Factors of Awakening in and of themselves.

Remaining mindful of The Seven Factors of Awakening is mindful acknowledgment of developing the Eightfold Path correctly. Mindfulness of The Seven Factors of Awakening may occur during meditation but should not necessarily be cultivated during meditation. The concentration developed during meditation will provide the spaciousness and focus to notice these seven factors and serve as continued direction.

357

Mindfulness of Four Noble Truths

"Furthermore, one remains mindful of the quality of the mind in reference to The Four Noble Truths.

"Remain mindful of knowing that 'This is stress, this is the origination of stress, this is the cessation of stress, and this is the Eightfold Path leading to the cessation of stress.'

"In this way one remains mindful of the quality of mind in and of itself internally and externally. One remains mindful of the phenomenon of the origination of qualities of mind and their arising and passing away. There is the knowledge of the maintenance of qualities of mind and their recollection - independent of and not clinging to anything in the world. This how one remains mindful of the Seven Factors of Awakening in and of themselves.

Here the Buddha is bringing together the Four Foundations of Mindfulness applied during meditation and remaining mindful of each factor of the Eightfold Path in Becoming Buddha. Emphasis is on the importance of remaining mindful of the impermanent nature of all phenomena clinging to qualities of mind - the arising and passing away of all self-referential thoughts and attached fabrications.

Notice how this last also relates directly to the Buddha's description of his awakening in the Nagara Sutta: 'I came to direct knowledge of fabrications, direct knowledge of the origination of fabrications, direct knowledge of the cessation of fabrications, direct knowledge of the Eightfold Path leading to the cessation of fabrications.'

The Effectiveness of The Four Foundations of Mindfulness

"Now, if anyone develops these Four Foundations of Mindfulness in this manner for seven years one could expect either complete understanding here and now or, if there is any clinging and maintaining remaining, in this present life.

"Let alone seven years, if anyone *(perfectly)* develops these Four Foundations of Mindfulness in this manner for six, or five, or four, or three, or two, or one year, for six months, or three months, for one month, for two weeks, for seven days, one could expect either complete understanding here and now or, if

359

there is any clinging and maintaining remaining, in this present life.

"Friends, this is the direct path for the purification of all beings, for the cessation of sorrow and regret, for the disappearance of pain and distress, for establishing the right method of practice, and for complete unbinding - in other words these Four Foundations of Mindfulness.

Perhaps the most important reference in all the Buddha's Dhamma is contained here. The opportunity to Become Buddha in this present life is often misunderstood in even the more traditional Buddhist schools, and directly contradicted in the modern Buddhist lineages. Most modern Buddhist schools claim it will take "endless lifetimes" to develop awakening.

Here the Buddha is stating clearly that through wholehearted engagement with the Eightfold Path anyone can Become Buddha in this present life. Whether seven days or seven years, through a well-concentrated mind and wholehearted mindful engagement with the Eightfold Path, Becoming Buddha is assured.

This is what the Buddha said. Hearing these words those assembled were gratified and delighted.

End of Sutta

Samadhi - Non-Distraction
Jhanas - Meditative Absorption

The Samadhi Sutta shows the proper use of Shamatha-Vipassana meditation practice within the broader framework of the Eightfold Path. The word meditation in modern Buddhist practice has many applications. "Meditation" is often used as contemplation or analysis. Topics popular for contemplation or analysis are suffering, emptiness, decomposition, conditionality, and many others. This over-emphasizes simple and direct teachings leading to distraction by analysis.

Often, too, meditation is used to describe a process of deity visualization and worship. Still other applications of meditation are used to develop a quality of mind of "nothingness" where an obscured but inherent "Buddha-Nature" is uncovered or "Buddha-Hood" realized.

363

Contemplation of Koans, or Hwadu practice, are not something taught by the Buddha and should not be considered meditation practice within the framework of the Eightfold Path.

The Buddha taught Shamatha-Vipassana meditation as one factor of the Eightfold Path for the purpose of developing the concentration necessary to support the refined mindfulness of the other seven factors of the path.

At its most profound and skillful usefulness, it is concentration developed within the framework of the Eightfold Path that directly brings cessation of all confusion, delusion, and unsatisfactory experiences.

The Samadhi Sutta

Anguttara Nikaya 4.41

The Buddha addresses those gathered: "Friends, there are four qualities that are developed from concentration. Concentration, when developed and practiced leads to:

1. Developing peace and calm here and now.

2. Developing useful knowledge and true vision.

3. Developing refined mindfulness and attentiveness.

4. Developing the cessation of craving, aversion, and delusion.

"How does the development of concentration lead to peace and calm here and now? When properly engaged in Shamatha-Vipassana meditation, one is withdrawn from sensuality and unskillful mental qualities. They enter and remain in the first jhana, delight and pleasure born of withdrawal and accompanied by focused thought and insight.

"As concentration deepens further they enter and remain in the second jhana. Focused thoughts and insight still. Delight and pleasure born of composure and inner poise arise.

"As concentration deepens further they enter and remain in the third jhana. Delight and pleasure

365

and the perception of pleasure and pain disappear. Equanimity and refined mindfulness increases and a peaceful mind prevails.

"As concentration deepens further they enter and remain in the fourth jhana. Mindful equanimity prevails. Greed and aversion disappear. This is the development of concentration that brings peace and calm here and now.

"And how does the development of concentration lead to developing useful knowledge and true vision? As concentration deepens distractions subside. Even the passing from day to night and night to day is free of disturbance. The mind is bright and spacious. This is the development of concentration that brings useful knowledge and true vision.

"And how does the development of concentration lead to developing refined mindfulness and attentiveness? As concentration deepens the impermanence of feelings is understood. As concentration deepens the impermanence of perceptions is understood. As concentration deepens the impermanence of thoughts is understood. This is the development of concentration that brings refined mindfulness and attentiveness.

"And how does the development of concentration lead to developing the cessation of craving, aversion, and delusion? As concentration deepens one remains attentive to the arising and passing away of The Five Clinging Aggregates. One knows the impermanence of form, of feelings, of perceptions, of mental fabrications, and of consciousness. This is the development of concentration that brings the cessation of craving, aversion, and delusion.

"Friends, these are the four qualities that are developed from concentration.

"Those who understand The Three Marks of Existence,

For whom there are no disturbances,

Free of desire, at peace,

This one has abandoned confusion, delusion, and disappointment."

End of Sutta

367

The Samadhi Sutta teaches the proper use of meditation and how the concentration developed through Shamatha-Vipassana meditation directly addresses developing understanding of Four Noble Truths, integration of the Eightfold Path, and cessation of greed, aversion, and deluded thinking.

The Samadhi Sutta shows that Right Meditation brings insight to the impermanence of Five Clinging Aggregates and insight to Three Marks of Existence.

The jhanas are not to be taken as mind states to achieve. The jhanas are simply an explanation of different levels of concentration. Much is made in the modern Buddhist commentaries regarding the importance of achieving these states and the intense effort needed to reach the more "advanced" levels. There is no relative importance to any of these states except to point to the experience of deepening concentration.

The Buddha explained these states to specifically downplay any sense of special achievements associated with the jhanas. They are simply states of mindfulness of deepening concentration that are common experiences to all who engage in whole-hearted development of the Eightfold Path.

All that is needed to experience these levels of concentration and absorption is Shamatha-Vipassana meditation within the framework of the Eightfold Path.

In the Sallekha Sutta, Majjhima Nikaya 8, the Buddha points out to Maha-Cunda, one of the senior monks, that he may have been placing too much emphasis on the levels of meditative absorption.

In this sutta, Cunda asked the Buddha if acquiring the absorption of the jhanas would bring final release.

The Buddha places the importance of the jhanas as a foundational aspect of Right Meditation and then describes the "Right Discipline" developed by the Eightfold Path as the way to develop complete release:

"In the Noble One's discipline it is not these [attainments] that are called 'ending clinging.' In the Noble one's discipline they are called 'peaceful abiding's.'

369

"But here, Cunda, is how ending clinging should be developed:

The following relates directly to being mindful of the Eightfold Path. It is not jhana development alone, or any other singular mediation practice that leads to awakening. Here the Buddha clearly shows it is through wholehearted development of the Eightfold Path that one Becomes Buddha.

- Remain Harmless.

- Abstain from killing living beings.

- Abstain from taking what is not given.

- Abstain from sexual misconduct.

- Abstain from false speech.

- Abstain from hurtful speech.

- Abstain from gossip.

- Abandon ill will.

- Abandon wrong view and develop Right View.

- Abandon wrong intention and develop Right Intention.

- Abandon wrong speech and develop Right Speech.

- Abandon wrong actions and develop Right Actions.

- Abandon wrong livelihood and develop Right Livelihood.

- Abandon wrong mindfulness and develop Right Mindfulness.

- Abandon wrong meditation and develop Right Meditation.

"In this way release from clinging can be accomplished."

The actual path the Buddha taught is what many modern "Buddhist" schools would consider too mundane and archaic teachings that can be dismissed in favor of over-emphasized meditative achievement and "mystical" insight.

In the Pancalacanda Sutta, Samyutta Nikaya 2.7, the Buddha teaches that jhana, meditative absorption or deepening concentration, is initiated with mindfulness:

"Even in a confining place (an un-awakened mind) it is found, the Dhamma is for the attainment of unbinding. Those who have gained (proper, refined) mindfulness are rightly well-focused" to experience jhana.

One enters the first level of meditative absorption beginning with the foundations of mindfulness. Being mindful of the breath-in-the-body, being mindful of feelings and thoughts arising and passing away, and being mindful of the present quality of mind, the first jhana develops and passes away. As meditation continues and concentration increases the other "levels" of meditative absorption develop and pass away.

In the Atthakangara Sutta, Samyutta Nikaya 56.11, a householder, Atthakangara, went to Ananda, the Buddha's chief attendant, and asked him if there is a single quality where one engaged in the Dhamma would find release.

Ananda replied: "When one has quieted the mind through mindfulness (of the breath) and has abandoned sensuality and unskillful qualities one enters and remains in the first jhana.

"Happiness born from abandonment accompanied by directed thought and reflection. They reflect with mindfulness and understand that this first Jhana is fabricated by intention. (The meditation method) being fabricated the first jhana is impermanent. Motivated by joy for the Dhamma and continuing shamatha-vipassana he goes beyond fabrications."

"As one continues with mindfulness imbued with good-will they enter the second, the third, and then the fourth jhana."

The second Jhana is simply a meditative state that is undirected or unfabricated. The meditation method has fallen away (temporarily) and one stays in peace and happiness for a period of time.

The Third Jhana is a (temporary) state of pervasive happiness and peace without the quality of acknowledgment of happiness and peace. It is a state of equanimity with awareness of an arisen state.

The fourth Jhana is a (temporary) state of unwavering equanimity and pure mindfulness.

373

These levels of concentration are developed as meditation practice deepens. These are not levels of meditation to achieve or to be held onto, they are fluid states. Each meditation session may include all three or even all four levels of jhana.

The jhanas are taught simply to be aware of different levels of mindfulness that occur as a result of a wholehearted practice of Shamatha-Vipassana meditation within the framework of the Eightfold Path.

The Jhanas are ordinary states of meditative absorption that, through integration of the Eightfold Path develop, profound concentration and extraordinary peace and refined mindfulness.

In another concise reference to the jhanas from the Anguttara Nikaya 4.124 the Buddha teaches that deepening mental absorption - concentration - is for recognizing and abandoning ignorance of Four Noble Truths and the ongoing personal experience of suffering - Five Clinging Aggregates:

"A Dhamma practitioner, when properly engaged in Shamatha-Vipassana meditation, they are withdrawn from sensuality and unskillful mental qualities. They enter and remain in the first jhana, delight and pleasure born of withdrawal and accompanied by focused thought and insight.

"They regard any phenomena connected with form, feelings, perceptions, fabrications, or consciousness as impermanent, stressful, diseased, painful, empty of self.

"As they enter deeper levels of meditative absorption - the second, third, and fourth jhanas, they regard any phenomena connected with form, feelings, perceptions, fabrications, or consciousness as impermanent, stressful, diseased, painful, empty of self."

There is nothing in the Buddha's Dhamma that promotes specialness in the development of jhanas, or meditative "Achievements."

The Buddha teaches that deepening levels of meditative absorption are for the establishment of concentration.

The concentration developed from Right Meditation supports refined mindfulness of the Eightfold Path.

The Eightfold Path provides the framework and guidance to recognize and abandon the craving and clinging rooted in ignorance of Four Noble Truths.

Profound understanding of Four Noble Truths unbinds one from the personal experience of Dukkha.

Profound understanding of Four Noble Truths unbinds one from Five Clinging-Aggregates.

The Yuganaddha Sutta
Right Meditation

Tranquility and Insight in Tandem

Anguttara Nikaya 4.170

In the Yuganaddha Sutta, Ananda teaches that that those that achieve lasting peace and happiness do so by developing shamatha and vipassana (tranquility & insight) in tandem.

In this sutta, Ananda, the Buddha's cousin and chief attendant known to have a word-perfect memory addressed a gathering:

"Friends whoever achieves the unbound state (awakened) does so by means of one of four paths:

"When one has developed insight (vipassana) preceded by tranquility (shamatha) their path is born. They follow that path (the Eightfold Path), develop the path and pursue the path. As they develop the path, their shackles are abandoned and their obsessions destroyed. They are unbound, awakened.

"When one has developed tranquility preceded by insight, their path is born. They follow that path (the Eightfold Path), develop the path and pursue the path. As they develop the path, their shackles are abandoned and their obsessions destroyed. They are unbound, awakened.

"When one has developed tranquility in tandem with insight, their path is born. They follow that path (the Eightfold Path), develop the path and pursue the path. As they develop the path, their shackles are abandoned and their obsessions destroyed. They are unbound, awakened.

"When one's mind has its restlessness (doubt and confusion) well under control their mind grows steady inwardly (tranquility) and settles down. Their mind becomes unified and well concentrated (leading to insight). As they develop the path, their shackles are abandoned and their obsessions destroyed. They are unbound, awakened.

"Friends whoever achieves the unbound state does so by means of one of four paths."

End of Sutta

The importance of this sutta is the emphasis on developing the foundation of a mind settled and well-concentrated. A well-concentrated mind supports the refined mindfulness necessary to develop the Eightfold Path. The Eightfold Path supports useful insight of The Three Marks of Existence.

A meditation practice focused solely on quieting the mind or attempting to reach a state of nothingness with the expectation that "Buddha-Mind" will spontaneously arise is not part of the Buddha's teaching. A technique such as this will likely develop a mind of nothingness with no useful insight. This is simply misusing the Dhamma for further distraction.

Using only vipassana meditation is not something the Buddha taught.

Using an analytical form of meditation and calling it "vipassana" or "insight" is not the intention of Shamatha-Vipassana meditation.

The insight gained in Shamatha-Vipassana meditation is insight into clinging and insight into Three Marks of Existence. This is done with a quiet mind dispassionately recognizing clinging to impermanent objects and views as they arise and pass away and releasing the attachment to them.

Analyzing one's own mental confusion and distractive views will only lead to an over-emphasis on confusion and distraction. This analytical method, often called "insight," uses quieting the mind only as a preliminary practice and then discarded. This method then uses this analytical "insight meditation" on all objects, events, views, and ideas that arise and never develops the non-distracted state - samadhi -that is the only useful purpose of meditation within the framework of the Eightfold Path.

The result of a practice with an over-emphasis on vipassana will usually lead to a focus on human problems from the viewpoint of "fixing" the problems through a combination of psychological principles (views) and out-of-context Buddhist principles.

It is easy to see how an overly analytical view of one's own mind will develop an overly analytical and complex fabricated "answer" to all fabricated problems.

The transformative power of the Dhamma lies in its simplicity and direct method of application free of distracting intentions and resulting distracting views.

Shamatha-Vipassana meditation practiced within the framework of the Eightfold Path develops the ability to recognize and abandon the shackles that keep one bound to confusion, stress and unhappiness.

Shamatha-Vipassana meditation practiced within the framework of the Eightfold Path avoids creating and chasing endless "insightful" fabricated views.

Shamatha-Vipassana meditation, properly developed within the guidance and framework of the Eightfold Path is the non-distracted foundation that supports the entire path of Becoming Buddha - the Noble Eightfold Path.

Shamatha-Vipassana Meditation Practice

Right Meditation

Introduction

The Buddha taught only Shamatha-Vipassana meditation throughout his teaching career. It is a remarkably simple technique with profound and transformative results.

Shamatha-Vipassana meditation is the foundation of the Eightfold Path.

Shamatha-Vipassana meditation is the initial establishment of the Four Foundations of Mindfulness.

Shamatha-Vipassana meditation is a meditation technique that anyone can integrate into their lives.

Shamatha-Vipassana meditation only requires

being mindful of the pure sensation of the breath in the body.

It is in its simplicity that Shamatha-Vipassana meditation will focus a distracted mind and end the feedback loop of self-referential views. Within the framework of the Eightfold Path, Shamatha-Vipassana meditation will develop the insight necessary to abandon confused and discursive thinking.

Developing trance-like states, distracting imagery, or visualizations is not the purpose of meditation.

The purpose of Shamatha-Vipassana meditation is to develop gentle and unwavering concentration. From a well-concentrated mind, insight into the arising and passing away of all objects, events, views, and ideas will develop. Distracting thoughts originating in clinging, craving, desire, and aversion, will fall away.

The initial difficulty for many beginning meditators is boredom. Boredom is a conditioned mind's need for continual distraction. As the practical benefits of meditation develop, joyful enthusiasm overcomes boredom.

Maintaining mindfulness of the breath brings a gentle focus to meditation, developing concentration.

Chasing mystical experiences or ego-driven analytical achievements is avoided.

Initially, short periods of meditation are effective in establishing a meditation practice. Attempting unrealistically long meditation sessions will often further conditioned thinking rooted in ignorance. Unrealistic methods will often develop unrealistic expectations. The framework and guidance of the Eightfold Path avoids these distractions.

There is no need to struggle with long periods of meditation. A few minutes of well-intentioned gentle practice is enough to begin to incline the mind towards samadhi.

Samadhi is the quality of mind of non-distraction, or deep and profound concentration.

Deepening concentration is the "goal" of meditation, not length of time. As gentle concentration deepens, the length of meditation sessions will naturally increase.

Shamatha means tranquil or quiet. Using the breath as a point of focus interrupts following one thought immediately with the next. As the mind quiets concentration increases.

The insight that develops through the Eightfold Path is not a distracting craving-insight into all mundane phenomena. A well-concentrated mind supports skillful insight into the core themes of the Buddha's Dhamma - Three Marks of Existence, Five Clinging-Aggregates, and Four Noble Truths.

Skillful insight may occur during Shamatha-Vipassana meditation. The Satipatthana Sutta shows that skillful insight more commonly occurs outside of formal meditation through mindfulness of the Eightfold Path *supported by the concentration developed during meditation.*

Rather than an aspect of direct inquiry into ordinary phenomena during meditation, *skillful insight is a product of a quiet and well-concentrated mind framed by the entire Eightfold Path.*

As seen in the Yuganaddha Sutta, developing tranquility and insight in tandem is for "developing the Eightfold Path so that the shackles of self-referential views are abandoned and self-obsessions destroyed."

The Buddha taught that what is held in mind determines experience. This is why quieting the mind and gaining insight into the nature of stress and clinging is so effective in developing awakening.

The purpose of the Buddha's teachings is to recognize and abandon craving and clinging rooted in ignorance of Four Noble Truths. It is craving and clinging rooted in ignorance that creates the feedback loop described in the Nagara Sutta.

Skillful insight into craving and clinging develops the refined mindfulness necessary to recognize and abandon all wrong views. Within the framework of the Eightfold Path, Right view develops as wrong views are recognized and abandoned.

Shamatha-Vipassana meditation returns the mind to a tranquil state not subject to reaction caused by conditioned thinking. Conditioned thinking causes continued wrong view which causes continued unskillful reaction. This reaction creates further conditioned thinking. This is another way of describing the feedback loop the Buddha describes in the Nagara Sutta. The insight developed into this process makes it possible to interrupt the cycle of discursive thinking.

This simple technique avoids the distraction of compulsively analyzing impermanent mental objects.

This would only continue ignorant views. The Buddha describes these views and what these views support as "like foam on the water."

It is foolish and unskillful to use meditation to further ignorance in this manner. Simply recognize distraction and return mindfulness to the breath. No further analysis of reactive thoughts or feelings is necessary or effective in interrupting this feedback loop.

Analysis of conditioned thinking during meditation will only strengthen conditioned thinking. What is held in mind will determine experience.

A meditation practice alone, without the guidance and framework of the Eightfold Path, will strengthen conditioned thinking while substituting more "acceptable" but still ignorant views.

This again is another example of being stuck in a feedback loop of self-referential views.

Having the intention to engage in a meditation practice to fix a broken or flawed self is not skillful use of meditation.

- Using meditation to realize a hidden Buddha-Nature is not skillful use of meditation.

- Using meditation to realize Buddha-Hood is not skillful use of meditation.

- Using meditation to seek pleasant mind states or mystical experiences is not skillful use of meditation.

- Using meditation to establish an imaginary mind-state of "nothingness" or "emptiness" is not skillful use of meditation.

- Using meditation in this way will create more self-referential conditioned thinking.

One can spend eternity in these distracting pursuits. Concentration supports the refined mindfulness necessary for recognizing and abandoning all wrong views.

Concentration supports the refined mindfulness necessary for integrating the Eightfold Path as the framework for developing awakened Right View.

Shamatha-Vipassana meditation will develop a non-distracted quality of mind. This brings the ability

389

to recognize and abandon all conditioned mind states. Ineffective "meditation" practices are abandoned.

As stated in the introduction, the Buddha practiced and mastered the most "advanced" meditation techniques of his time - both still practiced today - and rejected them as "not leading to the goal" and "not supporting unbinding."

The Buddha likened establishing a meditation practice to taming a wild elephant. In order for a young elephant to be useful, it must be able to focus and follow direction.

To tame a young elephant, a strong rope would be tied around the elephant's neck and to a strong post or tree. The elephant would immediately begin thrashing around, flapping its ears, stomping the ground, and making loud grunts and bellows, very unhappy to not be able to wander around, aimlessly engaging in any distraction that arose.

The more resistant the young elephant became, the stronger the rope held. Eventually the elephant would put aside its desire for continual distraction and sensual fulfillment and it would settle down.

In this metaphor, an untrained mind is the young elephant, the rope is mindfulness of the breath, and the strong post or tree is the breath.

As one begins to establish a meditation practice, the mind is often thrashing about, resistant to settling down. Thoughts insist on wandering aimlessly with strong desire to continue distraction by following one thought with another, continually describing their own self-created reality.

As mindful awareness of the breath develops the mind calms and concentration deepens. By utilizing the simple technique of Shamatha-Vipassana meditation it becomes possible to quiet a constantly distracted mind. With sustained gentle practice guided by the Eightfold Path, clinging, compulsive thinking settles down.

Returning to the metaphor, once the elephant has learned to remain mindful of the post, the rope is loosened and the elephant is finally free. Once tranquility and concentration deepens, the need to describe reality based on desirous thoughts driven by attachment and aversion is interrupted, and useful and skillful insight arises.

As concentration increases, integrating The Eightfold Path begins to clear "fetters" or "hindrances." Fetters are agitated mind states which can make quieting the mind much more difficult if not impossible. As practical insight into Right View, Right Intention, Right Speech, Right Action, Right Livelihood, Right Effort, and Right Mindfulness develops, fetters subside and Right Meditation becomes increasingly more effective.

In this way it is quickly seen that Shamatha-Vipassana meditation is one aspect of a complete path that develops profound wisdom, pure virtue, and unwavering concentration necessary for ending ignorance and for Becoming Buddha.

Meditation Posture

There is nothing magical or mystical about a meditation posture. The typical meditation posture of seated on the floor with legs folded against the torso is simply a way to sit comfortably during meditation. The meditation posture should be stable, relaxing and support a quiet and alert mind. It should provide a reasonable amount of comfort, avoiding physical distraction for the meditation period.

At first, any posture may prove uncomfortable, and the posture described below will become more comfortable with time. It is preferable to sit on the floor supported by a zafu (pillow made for meditation) placed over a zabuton (a larger, flatter mat to support the legs). The zafu should be from 6 to 8 inches thick and is often filled with cotton, buckwheat, or kapok.

When sitting on the zafu place your sit bones on the front third of the zafu and allow your hips to drop in front of you. With your legs straight in front of you, bend your right leg at the knee and place your right foot under your left thigh and near your left buttock.

Bend your left leg at the knee and place your left foot approximately in the crease formed by your right thigh and calf, resting on your calf. For more support you can place yoga blocks or a rolled towel under your knees.

This posture may be uncomfortable at first, but with time and patience this will prove to be a stable base with which to build a meditation practice on. This is known as the half-lotus or Burmese posture.

393

If you are particularly nimble, you may want to sit in the full-lotus position. The full-lotus is the same as the half-lotus except for placing the right foot on top of the left thigh and the left foot on the right thigh. There is nothing advantageous about the full-lotus over the half-lotus unless it affords you more stability and comfort.

From this stable base, keep your back straight but not stiff, not leaning forward or back. Align your ears with your shoulders and your nose with your navel.

Place your left hand on top of your right palm with the thumbs tips lightly touching forming an approximate egg-shape with the thumbs and forefingers.

Again, there is nothing magical or mystical about this hand placement. When done consistently it leads to quicker relaxation and lessens physical distraction.

An alternative to sitting on a zafu is to use a low bench called a seiza in a sitting-kneeling position usually over a blanket or zabuton.

If sitting on the floor proves too uncomfortable, it is acceptable to sit in a chair with your feet flat on the floor, your back straight but not stiff, ears aligned with your shoulders and nose aligned with your navel.

Lying down is the least effective regular meditation posture as it will usually lead to drowsiness. If lying on your back is the only choice due to injury or illness, make the best of it and avoid drowsiness. If drowsiness ensues, stop meditation and begin again when refreshed.

Shamatha-Vipassana Meditation Technique

To begin your meditation, take a few slow, deep breaths, exhaling fully. Remind yourself that now is the time for meditation. Gently close your eyes and gently close your mouth leaving a soft smile.

Breathing through your nose, notice your breath entering your body at the tip of your nose. Being mindful of the sensation of breathing in your body you may notice that the air is slightly cooler on the inhale and slightly warmer on the exhale. If you don't notice this temperature difference simply notice the flow of your breath.

Be mindful of your inhalation and your exhalation. Do not attempt to regulate your breathing in any way. However your body wants to breathe, place your mindfulness on the pure sensation of breathing.

Take a few minutes to sit with mindfulness of the breath. Notice that thoughts are flowing. Return your awareness to your breath.

As thoughts continue to arise, gently put your thoughts aside, not following one thought with another thought, and place your mindful awareness on your breathing.

As thoughts arise, gently put your thoughts aside and remain mindful of your breathing. This is being mindful of the breath, holding in mind your breathing.

This is the basic practice - being mindful of the breath in the body.

Remember that a trance-like state or the forced elimination of all thoughts is not a goal of meditation.

We are conscious beings - thoughts should be flowing.

The purpose of meditation is to not be distracted by thoughts.

When you find that you are caught up in your thoughts, return mindfulness to the sensation of breathing.

As thought constructs or physical feelings arise, dispassionately remain mindful of them for a few moments. Acknowledge the thought or feeling as impermanent and return your mindfulness to your breathing. You are now engaging in the "vipassana" part of Shamatha-Vipassana meditation of gaining useful insight.

What is useful insight? Simply that all thoughts, all experiences, are impermanent and empty of any lasting effect. Any further analysis will only further distract a distracted mind.

You are developing concentration and spaciousness between thoughts. By dispassionately experiencing thoughts while remaining tranquil, you are directly interrupting conditioned thinking. By remaining tranquil as thoughts arise, you are training

397

your mind to accept the people and events, including yourself, as they are. Dispassionate acceptance of thoughts as they are interrupts conditioned thinking.

It is the reaction caused by conditioned thinking that creates perception of an event. Understanding now reveals the means for freedom and liberation from suffering. Let everything that arises go and return your mindfulness to the pure sensation of breathing.

Notice the arising and the passing away of thoughts.

Notice the arising and the passing away of the breath.

As Shamatha-Vipassana meditation practice develops, the insight and spaciousness realized in sitting practice will become more and more apparent in your life off of your cushion.

You will find that you are more peaceful and less reactive.

You will find you are more present and mindful of who you are in the present moment.

You will find ever-deepening concentration.

Remember that you are not seeking a trance-like or blank mental state. No insight can arise in a trance. Shamatha-Vipassana meditation interrupts compulsively following one thought with another thought by being mindful of the sensation of breathing in the body.

Insight into The Three Marks of Existence through profound concentration is what distinguishes meditation taught by the Buddha from every other meditation technique.

Unless insight is developed, no freedom from conditioned thinking is possible. Until conditioned thinking is recognized and put aside, it will prove impossible to escape the suffering caused conditioned thinking.

Once conditioned thinking is recognized and abandoned the mind's natural spaciousness is realized free of clinging one thought immediately to the next.

If unpleasant thoughts arise, put them aside and return to the sensation of breathing in the body.

If pleasant thoughts arise, put them aside and return to the sensation of breathing in the body.

If visions arise, pleasant or unpleasant, grand or mundane, dispassionately put them aside and return to the sensation of breathing in the body.

Whatever arises during meditation practice is simply part of what is to be recognized as impermanent and put aside and return awareness to the breath.

There is a recording of a guided Shamatha-Vipassana meditation session at Becoming-Buddha.com

Establishing a Meditation Practice

The second and sixth factors of The Eightfold Path, Right Intention and Right Effort, greatly support meditation practice. The strong resolve of Right Intention is to recognize and abandon craving and clinging. Being mindful of Right Effort will provide the framework needed to develop and maintain a meditation practice.

Perhaps the most difficult challenge when beginning a meditation practice, and often as practice develops, is organizing life for practice. The busy-ness and nearly constant distractions of life are always creating the illusion of being too busy to practice. The irony is that it is often found that there is more time for the most important aspects of life when we do make the time for meditation practice.

Being mindful of Right Intention and Right Effort, make a commitment to practice. Put aside set times, preferably twice a day, for meditation practice. It is most skillful to sit as soon as possible after waking before becoming distracted or sidetracked by a daily routine. Simply doing this begins to diminish conditioned mind's desire to avoid quieting down.

Right Effort is keeping in fit physical, mental and spiritual condition as well. Getting enough rest, eating healthy, and physical exercise are all a part of Right Effort.

Any exercise is a support for meditation practice. Walking "meditation" is a very skillful way to combine exercise and meditation. Walking "meditation" is not a substitute for sitting meditation.

Nothing will bring the mind to a state of quiet receptivity necessary for insight to arise as will an effective sitting practice.

401

When doing walking meditation, walk slowly with hands folded in front of your abdomen or behind you. Avoid extremely slow walking - this is a modern form of asceticism. Maintain mindfulness of your breath and your walking, being aware of each step as your foot touches the earth.

Qigong is a very effective exercise that combines slow movements and mindful breath awareness. Qigong increases peaceful energy and builds flexibility, strength and well being. Some forms of yoga (asanas) can also build flexibility, strength and overall well-being though the underlying philosophy of yoga often contradicts the Buddha's teachings.

Once a decision to begin a meditation practice has been made, organizing life for practice is the first step in establishing an ongoing practice. Committing to meditation twice a day and, within reason, keeping to this schedule is itself part of practice.

The most skillful time to practice is when aversion to sitting arises.

Meditating when aversion to meditation arises diminishes the effects of conditioned thinking, including the conditioned thinking of aversion to meditation practice.

As stated previously, meditating upon arising in the morning is usually the most effective time to schedule a first sitting session. If possible, meditating approximately 12 hours later in the day will provide a skillful balance to practice. If the only other time for practice is just before bed, be mindful of drowsiness. If it is at times difficult to maintain alertness, try to adjust your schedule to earlier in the day.

If it is possible to set aside a room solely for meditation, keep the room clean and clutter free. The room should also be well ventilated and seasonally not too hot or cold. A candle to light during meditation and perhaps a small statue of the Buddha as a mindful reminder of awakening can be an initial point of focus, but are not necessary. If it is not possible to designate an entire room to your practice, a corner of a room that can be maintained as above will work just as well.

Developing a routine of place, time, posture and technique will greatly enhance commitment to practice and help subdue conditioned mind's desire to avoid the peaceful refuge of practice.

It is best to begin a meditation practice with just a few minutes of sitting at a time. By initially sitting for two or three minutes at a time you will not become disappointed or conclude that meditation is too difficult. As you become comfortable with two or three minutes of practice, gradually add a minute or two to your meditation time. Stay at this length of meditation practice until you are comfortable and feel it is time to lengthen your meditation practice again.

It is most skillful not to push yourself too hard and too fast, and also not to avoid increasing your practice time when appropriate. If you have a teacher or someone who has some experience in establishing a meditation practice, seek their counsel as well.

Establishing a mediation practice will be much more effective if done daily for short periods of time rather than long periods of meditation only occasionally.

Meditation practice is not an endurance test and should not create more stress by having too high expectations of yourself and your practice. The strongest impediment to establishing a meditation practice will prove to be your own judgments of your practice.

Joining a regular meditation group that stays focused within the framework of The Eightfold Path is an essential support to meditation practice.

If you are following the instructions, putting aside thoughts as they arise, not following a thought with a thought as best as you can, and returning your awareness to the sensation of breathing in your body, you are establishing a meditation practice.

Avoid judging yourself or your practice harshly. Always be loving and gentle with yourself and enjoy your practice.

Vitakkasanthana Sutta
Relaxation of Thoughts

Majjhima Nikaya 20

In this short but significant sutta the Buddha teaches five strategies for abandoning unskillful thoughts and for cultivating skillful qualities of mind.

By cultivating skillful qualities of mind and abandoning what has arisen from ignorance, one gains the ability to "think what they want whenever they want and does not think what is unskillful."

The Vitakkasanthana Sutta

The Buddha was at Savatthi, in Jeta's Grove, Anathapindika's monastery. He addressed those assembled: "When one is intent on developing awakening, there are five qualities of mind they should attend to:

1. When one's thoughts are unskillful and arising from craving and delusion they should be mindful of their unskillful thoughts in order to abandon unskillful thoughts. Once unskillful thoughts have been abandoned, they can now cultivate skillful thoughts guided by the Eightfold Path. With unskillful thoughts abandoned one's mind calms and concentration increases.

2. If unskillful thoughts driven by craving and delusion arise again one should be mindful of the suffering brought by these thoughts recognizing 'these thoughts are unskillful and will lead to more confusion, delusion, and stress.' Being mindful of the drawbacks of unskillful thoughts these thoughts can now be abandoned. With unskillful thoughts abandoned one's mind calms and concentration increases.

3. If unskillful thoughts driven by craving and delusion continue to arise while being mindful of the drawbacks of these thoughts one should

pay no attention to these thoughts. By mindfully withdrawing attention to unskillful thoughts these thoughts are abandoned and will subside. With unskillful thoughts abandoned one's mind calms and concentration increases.

4. If unskillful thoughts driven by craving and delusion continue to arise while being mindful of the drawbacks of these thoughts one should focus on relaxing the mental fabrications with regard to unskillful thoughts. With the relaxation of mental fabrications one's mind calms and concentration increases.

5. If unskillful thoughts driven by craving and delusion continue to arise while being mindful of relaxing the mental fabrications with regard to unskillful thoughts one should develop Right Intention in order abandon unskillful thoughts with continued refined mindfulness. With the intentional abandonment of unskillful thoughts one's mind calms and concentration increases.

"Now when a practitioner recognizes unskillful thoughts, understands unskillful thoughts...

409

"Paying no mind to unskillful thoughts...

"Attending to the relaxing of mental fabrications with regard to those thoughts ...

"And using Right Mindfulness and Right Intention to steady their mind, settle their mind, unifies their mind and concentrates their mind right within...

"This is a person with mastery of thought sequences.

"This person thinks what they want whenever they want and does not think what is unskillful.

"This practitioner has severed craving and has brought an end to suffering and stress."

End of Sutta

This sutta describes the simple process of first recognizing through refined mindfulness that unskillful thoughts are present. It should be noted here that those in attendance have already been introduced to the Four Noble Truths and are developing the Eightfold Path as their framework for Dhamma practice.

The Buddha emphasizes that unskillful thoughts arise due to craving and clinging. Notice the relationship to the Second Noble Truth, Five Clinging-Aggregates, and Dependent Origination. Be mindful of unskillful thoughts. When unskillful thoughts are recognized, abandon them. Cultivate skillful thoughts framed by the Eightfold Path. *This is the first strategy to use with unskillful thoughts.*

When unskillful thoughts reoccur, acknowledge the reoccurrence. Acknowledge that unskillful thoughts will continue confusion, deluded thinking, and suffering. *This is the second strategy to use with unskillful thoughts.*

When unskillful thoughts reoccur, acknowledge the reoccurrence. Acknowledge that unskillful thoughts will continue confusion, deluded thinking, and suffering. Withdraw attention from unskillful thoughts.

Here the Buddha is teaching to avoid analyzing the origination of unskillful thoughts. As a Dhamma practitioner one knows that unskillful thoughts originate in ignorance. Seeking "insight" at this point is rooted in ignorance and continues craving and

411

clinging. *Withdrawing attention from unskillful thoughts is the third strategy to use with unskillful thoughts.*

When unskillful thoughts reoccur, acknowledge that the reoccurrence is rooted in mental fabrications. Relax the thought - withdraw attention - to the mental fabrication. This relates directly to Dependent Origination.

Mental Fabrications are assumptions about yourself in relation to the world originating in ignorance.

Rather than hold tight to the fabrication, relax and let go of the fabrication. The Buddha instructs to directly avoid the compulsion for analysis of phenomena rooted in ignorance.

Relaxing thoughts attached to mental fabrications is the fourth strategy to use with unskillful thoughts.

When unskillful thoughts continue to reoccur a fifth strategy is to use the second factor of the Eightfold Path. Recognize that unskillful thoughts continue to arise. Acknowledge that these unskillful thoughts are rooted in craving and deluded thinking.

Develop the Right Intention to recognize and abandon craving and clinging immediately.

Acknowledge that intentionally abandoning unskillful thoughts will continue to refine mindfulness and continue to develop release and an awakened quality of mind. *Intentionally abandoning unskillful thoughts is the fifth strategy to use with unskillful; thoughts.*

Develop the Right Intention to recognize and abandon craving and clinging.

Abandoning craving and clinging roots out the cause of all unskillful thoughts, words, and deeds.

Intentionally recognizing and abandoning craving and clinging rooted in ignorance is the foundational task associated with Becoming Buddha.

413

Karma and Rebirth

- Karma is continuity of Dukkha within impermanence.

- Karma is the present unfolding of past intentional acts moderated by present mindfulness.

- Karma is the personal experience of Three Marks of Existence

"I am the owner of my actions, heir to my actions. I am born of my actions and related through my actions. My actions will determine the fortune or misfortune in my life." (Anguttara Nikaya 10.176)

Karma and Rebirth are closely linked concepts of the Buddha's teachings. Many modern schools claim the Buddha taught karma and rebirth only to relate to the prevalent beliefs of his time. They hope to show that Karma and Rebirth are not useful or relevant teachings. Understanding karma and rebirth is essential to Becoming Buddha.

The Buddha's teachings on karma and rebirth refuted many of the common beliefs of his time. Understanding Karma and Rebirth help clarify the purpose and experience of awakening.

Understanding Karma and Rebirth as they were originally presented and in the context of The Four Noble Truths brings insight and clarity to the Eightfold Path.

Understanding Karma and Rebirth and can help one recognize contradictory and confusing "Buddhist" teachings that are later-developed adaptations and accommodations to the original teachings.

Karma and Rebirth are conditions arising from ignorance. Karma means action. Karma is in no way punishment as a result of arbitrary judgments from a supreme being. Karma is not the consequences from a vague independent moral-ethical-spiritual system.

Karma is not a condition imposed on you. You alone are the cause of your karma and you alone are the cause of rebirth.

416

Karma should not be viewed simply as what is unfolding in your life. Karma is the present unfolding of past intentional actions moderated by your present state of understanding and quality of mindfulness.

As your present state of mindfulness and understanding animate your current thoughts, words, and deeds, your current actions are moderating the effects of past thoughts, words, and deeds.

What this means is the key a to developing the Dhamma.

Through mindfulness informed by wisdom and motivated by Right Intention, the unfolding of karma can be inclined towards release and awakening.

Developing understanding of the process of originating in ignorance resulting in confusion and suffering brings the ability to end ignorance through developing wisdom. By understanding the causes and conditions of suffering you can reverse the process.

Karma does not pre-determine life. Mindful and well-concentrated intention within the framework of the Eightfold Path develops release from craving and clinging and cessation of suffering.

417

"Whatever one continues to pursue with their thinking becomes the inclination of their awareness. Being mindful of Right Intention and abandoning thinking imbued with craving, clinging, and sensuality inclines the mind towards release." (Samyutta Nikaya 22.102)

All the events of life are not the result of individual karma. Most of what occurs in one's life is simply worldly conditions and described in the First Noble Truth and summarized as "There is stress." Reaction to impersonal events will create additional karma and further conditions conditioned mind.

Reaction arises from wrong views of self. It is wrong views that initiate and proliferate karma. Once all wrong views of self are abandoned, the establishment of further karma ends.

As with all the Buddha's original teachings, karma is taught in the context of The Four Noble Truths with the goal of the cessation of suffering.

In this context, karma describes the ongoing suffering rooted in ignorance and reinforced by wrong views and wrong intention.

"Karma should be understood (correctly). The cause of karma should be understood. The diversity (of the results) of karma should be understood. Cessation of karma should be understood. The path developing the cessation of karma should be understood." (Samyutta Nikaya 22.102)

Notice that these are the same words the Buddha uses to describe the truth of suffering. Karma unfolding, whether experienced as pleasure or pain, is an aspect of dukkha and originates in craving and clinging. This relates directly to Dependent Origination (ignorance resulting in suffering) and Right Intention.

The Buddha continues: "Intention is karma. With intention one does karma through thought, word, and deed. And what is the cause that initiates karma? Contact."

This again relates to Dependent Origination and the importance of unraveling the links of Dependent Origination. The ongoing process of ignorance resulting in confusion and suffering can be brought to an end through wisdom and ensuing right actions framed by the Eightfold Path (again, karma means action).

419

The Buddha continues: "And what is the cessation of karma? From the cessation of contact comes the cessation of karma. And how does one experience the cessation of contact? Through the Noble Eightfold Path."

This shows that the driving force to continue confusion and suffering is described by the Buddha as karma. This is to point out the importance of being mindful of all thoughts, words, and deeds.

This is the purpose of mindfulness in the context of The Four Noble Truths.

It is your actions that will determine your awakening or continued confusion and suffering. The framework for recognizing, understanding, and refining your actions is the Eightfold Path.

Through whole-hearted engagement with the Eightfold Path you are taking actions that directly influence the unfolding of your karma and incline your karma towards developing a life of lasting peace and happiness.

- Karma is your ego-personality's experience of craving and clinging within anicca.

- Karma is the direct experience of the results of ignorance.Understanding karma is understanding dukkha.

- Understanding dukkha inclines your mind towards abandoning craving and clinging and begins to unravel the links of Dependent Origination.

With awakened Right View no attachment to the ego-personality is present and any experience is simply an experience in the world that is dispassionately observed with mindful presence.

Any event that occurs in the phenomenal world is an opportunity to remain dispassionately present with a mind settled in equanimity.

- Once a reaction to an event has occurred, further karma is established.

- A mind settled in equanimity will cease creating additional karma.

"A fool and a wise person are both characterized by their actions. It is through the actions of one's life that reveals the fool or the sage. The fool engages in

421

three things: bodily misconduct, verbal misconduct, and mental misconduct. The sage engages in three things: good bodily conduct, good verbal conduct, and good mental conduct.

"Thus friends, train yourselves as a sage in thought, word, and deed." (Anguttara Nikaya 6.46)

Your experience of the unfolding of your karma is not predetermined. The state or quality of your mind in each moment determines your experience of karma unfolding. A reactive mind will further karma. A mind of equanimity will bring a peaceful experience of karma unfolding and avoid additional karma.

While it is more desirable to experience the effects of karma pleasurably, to have "good karma," all karma contributes to dukkha and rebirth. All karma is to be extinguished.

Holding the conscious intention to act in a certain manner to develop favorable karma will accomplish just that: develop additional karma. The result will be to forever perpetuate dukkha. This is why it is crucial to be mindful of Right View and the strong resolve, the Right Intention, to abandon all craving and clinging, and awaken.

Dukkha describes the underlying unsatisfactory experience of life in the phenomenal world. Karma describes your contribution to your experience of the underlying unsatisfactory experience. Your karma is your dukkha.

Intentional actions will determine the continuation or cessation of confusion and stress.

Altruistic or compassionate actions taken without wisdom can often generate further karmic entanglements. This can be very subtle and difficult to recognize. For example, if an underlying motivation and intention for compassionate action is to fulfill a view of what it means to be a "good" person, even a "good Buddhist," the resulting karma will reinforce an ego-personality.

Altruistic and compassionate actions that are an expression of an awakened mind will always benefit all with no karmic entanglements or consequences.

This is not to say that one should not act with compassion and in accordance with the framework of the Eightfold Path. The Eightfold Path provides guidance against continued self-identification and continued "I-making."

Holding the intention to establish and defend an ego-self leads to action and reaction that inevitably creates additional karma.

Acting with the (wrong) intention to establish a view of what a "Buddhist" should be or a "Buddhist practice" should be is a subtle but prevalent form of "I-making" that further establishes karma.

Holding in mind the intention to recognize and abandon craving and clinging will incline karma towards release. The life experience will naturally be more peaceful and meaningful.

Karma is the experience of self in this present moment. Who you see yourself to be is the result of karma or past actions unfolding in the present state of your mindfulness.

Karma is who you are in this moment in the phenomenal world. The more skillful your actions in the present, the more liberating will be your karma as life unfolds. Mindfulness of the Eightfold Path inclines you to Right Action.

By being mindful of the Dhamma and living with the integrity that arises from following The Eightfold Path, you directly impact karma in the

424

present moment. You will change the direction of your life by changing your intentional actions and reactions.

The Eightfold Path is the framework for clearly seeing your actions, reactions, and unfolding karma. Your actions and reactions change as your thoughts become virtuous, your mind becomes less distracted, and wisdom deepens.

Holding the intention to abandon all clinging, craving, desire and aversion diminishes the distraction of dukkha. Abandoning clinging interrupts the ongoing establishment and defense of your ego-self.

- Unskillful intentions and resulting actions will create additional karma.

- Right Intention will lead to cessation of unskillful actions and bringing an end to karma.

- Right Intention is holding the strong resolve to put aside all clinging, craving, desire and aversion.

- Right Intention arising from Right View generates the moral and ethical actions of Right Speech, Action and Livelihood.

425

- Right Intention arising from Right View informs a practice developing Right Effort, Right Mindfulness and Right Meditation.

- The virtuous aspects of The Eightfold Path lead to the abandonment of desire.

At Savatthi the Buddha said: "Monks, what a person wills, what they plan, what they dwell on forms the basis for the continuation of consciousness. This basis being present, consciousness has a lodgment. Consciousness being lodged there and growing, rebirth of renewed existence takes place in the future, and from this renewed existence arise birth, decay-and-death, grief, lamentation, suffering, sorrow and despair. Such is the uprising of this entire mass of suffering.

"Even if a person does not will and plan, yet if they dwell on something this forms a basis for the continuation of consciousness:... rebirth... takes place...

"But if a person neither wills nor plans nor dwells on anything, no basis is formed for the continuation of consciousness. This basis being absent, consciousness has no lodgment. Consciousness not being lodged there and not growing, no rebirth of renewed existence takes place in the future, and so birth, decay-and-death, grief, lamentation, suffering, sorrow and despair are destroyed. Such is the cessation of this entire mass of suffering." (Samyutta Nikaya 12.38)

Notice how this last passage relates to Dependent Origination. Remember that all of these teachings are to develop understanding of confusion and suffering and the cessation of future confusion and suffering.

- By gaining wisdom one no longer acts from ignorance.

- With no ignorance there is no basis for the establishment of mental fabrications or discriminating and discursive consciousness.

- With no consciousness established in ignorance there is nothing to sustain the Five Clinging-Aggregates.

- With no sustenance, the 12 Links of Dependent Origination unbind.

427

- With no sustenance, a moment free of delusion, confusion, and unsatisfactoriness, a moment free of dukkha is born.

- There will be no more births rooted in ignorance and subject to endless confusion and suffering.

- Lasting peace and happiness has been established through the Eightfold Path.

Unlike most religions, including many modern "Buddhist" religions, acting to gain favorable future experiences post physical death is contrary to the Dhamma. As has been seen, birth is the beginning of the experience of the "whole mass of suffering." As confusion and unsatisfactoriness is the underlying pervasive experience of life in the phenomenal world, the ending of karma and the cessation of future births is the purpose of the Dhamma.

An awakened mind settled in equanimity will produce no additional karma. As no additional karma is created, residual karma will simply ripen and fall away until complete liberation and freedom is realized.

The three defining characteristics of the phenomenal world are Anicca, Dukkha and Anatta.

Within the environment of impermanence Dukkha arises. Dukkha arises due to clinging, craving and aversion. Clinging arises from a misunderstanding of the nature of self.

What arises as "self" (shown to be anatta, not a self) is an impermanent combination of factors known as "The Five Clinging-Aggregates. These aggregates are described as clinging due to the nature of "self" to cling to thoughts, views, ideas, and objects that further define and describe self. It is craving and clinging rooted in ignorance that establishes a self and creates karma and the cycles of birth.

Anatta or "not-self" refers to the impermanent nature of the formation of a self that is subject to stress, disappointment and confusion.

The Buddha never taught that there is a self or that there is not a self. He avoided the issue as a focus on metaphysical questions would be a distraction from his stated purpose to bring "an understanding of dukkha and a cessation of dukkha. Nothing more."

He taught that what is commonly believed to be a self is not founded in Right View. It is a view of self

429

conditioned by ignorance that is to be abandoned if confusion and suffering is to end.

As the distraction of dukkha is always present to a deluded mind, then an awakened mind is a mind free of karma and free of the karmic manifestation of rebirth.

Once karma ceases there will be no more births. Without karma to create the unfolding need for continued existence, rebirth ends.

The Buddha's understanding and teaching on rebirth differ greatly from the Brahmanism of the Buddha's time and differs greatly with many of the mystical Buddhist religions. The Dhamma also differs greatly from the Hindu and Hindu-influenced beliefs that would arise well after the Buddha's passing.

Many religions, including some Buddhist religions, teach morals and ethics as a way of hopefully having ever more pleasurable future lives, but never abandoning conditioned thinking and continued I-making. This is continued clinging to an idea of an ego-self and is specifically what the Buddha was referring to when he said:

"This was the third knowledge I attained in the third watch of the night. Ignorance was destroyed; knowledge arose; darkness was destroyed; light arose — as happens in one who is heedful, ardent, & resolute. Birth is ended, the integrated life fulfilled, the task done. There is nothing further for this world." (Majjhima Nikaya 19)

Reincarnation is the belief that an individual and permanent soul travels throughout time as the same spiritual entity appearing in a different physical body, life after life.

This cannot be reconciled with the teachings of not-self, emptiness, Dependent Origination, Five Clinging-Aggregates and Karma.

The self that would reincarnate has been shown to be an impermanent aggregate of physical and mental factors sustained only in the present instant by craving and clinging.

Insisting on reincarnating this same entity is insisting on the continuation of karma.

The Buddha in describing Dukkha or suffering teaches: "Birth is suffering, sickness is suffering, old age is suffering." The Four Noble Truths directly teach

431

the cessation of suffering and the cessation of birth, death and rebirth.

The Buddha did not teach a way of manipulating a more pleasurable future birth, he taught a way of leaving the recurring cycle of dukkha behind.

This brings up the notion of annihilation. Annihilation is an extreme view rooted in the ignorance of anatta. It is an ego-personality's fear of annihilation that creates this doubt and reaction as the ego-personality is always vigilant about continuation. This creates a need of establishing the ego-self in the future.

The most skillful way of considering karma and rebirth is to view karma driving the birth of this present moment.

- Karma is the present unfolding of past intentional acts moderated by present mindfulness.

- In order to complete the path, to end craving and clinging and to bring Dukkha to cessation, giving birth to another moment of clinging to objects, views, and ideas is unskillful.

What is most skillful is to recognize the causes of continued confusion and suffering and to abandon those causes.

- The next moment holds the potential to be free of confusion and suffering.

- The next moment holds the potential for freedom from continued rebirth of anatta.

When you abandon craving and clinging your immediate future is free of confusion and suffering. The distracting questions rooted in ignorant views no longer arise. You are no longer experiencing the results of past karma and there is no longer any ongoing "birth" of confusion and suffering.

This is the most skillful way to consider birth, death, and rebirth. This moment holds the potential for the next moment' experience. Ignorance will bring more confusion and unsatisfactoriness.

Refined mindfulness and deep concentration, developed within the framework of the Eightfold Path, brings profound wisdom and understanding of The Four Noble Truths.

Wisdom in this moment brings a life free of ignorance, confusion, and stress.

It is a common reaction from an ego-personality insisting on continued establishment of "self" to continue to cling to form and resist or ignore the truth of ending rebirth.

- Anatta must establish itself in every object, event, view, or idea.

- The ego-self cannot accept any future thought or idea that does not include itself.

An awakened mind, free of craving and clinging, peacefully experiences life as life occurs with no limiting and stress-inducing self-referential thoughts or actions.

As stated, the Five Clinging-Aggregates are the vehicle for the "self" that experiences dukkha. This ego-self, or conditioned mind, is impermanent, or "empty" of any permanent and individually originated constituents.

There is no "self" and no karma other than a conditioned mind manifested due to specific causes and conditions arising in the phenomenal world.

The Buddha never taught emptiness as a mystical realm that somehow is both empty but includes the phenomenal world. As with all the Dhamma, emptiness is taught in relation to suffering and The Four Noble Truths. The Buddha taught that one should "empty oneself of clinging." He taught that The Five Clinging-Aggregates are "empty" of any permanence or substance. He taught that one should "empty" the world of self, to cease "I-making."

"Karma should be known. The cause by which karma comes into play should be known. The diversity in karma should be known. The result of karma should be known. The cessation of karma should be known. The path of practice leading to the cessation of karma should be known.' Thus it has been said. Why was it said?

"Intention, I tell you, is karma. Intending, one does karma by way of body, speech, & intellect.

"And what is the result of karma? The result of karma is of three sorts, I tell you: that which arises right here & now, that which arises later [in this lifetime], and that which arises following that.

"And what is the cessation of karma? From the cessation of contact is the cessation of karma; and just this Noble Eightfold Path - right view, right resolve, right speech, right action, right livelihood, right effort, right mindfulness, right concentration - is the path of practice leading to the cessation of karma.

"Now when a noble disciple discerns karma in this way, the cause by which karma comes into play in this way, the diversity of karma in this way, the result of karma in this way, the cessation of karma in this way, & the path of practice leading to the cessation of karma in this way, then he discerns this penetrative integrated life as the cessation of karma. With the cessation of karma comes the cessation of rebirth of The Five Clinging-Aggregates." (Anguttara Nikaya 6.63

Karma is the suffering of continually giving birth to another moment rooted in ignorance. Rooted in ignorance one can only become further ignorant.

The Eightfold Path provides the framework and guidance to be mindful of karma and to cease giving birth to another moment rooted in ignorance.

The Eightfold Path provides the framework and guidance to Become Buddha.

Five Hindrances
To Be Mindful Of

"Remain mindful of the quality of mind in reference to the five hindrances."

The importance of mindfully recognizing these Five Hindrances is emphasized by reference in the Satipatthana Sutta.

These common hindrances have caused much of the contradictions and confusion in modern Buddhism.

These Five Hindrances are the cause of well-intentioned Dhamma practitioners avoiding or giving up the path, and continuing conceit.

The second and sixth factors of The Eightfold Path, Right Intention and Right Effort, greatly support Dhamma practice. Maintaining the strong resolve of Right Intention and engaging in Right Effort will provide the framework needed to develop and maintain Dhamma practice.

Right Intention is holding in mind the intention to recognize and abandon craving, clinging, aversion and, delusional thinking. Right Intention is holding in mind the intention to awaken to the true nature of reality.

Being mindful of Right Intention and Right Effort, make a commitment to Dhamma practice. Put aside set times, preferably twice a day, for meditation practice. It is most effective to meditate as soon as possible after waking before becoming distracted or sidetracked by your daily routine. Doing this consistently begins to diminish conditioned mind's desire to avoid looking at itself.

An aspect of Right Effort (the sixth factor of the Eightfold Path) is keeping yourself in fit physical and mental condition. Getting enough rest, eating healthy, and physical exercise are aspects of Right Effort.

Any exercise is a support for Dhamma practice and walking "meditation" is a very skillful way to combine exercise and mindful movement. Keep in mind that there is no effective substitute for sitting meditation. Bringing the body to stillness greatly supports a calm and tranquil mind.

Tai Chi and Qigong are particularly supportive of Dhamma practice.

Five Common Hindrances to Practice

1. Sensory or Sensual desire.

2. Ill will.

3. Sloth, torpor, or drowsiness.

4. Restlessness and worry.

5. Doubt, uncertainty or skepticism.

The first hindrance to establishing a meditation practice is distraction from sensual desire. Distracted by the need for continual sensory engagement prevents developing concentration and encourages boredom.

Often this will arise as the belief that you are too busy to meditate.

Anyone can sit quietly for a few minutes twice a day and be mindful of their breath. This is all that is needed to begin a meditation practice.

441

Your mind, at first, may want to avoid meditation. When you meditate despite this common tendency, you begin to gain control of your mind and your life.

In meditation you may be distracted by an infinite number of craving thoughts. Whatever craving thoughts arise, recognize desire as a distraction. Remain mindful of the thought or thoughts, recognizing that they are a hindrance to practice. These thoughts are as impermanent as any other thought.

Dispassionately let thoughts go and return your awareness to your breathing. This is the basic practice and continued practice will diminish sensory desire and return the mind to its natural calm and well-concentrated state.

Ill will, or holding harsh judgments, anger, and resentments at others, or yourself, can make it almost impossible to practice. Recognize that the cause of the ill will is your own desire that the people and events of your life be different than they are, or that you perceive them to be.

If persistent thoughts of ill will arise, dispassionately stay with the thoughts for a moment or two, and return your mindfulness to the sensation of breathing.

As your awareness of the origins of ill will increase, maintain a mind of equanimity. As best as you can, remain free of judgment of the people and events of your lives. This takes Right Effort and consistent practice. With consistent meditation practice you can free yourself of the hindrance of ill will.

Practicing Metta Meditation, is a skillful aid in releasing harsh judgments. Practice metta whenever harsh judgments of yourself or others is making it difficult to quiet your mind. Once your mind has quieted using metta, resume Shamatha-Vipassana meditation.

There is a recording of Metta Meditation on Becoming-Buddha.com.

Sloth, torpor, drowsiness or laziness affect everyone at one time or another. It is most skillful to recognize this as aversion to practice. It is your ego's way of avoiding the freedom that will arise from consistent practice.

If drowsiness is an occasional problem, it is appropriate to rest for a while and then resume meditation. Check your posture. Lying down or not sitting up straight can contribute to drowsiness.

Drowsiness is another hindrance to practice that is to be dealt with through equanimity and persistence. Recognize that it is affecting you and your practice and stay with your practice. Drowsiness will fall away.

Restlessness and worry can be difficult hindrances to overcome. Persistence will show results. If restlessness and worry have risen to the level of anxiety, it may be best to meditate for shorter periods of time, and more often.

Remind yourself that just for the meditation period you will be putting aside restlessness and anxiety and maintain your awareness on your breath. Shamatha-Vipassana Meditation has proven to be a very effective way of putting anxiety causing thoughts aside and staying mindful of what is occurring. There is no restlessness, worry, or anxiety when being mindful of life as life unfolds.

Doubt, uncertainty and skepticism can be a hindrance at any stage of Dhamma practice. Doubt can deepen one's practice if the doubt is allowed to be a part of practice. Let doubt alone and mindfully continue with practice.

Other people's skepticism can be a hindrance as well. People that do not understand the Dhamma are often skeptical and threatened by what they do no understand.

The most effective way to work through uncertainty, doubt and skepticism is to engage in practice wholeheartedly without any unrealistic expectations.

Examine your motivations for practice. Is your intention for engaging in meditation practice to develop concentration?

Is your intention for engaging in meditation practice to "fix" an ego-self? Uncertainty and skepticism will arise if your view or intention is to fix a broken or flawed self.

Shamatha-Vipassana meditation practiced within the framework of the Eightfold Path is to mindfully develop concentration and develop awareness of craving, clinging, aversion, and desire.

Hindrances or distractions will arise. They will have no permanent effect on your practice if you

445

persevere. Hindrances are recognized mind states to be aware of. Be with them as dispassionately as possible.

As long as you continue with your practice, hindrances will arise and subside until they no longer are a part of your conditioned thinking.

By putting aside resistance to meditation practice you will strengthen your resolve and begin to diminish your mind's natural tendency to resist the quiet and spacious mind developed by a true and effective meditation practice.

Always avoid judging yourself or your practice harshly. Do the best you can and be gentle with yourself. Maintain a consistent Shamatha-Vipassana meditation practice within the framework of the Eightfold Path and you will develop lasting peace and happiness.

These five hindrances will arise just as often outside of meditation practice. Be mindful of the fleeting nature of the hindrances. Hindrances to awakening arise from ignorance of Four Noble Truths. Hindrances have no footing in an awakened mind.

One last thing. Joining a like-minded community of Dhamma practitioners well-focused on the Buddha's Dhamma greatly supports individual practice. Joining a community of Dhamma practitioners will provide structure to your practice.

A qualified teacher will notice if you are losing direction or focus. The community as a whole will support you with their own insights, and you will be able to support your sangha.

Concluding Suttas

The suttas in this final section of Becoming Buddha support key themes of the Buddha's teachings and provide additional clarity.

The Culavedalla Sutta is a teaching of a nun to her former husband on how self-identities are created and how they are recognized and abandoned.

The Sallatha Sutta further clarifies individual contributions to Dukkha arising from a misunderstanding of Three Marks of Existence.

The Kaccayayanagotta Sutta addresses the core themes of Dependent Origination, Five Clinging-Aggregates, the Eightfold Path, and becoming empty of ignorance. The miss-applied mystical and conceptual applications of "emptiness" that support modern non-dual doctrines are explained in relation to the Buddha's teachings on emptiness and in relation to ignorance of

Four Noble Truths.

The Four Suttas on Restraint teach the primary importance of developing restraint through the Eightfold Path.

- The Aparihani Sutta teaches restraint at the senses - at the point of contact originating I-making.

- The Bhikkhuvaga teaches this same theme in the context of the Eightfold Path and Five Clinging-Aggregates.

- The Pamadaviharin Sutta teaches restraint in the context of Dhamma practice and mindfulness.

- The Kummu Sutta teaches restraint directly in the context of craving.

The Ratana Sutta describes the skillful understanding that "taking refuge" can only be a true refuge if the meaning of Siddartha Gotama's awakening is acknowledged and the authenticity of his Dhamma is followed.

Finally, the third refuge, taking refuge in the sangha, can be a true refuge only if the individuals of the sangha actually follow the example and teachings that an awakened human being taught. This last is the profound responsibility of each member of a sangha who aspires to Become Buddha.

The last sutta is the Kalama Sutta. It is the last sutta presented to show the importance of individual direct experience of the Buddha's direct teaching rather than follow other dharmas simply because of associations or popularity. The confusion of false dharmas is not only a modern problem, but was prevalent even during the teaching career of the Buddha.

The Buddha's words from the Kalama Sutta:

"Now, do not go by reports, or legends, or traditions, or scripture, or conjecture, or inference, or analogies, or common agreement, or unexamined loyalty.

"When you know from your own experience that the qualities taught are skillful, shameless, unambiguous, and direct these teachings should be developed.

"When these teachings are praised by the wise they should be developed. When these teachings lead to unbinding and calm they should be developed."

Culavedalla Sutta

Majjhima Nikaya 44

The Culavedalla Sutta is a teaching presented by the nun Dhammadinna to her former husband, also a member of the first Sangha. The Buddha praised Dhammadinna as one of the most knowledgeable nuns of the Sangha.

This is another example of the importance of women in the early monastic tradition of the Buddha's Sangha. Visakha, the questioner, is also well-established in the Dhamma.

Visakha is seeking clarity on Anatta and how Anatta continually establishes itself through clinging in all phenomena.

As has been seen in the section on Impermanence,

453

Not-Self, and Dukkha, Anatta, is the word used to describe wrong views believed to be a "self."

"Dhammadinna, what is self-identification as described by the Buddha?"

"Visakha, the Buddha teaches that self-identification is established by clinging to form, by clinging to feeling, by clinging to perception, by clinging to fabrications, and by clinging to consciousness. These Five Clinging-Aggregates are the self-identification taught by the Buddha."

Anatta seeks to continually establish itself in every form, feeling, perception, mental fabrication, indeed in every thought. Misunderstanding anatta to mean no-self and to minimize the importance of understanding anatta by misapplying emptiness to anatta negates the Buddha's teachings. In this sutta anatta is presented in a clear and direct way as the central understanding to be developed.

Visakha continues: "Your answer is very helpful. What then is the origination of self-identification to form, feeling, perceptions, fabrications, indeed in every thought?"

"It is craving, Visakha, that brings continual establishment of anatta, craving born of clinging

454

accompanied by passion and by delight. Craving for sensual pleasure, craving for continued establishment in this world and other realms. This is the origination of self-identification as taught by the Buddha."

Continued establishment in other realms is often presented as craving for non-becoming. This is part of a doctrine of self that seeks to establish anatta as a "soul" that migrates through endless life and death cycles maintaining the identity of the current (impermanent) self-identification.

Another example of craving for non-becoming is attempting to establish an inherent "Buddha-Nature" in a type of Buddhist heaven or in a conceptual environment of "emptiness." These beliefs, common in modern Buddhism, directly contradicts the Buddha's teachings on anatta and leads to continued confusion and suffering.

All views of "self" rooted in ignorance can only lead to becoming further ignorant, whether in this life or another, whether in this realm or another.

Visakha: "What then is the cessation of self-identification?"

"The renunciation and remainder-less fading away of the very craving, born of clinging, that originates the continual establishment of anatta. This is the cessation of self-identification as taught by the Buddha."

"What then, dear lady, is the path, or the practice, leading to the cessation of self-identification that is taught by the Buddha?"

"Friend Visakha, it is precisely the Noble Eightfold Path of Right View, Right Intention, Right Speech, Right Action, Right Livelihood, Right Effort, Right Mindfulness, and Right Meditation. The Buddha teaches this Eightfold Path to develop the virtue, the concentration, and the wisdom required to abandon self-identification, to abandon clinging."

"Is clinging the same as the Five Clinging-Aggregates?"

"Clinging is not the same as the Five Clinging-Aggregates, Visakha, nor is it separate. It is the nature of the Five Clinging-Aggregates to cling. It is the function of the Five Clinging-Aggregates to cling. It is the nature of anatta to cling. It is the function of anatta to cling."

Visakha: "How does self-identification develop?"

"Those uninstructed in regard to the Dhamma, run-of-the-mill people, with no regard for noble ones or those of integrity are deluded. They believe that form to be the self, or that the self possesses the form.

"They are further deluded to believe that their (self-referential) feelings are the self, that their perceptions (of self) defines the self, that their fabrications that further establish the self, to be the self.

"They assume that their self-referential thoughts establish a self. Each of these Five Clinging-Aggregates are impermanent and arise from ignorance. They are anatta, they are not a self."

"How does self-identification not develop?"

"Those well-instructed in regard to the dhamma, with regard for the noble one's and those with integrity, well-disciplined in their practice, do not believe form to be the self.

"They do not believe that feelings establish or define a self, or that perception defines a self.

"They are free of mental fabrications, having no foundation for fabrications.

"They do not assume that thoughts establish a self or that the self possesses thoughts.

"They do not assume that consciousness is the self or that the self possesses consciousness.

"There is no "self" attached to any of these Five Clinging-Aggregates."

The Buddha's original teachings are grounded in Dependent Origination, expressed through The Four Noble Truths, and directly experienced through The Eightfold Path.

Dependent Origination shows that from ignorance, through 12 observable causative links, stress, confusion, and delusion develops.

Those well-instructed in the Buddha's dhamma, free of anatta, have developed a non-distracted mind bringing useful insight into reality. Wisdom has replaced ignorance. Fabrications (and deluded beliefs) have ended.

Visakha then asks if the Eightfold Path is fabricated or unfabricated and Dhammadinna replies that the Eightfold Path is fabricated.

The Eightfold Path is fabricated, arising from form, feelings and perceptions, as it is a teaching developed within the sphere of the impermanent, phenomenal world.

The intention of the Eightfold Path is that it bring understanding to those under the delusion that their belief in self requires clinging to what is in reality, anicca, impermanent.

The Eightfold Path is a path of skillful means to developing the unfabricated quality of mind of release from clinging. Once cessation of clinging mind is accomplished, when awakening has occurred, the Eightfold Path is abandoned.

An awakened being has integrated the three characteristics of wisdom virtue, and concentration. The arahant remains harmless to themselves and others, their mind resting in equanimity.

Visakha then inquires if the qualities of virtue, concentration, and wisdom are developed through the Eightfold Path or do these 3 qualities inspire the Eightfold Path.

"Visakha, the Eightfold Path is inspired by the qualities of virtue, concentration, and wisdom. Right Speech, Right Action, and Right Livelihood inspire the development of heightened virtue. Right Effort, Right Mindfulness, and Right Meditation inspire the development of heightened concentration, and Right View and Right Intention inspire and develop heightened Wisdom."

The Buddha consistently characterized the Eightfold Path as a path combining the three qualities of wisdom, virtue, and concentration and that all three characteristics are necessary for awakening to occur. Over-emphasizing one quality over the other two would not develop a fully-integrated or fully-awakened human being.

This is an important understanding as much of modern Buddhism will focus mostly on compassionate engagement, or scholarly study, or "mind-only" practice of primarily meditation, with little or no engagement with the Four Noble Truths.

This sutta brings to mind the actual path the Buddha taught as the path to awakening. Modern applications of mindfulness alters the intention of Right Mindfulness and Right Meditation.

The Buddha used mindfulness not as another way to maintain distraction by being mindful of all impermanent phenomena. He did not use mindfulness to seek endless insight into temporary states of mind. As shown in the Vitakkasanthana Sutta, this type of compulsive insight seeking is to be recognized and abandoned.

As has been seen in the Satipatthana Sutta, the Buddha teaches mindfulness of what occurs during meditation so to deepen concentration. He then teaches to be mindful of Five Hindrances, the Five Clinging-Aggregates, the Six-Sense Base, the Seven Qualities, and Four Noble Truths.

Often modern meditation and mindfulness practices dismiss the framework of the Eightfold Path for a conceptual application of "mindfulness meditation."

Visakha: "What is concentration and what is the framework for Right Concentration, what are the requisites and how is it developed?"

"Samadhi, non-distraction is concentration. The framework for Right Concentration is the Four Foundations of Mindfulness:

- Being mindful of the breath in the body.

- Being mindful of feelings arising and fading away.

461

- Being mindful of thoughts occurring and fading away.

- Being mindful of the present quality of mind.

"Right Effort provides the requisites for Right Concentration. You should always endeavor with skillful desire and persistence for the non-arising of unskillful qualities and to abandon unskillful qualities that have yet arisen.

"Visakha, always endeavor, with great desire and persistence, to generate skillful qualities that have yet arisen and to maintain skillful qualities that have arisen."

"What are fabrications, dear lady?"

Dhammadinna: "There are three: Bodily fabrications, verbal fabrications, and mental fabrications.

In-and-out breaths are bodily fabrications as breaths are generated from the Clinging-Aggregate of form.

Feelings and perceptions are mental fabrications as they are generated by the Clinging-Aggregates of feelings and perceptions.

Conditioned and discursive thought and evaluation are verbal fabrications as they are generated from the Clinging-Aggregate of consciousness.

"How then does the attainment of cessation of feelings and perceptions develop?"

"A well-informed person who has developed understanding through the Eightfold Path does not have a thought of attainment. Rather, their refined mind leads to the cessation of feelings and perceptions. Verbal fabrications cease, then bodily fabrications, and finally mental fabrications."

This process relates directly to Right Speech and verbal fabrications, Right Action and bodily fabrications, and the three concentration factors and the cessation of mental fabrications. Of course the entire Eightfold Path is a mutually supportive practice of developing cessation.

Mindfulness of Right Speech is often the initial insight into clinging, conditioned mind gained when developing understanding through engagement with the Eightfold Path. With mindfulness of Right Action a mind deluded by its own fabrications is gently led to insight and abandoning clinging. As samadhi deepens mindfulness of virtue and developing wisdom increases.

Dhammadinna continues: "When a well-informed person emerges from the cessation of feelings and perceptions they are empty of clinging, free of self-identification and conditioned mind. The well-informed person's mind inclines to seclusion and away from delight and entanglement (with the world)."

The Buddha describes an awakened human being as "unbound" from clinging. He describes the quality of mind of an awakened human being as "calm." This may seem rather simplistic and mundane. In the context of Four Noble Truths it is clearly seen that the endless cycle of wandering through samsara has been brought to cessation. Rather than seeking further establishment of anatta, the remainder of life can be lived in lasting peace and contentment.

Visakha asks: "How many kinds of feelings are there?"

"There are only three types of feelings, Visakha. There is pleasant feeling, painful feeling and neutral feeling.

- Pleasant feeling that changes becomes painful.

- Painful feelings that change become pleasant.

- Neutral feelings may change as well, to either pleasure or pain.

- All feelings are subject to anicca (impermanence).

"Pleasant feelings can give rise to passion-obsession. Painful feelings can give rise to resistance-obsession. Neutral feelings can give rise to ignorance-obsession.

"When a well-informed person is withdrawn from the obsession of sensual fulfillment and withdrawn from unskillful qualities, through meditative absorption, they abandon passion and passion-obsession. Yearning for final liberation, resistance obsession is abandoned. Deepening meditative absorption, ignorance obsession is abandoned."

"Dear lady, what then lies on the other side of ignorance?"

"Clear knowing (useful insight) lies on the other side of ignorance. And, Visakha, with clear knowing comes release (from clinging). From release from clinging comes complete unbinding."

The stated purpose of the Buddha's Dhamma is the cessation of Dukkha by releasing clinging to ignorance. The result of unbinding from ignorance is a life of lasting peace and contentment.

When anatta has been abandoned lasting peace and contentment would be seen as the only realistic goal anyone could hope to develop. When the ego-personality is still clinging to a doctrine of self, lasting peace and contentment will not be enough to satisfy the craving of anatta.

Tracing back to the Second Buddhist Council and continuing today, the Buddha's Dhamma has been adapted to accommodate wrong views, to accommodate anatta. Providing imaginary concepts for the ego-personality to further establish itself continues confusion, deluded thinking, and ongoing disappointment.

Self-referential doctrines that include the notions of an inherent Buddha-Nature, awakening to "Buddha-Hood", inter-being, and acquiring Buddhist "heavens" of various descriptions and requirements continues Dukkha.

Visakha, despite his understanding, continues to cling to the need to establish a "self" after liberation.

"Dhammadinna, what then lies on the other side of unbinding?"

"Visakha, your clinging-mind has demanded too many answers and your question will lead to only more confusion and suffering. The Buddha's path, the Eightfold Path, culminates in unbinding. Is this not enough? If you wish, go to the Buddha and ask him. Let his answer be enough."

Visakha was delighted in Dhammadinna's teachings. He bowed to her and left for the Buddha. Finding the Buddha nearby, he sat to one side of the Buddha and recounted what Dhammadinna told him.

The Buddha replied, "Dhammadinna is very wise and of great discernment. I would have answered your questions exactly as she has. This is how you should remember these teachings."

Visakha, was pleased by the Buddha's confirmation.

End of Sutta

This sutta presents a complete teaching on the process of delusion that begins with self-identification. This sutta teaches the actual experience of developing useful insight. Dhammadinna teaches the Eightfold Path to be developed to end clinging to objects, events, views, and ideas, and complete unbinding.

As a well-informed and highly regarded member of the Buddha's Sangha, Dhammadinna presented the dhamma in a clear and direct way and free of any ego-influenced individual view.

Her integrity preserved the dhamma and provided the skillful means for Visakha to also awaken.

Sallatha Sutta
The Two Arrows

Samyutta Nikaya 36.6

Individual Contributions To Suffering

The Sallatha Sutta is a key teaching as it clearly explains what for many is a confusing aspect of the Dhamma. The Buddha teaches that awakening is "understanding stress and unhappiness, abandoning the cause of stress and unhappiness, experiencing the cessation of stress and unhappiness, and developing the Eightfold Path leading to the cessation of stress and unhappiness."

Understanding the First Noble Truth is understanding that as a consequence of living in the phenomenal world, there will be stress and unhappiness, there will be suffering. Unsatisfactory experiences are unavoidable aspects of human life.

Attempting to negate stress is aversion

to what is simply present. Creating beliefs of a better life after physical death as compensation for the suffering present in life creates more confusion and delusion. This type of aversion arises due to clinging, or wanting any experience to be different than what occurs. Due to anicca, impermanence, and uncertainty, there is an underlying unsatisfactory nature to human life. There is stress and unhappiness in life.

The Sallatha Sutta

A question is put to the Buddha as to what is the distinguishing factor between a well-instructed dhamma practitioner and those that have no understanding of the Four Noble Truths.

The Buddha responds: "Friends, an ordinary uninformed person feels feelings of pleasure, feelings of pain, and neutral feelings. One well-informed of the Four Noble Truths also feels feelings of pleasure, feelings of pain, and neutral feelings.

"When through the six-sense base an uninformed person experiences a feeling of pain they are sorrowful, they grieve, they become distraught and irate. The uninformed feels two pains: the pain of the experience and the pain caused by the reaction arising from clinging.

"This would be like being hit with an arrow and then, by request, being hit again by an arrow.

The six-sense base are the five physical interpreted though consciousness.

"As the person is experiencing pain, resistance occurs leading to resistance-obsession. As the person experiences pleasure, delight in pleasure occurs leading to pleasure-obsession. Reaction (feelings) bring obsession as the uninformed does not discern what is actually present: the origination, the allure, the drawback, or the passing away of the feeling."

The first arrow is simply the stress and unhappiness that occurs in the phenomenal world. The second arrow is the stress and unhappiness caused by ignorance giving rise to clinging, craving, desire, and aversion. In other words wanting the people and experiences of life to be different than what occurs compounds the initial pain of an experience.

The Buddha continues: "Sensing pleasure or pain the uninformed joins with it. The uninformed is joined to birth, aging, sickness, death and joined with sorrows, regret, grief, pain and despair. Through reaction to experience, the uninformed furthers their confusion and suffering.

Now the Buddha teaches how a person well-informed of The Four Noble Truths and understanding stress and unhappiness responds to the unfolding of dukkha:

"The well-informed person, when stress arises, has no resistance. With no resistance, no resistance-obsession is formed. With no delight in sensual pleasure, no pleasure obsession occurs.

"The well-informed person discerns what is actually present and understands its origination, its allure, its drawbacks and its passing away. He remains disjoined from pleasure and pain.

"This is the distinction between those uninformed and those well-informed of the Four Noble Truths.

End of Sutta

The Four Noble Truths bring an understanding of life as life occurs. The Four Noble Truths bring understanding of the cause of furthering stress, unhappiness, and confusion.

The Buddha's direct teachings are not salvific, offering the promise of a better future life as a reward for "proper behavior." The Buddha's direct teachings develop the experience of lasting peace and contentment in this human life.

This understanding is a key difference between what the Buddha taught and the beliefs of his time arising from the Vedas. The Vedas are the scriptural doctrine that modern Hinduism resets on.

The Vedas inspired the teachings of Alara Kalama and Uddaka Ramaputta that the Buddha studied and rejected. (See Introduction)

The modern Buddhist religions that promote salvation as reward or compensation for suffering have more in common with the Vedas than the Buddha's Dhamma.

Salvation is a notion common to most religions, including many modern "Buddhist" religions. Salvation dismisses awakening for future reward.

The Buddha teaches that lasting peace and contentment can be had in this present life through wholehearted development of the Eightfold Path.

There will be stress and unhappiness, disenchantment and disappointment. Stress is simply part of life. Developing radical acceptance of things as they are develops a calm and peaceful mind.

With no passionate desire that the events of life be any different than what occurs, despite impermanence and uncertainty, the mindful experience of life remains stress-free, purposeful and peaceful.

The Four Noble Truths bring lasting peace and happiness in this present life through the understanding of life in the ever-changing phenomenal world. What may occur after death is of no concern as skillful behavior - moral and ethical behavior - is a stress-free expression of an awakened, fully mature, human being.

The "reward" of mindful living is a life free of clinging to ignorant views, a life of having Become Buddha.

Kaccayanagotta Sutta

Samyutta Nikaya 12.15

Right View, Becoming Empty of Ignorance

The Buddha consistently described an awakened human being, an Arahant, as unbound, or released from clinging. Due to ignorance, self-referential identities are created by clinging to objects, events, views, and ideas.

The Buddha never taught that all things are interdependent, interconnected, or "inter-be." These are conceptual strategies of continued I-Making rooted in ignorance of Four Noble Truths.

The notion of a grand cosmic "oneness" was consistently dismissed by the Buddha as "a thicket of views that do not lead to   disenchantment, dispassion, cessation, to calm, direct knowledge, to full Awakening, to unbinding." (Majjhima Nikaya 72 and many others.)

The Eightfold Path develops the compassion and wisdom to free all beings from clinging to the world by freeing oneself from clinging to wrong views.

The Kaccayanagotta Sutta is a teaching on Right View and also a clear explanation of the common misunderstandings of "emptiness" and non-duality.

The common applications of emptiness and non-duality are extreme (wrong) views of existence and non-existence.

These continued wrong views create a deluded doctrine of emptiness and non-duality by fixating on these views as if they are the only views possible.

When the Buddha's teachings are fully developed, it is clear that all things in the impermanent phenomenal world are discrete in a practical sense.

The Kaccayanagotta Sutta is another teaching on Dependent Origination. It shows the relationship between the "middle way" of the Eightfold Path and Dependent Origination.

The Kaccayanagotta Sutta presents the foundational teachings of the Buddha in the context of developing emptiness of clinging and emptiness of ignorance.

Notice that there is nothing in the direct teachings of Dependent Origination that would imply a doctrine of interdependence, interconnectedness, or inter-being. These are non-dual teachings rooted in ignorance and wrong view. The "world" in this sutta is metaphor for confused and deluded views that result in unsatisfactory experiences, or Dukkha.

The insistence on a non-dual doctrine obscures reality and contradicts Right View and the entire Eightfold Path. As seen here the Buddha shows that a non-dual doctrine is an extreme (wrong) view rooted in ignorance of Four Noble Truths.

The Kaccayanagotta Sutta

The Buddha was staying at Savatthi, at Jeta's Grove, Anathapindika's monastery. The monk Kaccayana Gotta approached the Buddha with a question: "I don't understand Right View. Can you teach me how Right View relates to the world?"

"Kaccayana, the confusion and deluded thinking in the world arises from polarizing views. There is the view of (permanent) existence and a view of (permanent) non-existence.

"When the origination of confused and deluded thinking is understood and abandoned, from Right View it is seen that *(nihilistic)* 'non-existence' does not occur.

"Furthermore, when the cessation of confused and deluded thinking is understood and abandoned, from Right View it is seen that *(permanent)* 'existence' does not occur.

"The world is sustained by attachments, by clinging to conditioned thinking and wrong views rooted in ignorance (of Four Noble Truths).

"One who has developed Right View no longer clings to attachments, or fixated (conditioned) thinking, or self-obsession.

"It is understood that stress arising is stress arising. It is understood that stress passing away is stress passing away. In this, their knowledge is independent of other views. This is how Right View relates to the world.

"The view that everything exists is a wrong view and the view that nothing exists is another wrong view. My Dhamma avoids extreme views. I teach from the middle, I teach the Eightfold Path as the middle way that avoids extreme views.

"The middle way shows that suffering originates and is dependent on ignorance:

- From ignorance (of Four Noble Truths) as a requisite condition come fabrications.

- From fabrications as a requisite condition comes consciousness.

- From consciousness as a requisite condition comes name-and-form.

- From name-and-form as a requisite condition comes the six sense-base.

- From the six sense-base as a requisite condition comes contact.

- From contact as a requisite condition comes feeling.

- From feeling as a requisite condition comes craving.

- From craving as a requisite condition comes clinging and maintaining.

- From clinging and maintaining as a requisite condition comes becoming.

- From becoming as a requisite condition comes birth.

- From birth as a requisite condition comes aging, sickness, death, sorrow, regret, pain, distress and despair.

"Such is the origination of extreme views and the entire mass of confusion, delusion, and stress.

"Now,

- From the remainderless fading & cessation of that very ignorance comes the cessation of fabrications.

- From the cessation of fabrications comes the cessation of consciousness. (conditioned thinking)

- From the cessation of consciousness comes the cessation of name-&-form.

- From the cessation of name-&-form comes the cessation of the six sense media.

- From the cessation of the six sense media comes the cessation of contact.

- From the cessation of contact comes the cessation of feeling.

- From the cessation of feeling comes the cessation of craving.

- From the cessation of craving comes the cessation of clinging and maintaining.

- From the cessation of clinging and maintaining comes the cessation of becoming.

- From the cessation of becoming comes the cessation of birth. From the cessation of birth,

481

then aging & death, sorrow, regret, pain, distress, & despair all cease.

"Such is the cessation of this entire mass of stress and suffering."

"Now this, monks, is the noble truth of stress:

- Birth is stressful.

- Aging is stressful.

- Death is stressful.

- Sorrow, regret, pain, distress, & despair are stressful.

- Association with the unbeloved is stressful.

- Separation what is loved is stressful.

- Not getting what is wanted is stressful.

- In short, The Five Clinging-Aggregates are stressful.

"And this, monks, is the noble truth of the origination of stress:

"The craving that makes for further becoming - accompanied by passion & delight, relishing now here & now there - i.e., craving for sensual pleasure, craving for becoming, craving for non-becoming.

"And this, monks, is the noble truth of the cessation of stress:

"The remainderless fading & cessation, renunciation, relinquishment, release, & letting go of that very craving.

"And this, monks, is the noble truth of the way of practice leading to the cessation of stress:

"Precisely this Noble Eightfold Path - Right View, Right Intention, Right Speech, Right Action, Right Livelihood, Right Effort, Right Mindfulness, Right Meditation."

End of Sutta

Everything the Buddha taught for the forty-five years of his teaching career was taught in the context of the Four Noble Truths.

The First Noble Truth states that Dukkha occurs as a common consequence of human life.

The Second Noble Truth teaches craving originates and clinging perpetuates Dukkha. Craving for self-establishing existential experiences arises from a misunderstanding of Three Marks of Existence.

All phenomenal experiences carry the Three Marks Of Existence. All phenomenal experiences are subject to confusion, delusion, and suffering. It is craving for and clinging to phenomenal existence that originates and perpetuates suffering. Establishing self in everything that occurs through self-referential views is clinging to phenomenal existence.

The Third Noble Truth states that the cessation of confusion, delusion, and suffering is possible.

The Fourth Noble Truth states that it is the Eightfold Path that develops the cessation of dukkha.

The Eightfold Path is the path the Buddha taught to overcome the common human problem of wrong or ignorant views developing conditioned thinking.

Conditioned thinking are ongoing thoughts "conditioned" by ignorant views. Ignorant views can only develop further ignorant views unless the proper framework for recognizing and abandoning ignorant views is developed.

The purpose of the Eightfold Path is to provide the framework and guidance necessary to recognize and abandon wrong views ignorant of Four Noble Truths.

Much of the modern Buddhist views of emptiness are formed by ignorant views that arose from the individual and cultural influences that have altered the direct teachings of the Buddha.

The first factor of the Eightfold Path is Right View. Right View is ultimately viewing the world empty of any notion of a permanent self - "there is no me here, this is not me, this is not mine."

Most modern Buddhist teachings present a doctrine of no-self residing in emptiness or a vast cosmic void - this is simply more "I" making. This contradictory view is what necessitated the split in the later-developed Mahayana Buddhist schools.

This contradictory view of emptiness then necessitates the alteration of the Buddha's teachings on Dependent Origination. Conceptual "emptiness" is now the repository for everything that contradicts the Buddha's direct teachings. This conceptual "emptiness" most significantly dismisses the Buddha's actual teachings on emptiness.

The Buddha's teaching on the origination of confusion, deluded thinking, and ongoing stress are clear and direct. Dependent Origination as presented in this sutta and many others shows that it is ignorance of Four Noble Truths that initiates the 12 causative links of Dependent Origination.

The Buddha taught that the personal experience of suffering - Five Clinging-Aggregates - are impermanent and "empty" of anything that should be seen as "self." He did not teach that there is no "self." He simply taught that the mental fabrications rooted in ignorance used to define and describe a "self" are wrong views.

He taught an Eightfold Path to recognize and abandon wrong views. He taught an Eightfold Path to *become empty of ignorance - empty of wrong views.*

Altering, adapting, or dismissing Dependent Origination to allow for the many confusing contradictions of modern Buddhism also dismisses Four Noble Truths as the foundation for the Buddha's Dhamma.

Right View teaches that within the ever-changing environment of the phenomenal world there cannot be found a permanent and substantial "me."

Right View develops from understanding the emptiness of Dukkha being a personal experience.

Stress and unhappiness arise due to a lack of understanding of Four Noble Truths. From this ignorance an attempt to establish a substantial and permanent self follows. Impermanence does not support a "permanent" establishment of "self." The attempt at establishment of self is rooted in ignorance and results in confusion, deluded thinking, and ongoing disappointment.

In this way, it is appropriate to see emptiness as a noun. Ignorant views seek to establish an environment of emptiness that a "self" is somehow a part of. This arises from the compulsive need to continue to establish a view of self in some realm, now the realm of emptiness. This is the foundational teachings of many modern Buddhist "sutra's." This wrong view can be traced to the Second Buddhist Council and the desire of the Mahasanghikas for a mystical Buddhism.

The feedback loop of self-referential views stuck in consciousness rooted in ignorance must be further ignored to establish the extreme view of "nothingness" or "emptiness" or "non-duality."

This is what the Buddha referred to in the Nagara Sutta:

"Then I had the thought: This consciousness turns back at name-&-form and goes no farther. It is to this extent that there is birth, aging, death, falling away and returning. This is where ignorance is established. Name-&-form (self-referential views) is the requisite condition that brings consciousness and consciousness is the requisite condition that brings name-&-form."

Any nihilistic dismissal of self, or permanent establishment of self in realms of nothingness or emptiness continues to ignore the feedback loop of wrong views turning back on consciousness rooted in ignorance.

An understanding of Dependent Origination and Four Noble Truths brings wisdom. Wisdom allows one to *become empty of ignorance*:

"And this, monks, is the noble truth of the way of practice leading to the cessation of stress:

"Precisely this Noble Eightfold Path - Right View, Right Intention, Right Speech, Right Action, Right Livelihood, Right Effort, Right Mindfulness, Right Meditation."

"Such is the cessation of this entire mass of stress and suffering."

What *Becomes* when all views of self are abandoned, when all clinging to objects, events, thoughts, and views are abandoned? A human being accomplished this and lived a full and effective and deeply meaningful life. Most importantly he taught others to develop his authentic path and Become Buddha.

Not fixing a view of self onto anything conceptual or actual allows for the awakened experience of entering the stream as in a "stream enterer." Ceasing to define or identify "self" with what is unfolding - what one has, what may be lost, what is arising that increases desire, what is arising that brings aversion - allows for entering the Dhamma stream of awakening.

This is not the same as being compulsively focused on the present moment which has become a kind of modern worship. There is no actual point in time that can be called the present moment.

The process of awakening is a continuing process. Through wisdom the understanding is gained to let go of all attachments and entanglements and be mindful of life as life occurs.

As Karma unfolds, there will still be rebirth in each present moment that is subject to disappointment. This is an unsatisfactory experience from the view of an ego-self.

When an awakened, fully mature, state of mind has been achieved, reaction to life's experiences cease to be satisfying, or disappointing, or neutral. An awakened, fully mature mind rests in ongoing equanimity.

When developed and fully integrated, the Eightfold Path shows that fixed views are also views that "fix" a self within these fixed views. This is also often referred to by the Buddha as "a confining space." The Buddha's teachings bring understanding and release from fixed views and develops the understanding of the potential of each moment to incline refined mindfulness towards awakening, towards full human maturity.

Each moment holds the potential to cease becoming rooted in ignorance and develop the requisite conditions, through the Eightfold Path, to become empty of all ignorant views and live a human life from the peace and freedom of Right View.

Each moment holds the potential to Become Buddha.

The Wisdom Of Restraint
Four Suttas

There is a popular phrase that shows that the modern view of the purpose of life for many is acquisition and a consumer-driven way of life. "Life is a banquet - don't leave the table hungry." This phrase is likely an adaptation of a quote from Aristotle who lived approximately 150 years after the Buddha: "It is best to rise from life as from a banquet, neither thirsty nor drunken."

Notice how the adaptation to Aristotle's quote dismisses restraint in favor of consumption and continually seeking to satisfy the senses. Rephrasing the modern adaptation to reflect restraint might be "Life is a banquet - take only what is necessary."

Modern life encourages constant engagement with the world and in many subtle ways discourages restraint. Activism and "engaged Buddhism" arising from a lack of restraint and wisdom lead to increasing isolation and divisiveness.

Many today feel overwhelmed by the demands of life and the busyness of their lives. Often what is creating the busyness is a lack of restraint and a "wrong view" of what is realistically skillful and necessary to associate with. Solitude and disengagement are essential aspects of the Dhamma and are easily developed through proper restraint.

It is mindful restraint at the Six-sense base that develops awakening, or full human maturity. The Six-sense base are the five physical senses and interpretive thinking. In this way, the teachings on restraint directly relate to Dependent Origination in a very practical way.

Dependent Origination shows that:

- From ignorance as a requisite condition come fabrications.

- From fabrications as a requisite condition comes consciousness.

- From consciousness as a requisite condition comes name-and-form.

- From name-and-form as a requisite condition comes the six sense-bases.

- From the six sense-bases as a requisite condition comes contact.

- From contact as a requisite condition comes feeling.

- From feeling as a requisite condition comes craving.

- From craving as a requisite condition comes clinging and maintaining.

- From clinging and maintaining as a requisite condition comes becoming.

- From becoming as a requisite condition comes birth.

- From birth as a requisite condition comes aging, sickness, death, sorrow, regret, pain, distress and despair.

As the fifth link in the 12-link chain of dependencies, the six-sense base follows from initial ignorance of Four Noble Truths.

495

The interpretation of contact at the senses is rooted in ignorance.

Further assumptions made by contact can only continue confusion and deluded thinking.

Whatever follows from ignorance will be tainted by the fabrications or conditioned thinking initiated from ignorance of Four Noble Truths.

It is imperative to recognize the ongoing process of using sensory stimulus to continue establishment of a permanent self through discursive self-referential thinking.

Recognizing this process of "I-making" or "Selfing" develops the ability to be mindfully present with what is occurring. Recognizing and abandoning I-making interrupts life unfolding from a view rooted in initial ignorance.

Each of the following suttas teaches restraint with different applications. In the Aparihani Sutta restraint is presented as a guard against losing the Eightfold Path.

The Aparihani Sutta

Not Losing the Way

Anguttara Nikaya 4.37

The Buddha teaches those gathered:

"Having developed four qualities a Dhamma practitioner cannot lose the way and is free of clinging to views. When one has fully integrated the Eightfold Path they are:

- Established in virtue.

- They guard the six-sense base.

- They know moderation in eating.

- They are devoted to mindfulness.

"And how does one establish virtue? They are continually mindful of the precepts and the various factors of the Eightfold Path. They understand the danger in even the slightest unskillful actions.

"And how does one guard the six-sense base? On seeing form, they do not grasp at fabrications that would further greed and distraction. They practice restraint at the eye.

"Furthermore,

"On hearing a sound they practice restraint at the ear,

"On smelling, an aroma they practice restraint at the nose,

"On tasting a flavor they practice restraint at the tongue,

"On feeling a tactile sensation they practice restraint at the body,

"On cognizing an idea they practice restraint at the intellect, they do not grasp at fabrications.

"This is how one guards the doors to the six-sense base.

"And how does one establish moderation in eating?

"They understand nourishment skillfully.

"They do not eat for entertainment or distraction.

"They do not eat for intoxication.

"They do not eat to grow large or for beautification.

"They eat simply for the survival of the body so that the integrated life can be lived.

"They abandon craving for food and for mindless eating.

"And how does one establish mindfulness as a quality?

"Whether resting, sitting or moving about, they cleanse their mind of anything that is a distraction. This is how one establishes mindfulness.

"Having established these four qualities this Dhamma practitioner will not lose the Eightfold Path.

"Established in virtue,

"Restrained with the six-sense base,

"Established in moderate eating,

"Established in mindfulness,

499

"Forthright and inspired,

"The qualities for unbinding develop,

"Delighting in refined mindfulness,

"Knowing the danger of mindlessness,

"They stay true to the Eightfold Path,

"And remain free of deluded views."

End of Sutta

In this sutta, the Buddha teaches the importance to develop the virtuous factors of the Eightfold Path of Right Speech, Right Action, and Right Livelihood to recognize and abandon unskillful thoughts, words, and deeds. The concentration developed through Shamatha-Vipassana meditation supports the refined mindfulness that brings the ability to guard the six-sense base.

In the Bhikkhuvaga discourse, the Buddha continues the theme of restraint and also addresses the Three Defilements of greed, aversion, and deluded thinking. The Bhikkhuvaga is from a section of the

500

Dhammapada which is a collection of short texts from the Khuddaka Nikaya. (Dhp 360 to 382)

The Buddha teaches restraint at creating a Dhamma diminished by rites and ritual. He further teaches restraint at attempting to establish a self in non-physical realms.

Here the Buddha is painting a picture of an awakened, fully mature human being living a life of peace and happiness free of entanglements with the world.

501

Bhikkhuvaga

To a Monk

"Skillful is restraint at the eye, at the ear, at the nose, and at the tongue.

"Skillful is restraint at the body, skillful is restraint in speech, skillful is restraint in thought. Restraint in all experiences is skillful. One restrained in the world is free from confusion, delusion, and disappointment. *(Free of Dukkha)*

"Those who have full control over their hands, their feet, and their tongue are delighted with their understanding. They are well established in meditative absorption. They are content in solitude, free of entanglements. They are called Dhamma Practitioners.

"Those who have control of their tongue are moderate in speech. Unassuming they explain the Dhamma with integrity and by example - their words are useful and pleasing.

"Those that abide in the Dhamma, who delight in the Dhamma, are   mindful of the Dhamma, they do not lose the Dhamma.

"Those free of aversion of what has occurred to them and free of craving for what has occurred to others will be able to attain meditative absorption.

"Those that are calm even when receiving little, pure in livelihood and determined in their Dhamma practice are exalted by the wise.

"Those with no clinging to thoughts or feelings, free of regret from what is not present, they are true Dhamma Practitioners.

"Those who abide with compassion for all beings and devoted to the Dhamma will achieve unbinding (Nibbana) and the bliss of the cessation of all conditioned thinking.

"Empty of all conditioned thoughts, free of craving and aversion, they achieve unbinding.

"Abandon the five lower fetters of self-referential views, of doubt, of belief in rites and rituals, of lust, and of ill-will. Abandon conceit, restlessness, and ignorance and abandon the fetters of craving to establish a self in peace and equanimity. Cultivate the skillful faculties of conviction, persistence, refined mindfulness, concentration, and wisdom. Overcoming the fetters one has crossed to the far shore *(of lasting peace and contentment).*

"Develop concentration through meditation. Do not be mindless and allow your mind to be distracted by sensual pleasure. The world's bait is like a red-hot ball of iron. Do not swallow it and then cry how painful it is!

"There is no concentration for those that fail to develop insight. *(Into impermanence, not-self, and disappointment)*

"There is no insight for those that fail to develop concentration.

"Those who have developed *(through the Eightfold Path)* concentration and insight in tandem are close to Nibbana.

"Those who abide in solitude, free of worldly entanglements, with a calm mind, who understand the Dhamma through tranquility and insight, in them arises delight that transcends all human delight!

Notice the reference again to tranquility and insight in tandem.

505

"Those that see with true insight the rise and fall of all conditioned things and of the Five-Clinging Aggregates, they are full of joy and lasting happiness. This is called the Deathless State as there will be no rebirth of confusion, delusion, and disappointment. The task (of unbinding) has been accomplished.

The "Deathless State" refers to the death of Karma. The present moment is empty of Dukkha.

"Restraint of the senses, contentment in the Dhamma, and restraint of unskillful behavior, these form the foundation of a well-integrated life.

"Associate with those who are engaged in the Noble search, who have passion for the true Dhamma, who are pure in thought, word, and deed, who are pleasant and refined in their behavior. Full of joy, unbinding will occur.

"Just as a jasmine creeper sheds its withered flowers, so should you shed greed, aversion, and deluded thinking!

'Those well-composed, calm and pleasant in thought, word, and deed, free of worldly entanglements, can be truly known as serene.

"It is by self-understanding that one can scrutinize themselves and restrain themselves. With the Six-sense base well-guarded with refined mindfulness one will always live in peace and happiness.

"Be your own protector. Be your own refuge. What other refuge could there be? Restrain yourself as a rider restrains his horse.

"Full of joy and conviction in the Dhamma the peaceful state is developed and conditioned thinking ends.

"Those that develop the Dhamma illuminate the entire world as a bright moon free of clouds."

End of Sutta

The Bhikkhuvaga discourse shows that restraint develops a true understanding of "emptiness" and the effect restraint has on the entire world.

In the Pamadaviharin Sutta, the Buddha shows the value of restraint in abandoning mindlessness and developing the refined mindfulness of the Eightfold Path.

Pamadaviharin Sutta
Dwelling in Mindlessness

Samyutta Nikaya 35.97

"Friends, pay close attention! I will teach you about one who dwells in mindlessness and one who dwells in mindfulness.

"And how does one dwell in mindlessness? When one is unrestrained at the eye the mind is agitated and distracted by mental fabrications. When agitated and distracted there is no joy and no passion for the Dhamma.

"Lacking passion for the Dhamma there is no serenity. There is only disappointment and distraction. When the mind is distracted, there can be no Dhamma. Lacking the Dhamma there is only mindlessness.

"When one dwells unrestrained over the ear, or the nose, or the tongue, or the body, the mind is agitated and distracted. There is no joy and no passion for the Dhamma. Lacking passion for the Dhamma there is no serenity. There is only disappointment and distraction. When the mind is distracted, there can be no Dhamma. Lacking the Dhamma there is only mindlessness.

"When one dwells unrestrained of thoughts the mind is agitated and distracted by ideological fabrications. There is no joy and no passion for the Dhamma. Lacking passion for the Dhamma there is no serenity.

"There is only disappointment and distraction. When the mind is distracted, there can be no Dhamma. Lacking the Dhamma there is only mindlessness.

"This is how one dwells in mindlessness.

"And how does one dwell in mindfulness? When a Dhamma Practitioner dwells in restraint with eye, with nose, with the ear, with the tongue, and with the body, the mind is not agitated or distracted by mental fabrications.

"There is joy and passion for the Dhamma. There being passion for the Dhamma there is serenity. There is contentment. The Dhamma is present moment-by-moment and they dwell in mindfulness.

"When one dwells well restrained of thought's the mind is not agitated or distracted by ideological fabrications. There is joy and passion for the Dhamma.

"There being passion for the Dhamma there is serenity. There is contentment. The Dhamma is present moment by moment and they dwell in mindfulness.

"This is how one dwells in mindfulness."

End of Sutta

The Kumma Sutta uses metaphor to show how the Dhamma is a protection against the mindlessness that arises from unrestrained desire and the peace and happiness that develops directly through restraint.

Kumma Sutta

The Tortoise

Samyutta Nikaya 35.199

In the Kumma Sutta the Buddha uses metaphor to teach the importance of restraint in thought, word, and deed.

"Once there was a tortoise foraging for food. A jackal was also foraging nearby. The tortoise noticed the Jackal and withdrew into its shell. The jackal also noticed the tortoise and went to the tortoise, hovering around and thinking 'as soon as the tortoise comes out of its shell I will eat it.' The tortoise remained in its protective shell and the jackal eventually lost interest and looked elsewhere for a meal.

The Buddha teaches: "Just as a jackal hovers around hoping for a meal, Mara hovers continuously hoping to create confusion, delusion, and disappointment by contact with the eye, or the ear, or the nose, or the tongue, or the body, or through the intellect.

The metaphor of the malevolent god Mara is used throughout the Sutta Pitaka to portray ongoing thinking rooted in ignorance.

"On seeing form with the eye, or hearing a sound with the ear, or smelling an aroma with the nose, or tasting a flavor with the tongue, or a tactile sensation with the body, if you have no restraint at these senses unskillful qualities such as greed, aversion, or deluded thinking will arise and suffering will follow. Guard the senses with restraint.

"Do not crave for or cling to any thought, or idea, or mental fabrication without restraint. If you have no restraint with regards to thoughts, ideas, or mental fabrications, unskillful qualities such as greed, aversion, or deluded thinking will arise and suffering will follow. Guard the senses with restraint. Guard your thinking with restraint.

"When you abide with the six-sense base well-guarded, Mara (confusion, delusion, and disappointment) has no opportunity for further

514

distraction and will lose interest just as the jackal lost interest with the tortoise.

"Like a tortoise well-protected in its shell, a wise disciple, restrained, independent, harmless to all, free from ill-will, is totally unbound.

End of Sutta

These four suttas show the importance of restraint in the Dhamma. The Four Noble Truths show that all manner of disappointment and suffering arises from craving and clinging. It is mindful restraint that brings the ability to recognize and abandon craving and clinging.

It is the refined mindfulness of the Eightfold Path that provides the framework for developing restraint of a self-referential ego-personality and brings a calm and peaceful life.

Bringing to cessation grasping after objects, events, views, and ideas develops a gentleness and lasting peace to life as life occurs, free of the distraction caused by an insatiable self-referential ego-personality.

Restraint is the ongoing quality of mind of an awakened, fully mature human being.

Restraint is the quality of mind of one who has developed the Dhamma and Become Buddha.

Ratana Sutta
True Refuge

Samyutta Nikaya 2.1

Nearly all schools of Buddhism refer to "The Three Jewels. The Three Jewels are also called "The Three Refuges." Refuge is a protection or a shelter from hardship or danger. Refuge is a source of comfort and peace.

The Three Jewels are:

1. The Buddha.

2. The Dhamma.

3. The Well-Focused Sangha.

In Buddhism when one takes refuge one is taking refuge in these precious jewels. The ritual of taking refuge is a formal, and usually public statement of holding the intention to have the example of the Buddha and his teachings of the dhamma be the framework   for   awakening. This, along with supporting and receiving the support of a community of dhamma practitioners, the sangha, is The Three Refuges.

The teaching known as the "Jewel Discourse" or the "Ratana Sutta" was given in the city of Vesali at a time of widespread famine and spreading disease. There were many dead bodies as the conditions overwhelmed the ability to properly dispose of bodies. The local citizens sought out the Buddha's help, who was nearby in Rajagaha.

The Ratana Sutta

The Buddha arrived in Vesali a short time later with a large number of monks, including Ananda. Just before the Buddha's arrival torrential rains helped the situation somewhat by cleansing the landscape of rotting corpses and clearing the air and water.

The Buddha presented this teaching to an entire city overcome by physical and emotional suffering.

Prior to his presenting this discourse he instructed his attending monks to walk through the city and do what they could to ease the physical suffering of the citizens and to individually present this teaching. At the formal teaching the Buddha then presented a way to bring true refuge from the stress and suffering of the world and to put an end to all dukkha:

"May all beings assembled have peace of mind.

"May all beings assembled listen mindfully to these words.

"May you all radiate goodwill and loving-kindness to all who offer help and understanding to you.

"Understand this:

"There is no more precious jewel, no more refuge, no more comfort, than the Buddha. As woodland groves in the early heat of summer are crowned with blooming flowers, so is the sublime Dhamma leading to the calm and peace of nirvana.

"The peerless and excellent awakened one, the teacher of true understanding, the teacher of the Noble Path is the Buddha, The one who has awakened."

Here the Buddha is not teaching worship of himself. The Buddha often referred to himself as the "Tathagata," the one who has gone forth. The Buddha had gone forth from distraction and ignorance, stress and suffering, to well-concentrated wisdom.

The Buddha liberated himself from clinging to all objects and views. Through his own efforts, Siddhartha Gotama awakened to become a Buddha. The Buddha is here offering himself as the example of one going forth on the Eightfold Path and awakening.

Taking refuge in the Buddha is understanding that all human beings can go forth from ignorance and attain wisdom and Right Understanding. There is great protection and comfort in understanding that liberation and freedom is possible for all human beings.

The Buddha continues:

"There is no more precious jewel than the teachings of the Buddha, the Dhamma. Understanding this brings true liberation and freedom.

"The Buddha, calm and mindful has experienced the cessation of clinging and desire. The Deathless state of nirvana has been attained.

"The Buddha teaches the Noble Eightfold Path that unfailingly brings concentration, liberation and freedom. There is no more precious jewel than the Buddha's dhamma."

The Buddha is describing the precious jewel of taking refuge in the path of liberation and freedom. In this setting in Vesali, the Buddha is teaching that once practical needs have been taken care of to turn one's attention to being mindful of the teachings of the Buddha.

The Buddha continues:

"There is no more precious jewel than the Sangha. Understanding this brings true liberation and freedom.

"The virtuous ones who bring the Dhamma, they are the Jewel of The Sangha.

"Those with steadfast minds, free of clinging, they are the jewel of the Sangha.

"Those that understand with wisdom The Four Noble Truths, they are the jewel of the Sangha.

"Those that gain true insight and abandon self-delusion, doubt, and indulgence in meaningless rites and rituals, they are the jewel of the sangha.

"Those beyond despair and evil-doings, They are the jewel of the sangha.

"Those whose understanding arises from the support of the sangha, who can no longer conceal the truth from themselves due to the sangha, they are the precious jewel of the sangha.

"Those whose karma is extinguished, the future of no concern, with rebirth ending, due to the support of the sangha, this is the precious jewel of the sangha."

End of Sutta

The example of the Buddha's life, the teachings of the Buddha, the Dhamma, along with the support of the Sangha, provides refuge from the suffering of distraction and ignorance arising from dukkha. Being mindful of the three jewels concentrates the mind to what is of utmost importance.

Taking Refuge in the Three Jewels is taking great comfort in understanding that awakening is possible for any human being. The example of the Buddha's life shows that.

There is great comfort in realizing that the way of liberation is a path accessible and integrated by anyone, the Eightfold Path.

There is great comfort in knowing that we do not engage in the path of liberation and freedom alone. Wisely associating with others well-focused on the Buddha's direct teachings is of primary importance. Who or what is associated with determines one's experience.

The Buddha often said that the most important aspect of practice is the sangha. The support and commitment that gained from a Sangha well-focused on Four Noble Truths provides the encouragement and strength to continue, even when distraction and aversion arise.

Holding in mind the Three Jewels provides continual direction for mindfulness.

Taking refuge in the Buddha, The Dhamma and the Sangha also provides a framework for mindful expression of joy and freedom.

Taking refuge in the Buddha, The Dhamma and a well-focused Sangha is Becoming Buddha.

523

The Kalama Sutta
Authentic Dhamma

Anguttara Nikaya 3.65

Becoming Buddha concludes with The Kalama Sutta. This sutta shows the restraint necessary to avoid continuing the ignorance of the Mahasanghikas at the Second Buddhist Council.

It is a self-referential ego-personality that would abandon restraint and grasp at doctrines, rites, and rituals rooted in ignorance of Four Noble Truths.

In the Kalama Sutta the Buddha directly addresses greed, aversion and deluded thinking. He teaches this to show how other teachings fail to address these defilements. Often these other "dharmas" promote deluded thinking and behavior.

The Buddha uses the qualities of generosity, non-clinging and well- concentrated refined mindfulness developed through The Eightfold Path as the framework for Dhamma practice. The Buddha points out that by awakening one becomes "mindful and imbued with equanimity, free of ill-will, undefiled and pure."

The Buddha consistently presented Four Noble Truths and the Eightfold Path as unique and distinct.

The Buddha never taught the Eightfold Path as a common teaching that could or should be integrated into other "dharmas."

It is the insistence that the Buddha's teachings can and should be accommodated to individual and cultural beliefs that have resulted in confusing, contradictory, and ineffective "dharmas."

He instructed the Kalama's to not "go by other's accounts, or by legends or traditions. Do not follow scriptures (later developed texts) or logical conjecture (conditioned thinking). Do not form conclusions through inference, analogies, or common agreement."

His admonition here to "question everything" must also be seen in the context in which he made this statement. This phrase is often gleefully and compulsively taken by many today as license to practice anything and everything and call it "Buddhist practice." Taken in the context he said this it is clear that the Buddha is telling the Kalama's to compare other teachings to his Dhamma through direct experience.

One must develop the Dhamma to know the practical effectiveness of the Dhamma. Once a practical knowledge of the Dhamma is developed, he taught to decide if other "dharmas" are consistent with his dhamma, and effective. He also provides very skillful guidance how to precisely determine what his Dhamma is based on.

Another way that many have adapted his admonition to "question everything" was in reference to him telling students that "when uncertain, confused, or doubtful *to question me directly*" conveniently leaving out the part where the Buddha emphasizes to be addressed directly.

This should be obvious that there could be no useful answer by asking someone who has dismissed the Dhamma. They are confused by their own insistence that the Dhamma should be adapted to fit desired answers to questions that are rooted in ignorance and taken out of context.

The Buddha encouraged others to question his teachings directly to him so that he could provide an answer in the proper context. He was not interested in engaging in endless debate or to convince someone of his Dhamma. The Buddha's response was only to provide guidance within the proper context.

Of course, since the Buddha's passing, we can no longer question him directly. We are indeed fortunate that we can look to the only written record of his teachings still existing today, or question a teacher that has actually studied his teachings as preserved in the Sutta Pitaka.

The Kalama Sutta

The Buddha was walking with a large group from the sangha. They arrived at Kesaputta, the town of the Kalama's. The Kalama's have heard that the Buddha was an awakened human being who teaches a complete path that is admirable in the beginning, in the middle and in its conclusion.

The Kalama's went to the Buddha and told him of the many teachers that come through their town all claiming to have taught the one true "dhamma" while ridiculing other teachers and their teachings. "How are we to know which is a useful and effective dhamma, and what is not."

The Buddha replies:

"Of course you are uncertain and filled with doubt. When there are reasons for doubt uncertainty will follow.

"Do not go by reports, or legends, or traditions, or scripture, or conjecture, or inference, or analogies, or common agreement, or unexamined loyalty.

"When you know from your own experience that the qualities taught are unskillful, shameful, confusing, and distracting these teachings should be abandoned.

I found much that was confusing and distracting in modern Dharmas, and occasionally quite shameful.

"When these teachings are criticized by the wise they should be abandoned. When these teachings lead to harm and suffering they should be abandoned.

"What do you think, Kalamas - when the three defilements of greed, aversion and deluded thinking arise in a person do they arise for benefit or for harm?"

"The defilements always bring harm."

"And when a person is driven by the defilements, their mind possessed, they kill other beings, they take what is not given, they take another's spouse, they lie and induce others to lie, all of which create long-term harm and suffering for themselves and others.

Unfortunately, the Buddha here could be referencing too many modern "Buddhist" teachers whose substance and sexual addictions are excused away with continued ignorance.

"What do you think, Kalama's - are these defilements skillful or unskillful, shameful or shameless, criticized or praised by the wise?"

"The defilements are unskillful, shameful, and criticized by the wise."

"When the defilements are acted upon do they lead to long-term suffering for one's self and others, or not?"

"They always lead to long term suffering for one's self and others."

"So as I said 'Do not go by reports, or legends, or traditions, or scripture, or conjecture, or inference, or analogies, or common agreement, or unexamined loyalty.

"When you know from your own experience that the qualities taught are unskillful, shameful, confusing, and distracting these teachings should be abandoned.

"When these teachings are criticized by the wise they should be abandoned. When these teachings lead to harm and suffering they should be abandoned.

"Now 'do not go by reports, or legends, or traditions, or scripture, or conjecture, or inference, or analogies, or common agreement, or unexamined loyalty.

"When you know from your own experience that the qualities taught are skillful, shameless, unambiguous, and direct these teachings should be developed.

"When these teachings are praised by the wise they should be developed. When these teachings lead to unbinding and calm they should be developed.

"What do you think, Kalamas - when the defilements do not arise in a person is this for their long-term welfare and happiness and for others long-term welfare and happiness?"

"For everyone's long-term welfare and happiness."

"And this person, free of the defilements, does not kill living beings or take what is not given, or take another's spouse, or lie or induce others to lie. So what do you think - are these qualities skillful, shameless, and praised by the wise?"

"They are, sir. When developed and acted on they bring long-term welfare and happiness to one's self and others."

"Now, Kalama's, one who follows the Dhamma, free of greed, aversion or deluded thinking, alert and mindful of the path, experiences their life imbued with good will.

"Everywhere they go their mindfulness is imbued with good will, with gratitude, with a mind resting in equanimity.

"They are abundant and free from all agitation towards themselves and all humanity.

"When one follows the Eightfold Path, free from greed, aversion, and deluded thinking, undefiled and pure, there are four qualities they will naturally develop:

They will give rise to pleasant experiences in the present.

They will give rise to pleasant experiences in the future.

If harm is done with no intention, no suffering will touch them.

If they remain harmless than they can know that they are pure and no suffering will touch them.

"These are the four qualities naturally developed in one free of the defilements from following the Dhamma."

533

"Great Teacher, you have shown a way to those who were lost. Through clear reasoning, you have made the Dhamma clear and taught us how to know a true Dhamma.

"We take refuge in you the Great Teacher, in your Dhamma and in your Sangha. Please remember that from this day forward we have taken refuge."

End of Sutta

There continues to be strong desire to accommodate the Buddha's direct teachings to fit cultural and individual traditions and hardened beliefs. The Buddha taught to avoid the desire to make his teachings fit self-referential views.

He taught Four Noble Truths including an Eightfold Path as the framework to recognize conditioned thinking rooted in ignorance, to abandon clinging, and develop a life of lasting peace and contentment.

The Buddha taught a unique, distinct and direct Eightfold Path. He also taught that recognizing differences in philosophies was primary and not intolerant or in any way divisive or discriminatory.

He taught that recognizing the differences between what he taught and what others taught was essential in developing becoming empty of ignorance.

Anyone seeking the truth of their own existence should and must be encouraged to abandon that which proves to be distracting from that search.

Maintaining a refined focus is the essence of refined mindfulness of the Dhamma. Concentration and refined mindfulness will prevent the confusion and continuing distraction of attempting to incorporate all things into a necessarily and wisely refined, complete, and specific Dhamma.

The Buddha taught an Eightfold Path to be the guiding framework for developing awakening, for developing full human maturity, for Becoming Buddha.

Peace.

Closing Words

Thank You for reading my book. I am honored that you have done so. My skillful wish is that you have found this book helpful in developing understanding of the simple and direct teachings of the Buddha.

Always be gentle with yourself and others and enjoy your developing freedom from ignorance.

I would greatly appreciate your questions or comments at Becoming-Buddha.Com. Please feel free to contact me at any time.

For more Dhamma articles and recorded Dhamma talks and videos, please visit Becoming-Buddha.Com.

Cross River Meditation Center is in Frenchtown, New Jersey, which is about an hour and twenty minutes from mid-town Manhattan and Center City Philadelphia. If you are in the area, please join our

Sangha at one of our classes. For my Dhamma classes and retreat schedule, please visit CrossRiverMeditation.com.

If you have found this book helpful, please consider writing a review and posting it at Amazon.com.
(https://www.amazon.com/dp/B071DGYFR3)

Thank You,

Peace.

About The Author
John Haspel

At an early age I became disappointed, unsettled and confused with my life. The purpose of life seemed to be the acquisition of things and superior labels. External phenomena such as gender, skin color, religious and political beliefs, body type, scholastic achievements, financial status, and an almost endless list of temporary states appeared to define a person's value and usefulness. Life was uncertain and nothing could bring certainty.

The competitiveness for the acquisition of things and superior labels seemed pointless and rife with struggle. No achievement or acquisition could bring lasting peace and happiness. I often blamed myself for my confusion and growing frustration.

While in an alcohol and drug rehab

at the age of nineteen, a family member gave me two books that would point my thinking in a new direction. I read Siddartha by Hermann Hesse, and Think on These Things by Jiddu Krishnamurti.

While I understood little of what I read, I was able to recognize a new way to view the world. I did not realize at the time that I was beginning to question my views of the world and myself.

I would drink and drug for another six years. Now twenty-five, and near death from the effects of alcohol and drug abuse, I took the 12 Steps of the Alcoholics Anonymous program of recovery as the 12 steps were originally presented. One of the 12 steps, step 11, emphasizes the need to develop spiritually through prayer and meditation.

Having been brought up in a Christian household I understood prayer (or thought I did) but I had no understanding of meditation. As I knew nothing of meditation, I wanted to dismiss it.

Fortunately, meditation was presented to me as necessary if I was to recover. I remembered the emphasis that the Buddha and Krishnamurti placed on meditation. I sought out meditation teachers.

I first learned Transcendental Meditation and practiced the TM technique for 4 years. I eventually became disappointed with this technique. TM did not seem to be able to provide any framework for developing understanding of the confusing nature of life. TM only developed a measure of concentration. The Hindu rituals and dogma loosely associated with TM created more confusion for me.

The need to be able to afford the more "advanced" levels of TM, or not be allowed the teachings was off-putting. This seemed just another aspect of the competitiveness and "bottom line" mentality that is all part of the confusing nature of the world.

I settled on Buddhism and studied and practiced in the Tibetan schools for many years. I attended many retreats and special teachings and learned of the beauty and depth of these teachings.

The more I studied and practiced, the more elusive understanding became. The more I learned, the more confused I became. The more I learned, the more I was asked to take on faith.

This seemed contrary to what a Buddha would teach. I had to admit, though, that after many years of "Buddhist" study I likely knew little of what the Buddha actually taught. Ultimately I left Tibetan Buddhism.

I then spent some time simultaneously studying in the Zen schools (Zen, Chan, Soen) and in the New Kadampa Tradition sect. A few years into the NKT sect, I found their teachings to have little to do with the teachings of the Buddha.

The NKT seemed to have their own contrary philosophy by professing worship of a worldly deity, Dorje Shugden, and an intense hatred for the Dalai Lama. Neither seemed consistent with a Buddha would teach.

I then put my efforts into the various Zen schools. My initial impression of Zen Buddhism was that it is a less dogmatic or less mystical teaching.

After extensive study, many sesshins, retreats, and diligent practice, I found that I was still not developing understanding or finding anything that would likely lead me to understanding.

I found nearly as much dogma and nearly as much mysticism in the Zen schools. The Four Noble Truths seemed to be treated more as an anachronism rather than the defining understanding of a Buddha's teachings.

Through all these different teachings and association's, it seemed that "becoming" a Tibetan Buddhist, or a Zen Buddhist, or Chan or Soen Buddhist, or an NKT Buddhist, or to "Inter-be," was more important than actually developing useful understanding and Becoming Buddha.

There was much more emphasis on adapting to, and adopting, the individual and cultural embellishments to the original teachings as there was in developing an understanding of the nature of confusion, delusion, and suffering.

In these later-developed schools it was first necessary to learn the dogma, rituals, and methods of each school, no small matter, and then engage with their particular teachings for "many lifetimes" in order to gain any understanding. There exists a subtle, and often not so subtle, elitism within most of these schools.

I came to understand that the Buddha did not teach any of these individual or cultural embellishments as part of his Dhamma.

After careful and intensive study, I became convinced that these later schools would not be able to develop in me the Buddha's stated goal of release from all clinging views and resulting suffering.

I then looked to the Theravadin school. I found much of what I was looking for in "the teachings of the elders" but I found that the mystical aspects rooted in the Abhidhamma practiced by many Theravadins confusing and not helpful to developing understanding.

I found the modern meditation practice of the "Vipassana" movement, considered a sub-school of Theravada, to be stripped of most of the Buddha's original teachings in favor of an exhaustive and hybridized meditation technique.

This was my experience. Many people have gained a measure of belonging and comfort from these schools, and the many other modern "Buddhist" schools. I did not.

Many years of extensive study and practice left me more confused and frustrated. I had put in the time and studied with many of the foremost modern teachers. I read the writings of all the great Mahayana teachers. Yet I was more confused as to what the Buddha taught than when I first began studying the Dhamma 25 years prior.

I decided that I would try to separate what the Buddha likely taught from what developed later. I learned that the original teachings of the Buddha were still available and preserved in a set of books called "The Pali Canon."

As I studied the Sutta Pitaka, in particular the translations by Thanissaro Bhikkhu and, to a lesser degree, the books by Bhikkhu Bodhi, it became clear that the Buddha taught that he was a human being who through his own Right Effort "awakened" to the truth of his existence.

The Buddha taught a Dhamma that any human being could engage with. The path he taught was an Eightfold Path of developing heightened wisdom, virtue and concentration. The Buddha taught that nothing needed to be taken on blind faith.

The Buddha taught that with conviction arising from a basic understanding of the Four Noble Truths, a "Right View" of the world could be achieved.

I found that there were no "special" or "advanced" rituals, chants, initiations, or empowerments necessary to develop understanding.

The Buddha taught a specific meditation technique with specific goals. This meditation technique, Shamatha-Vipassana meditation, was to be practiced within the framework of the Eightfold Path if it would contribute to and support awakening.

I found that the Buddha described awakening not as finding an essential inner nature, or "Buddha-nature" but as unbinding from all views that developed from a doctrine of "I." The Buddha described the state of mind of an awakened human being not as "Buddha-nature," or "Buddha-hood," but as released, unbound, and calm.

I found that the Buddha awakened to Dependent Origination. Here he taught that it is ignorance of Four Noble Truths that lead to all manner of confusion, deluded thinking, and ongoing disappointment.

I found my confusion, deluded thinking, and disappointment rooted in this same ignorance.

I found that what I had previously thought of as my "self" was an impermanent and insubstantial creation of my own ignorance. This "self" was a composition of five psycho/physical aggregates that cling together, and cling to phenomena.

It is these Five Clinging-Aggregates that I have projected a doctrine of self onto and into. It is this impermanent "self" that is prone to confusion and suffering.

This cleared much of the confusion of other "dharmas" that taught a continued doctrine of self within a cosmic environment of inter-being, interdependence, and interconnection clinging to other conditioned objects.

I found that I did not have to reconcile my understanding of the Buddha's teachings with every other philosophy or "spiritual" teaching, "Buddhist" or otherwise.

I developed this understanding by learning that the Buddha felt no such compulsion to reconcile the

Dhamma to the prevailing beliefs or religions of his day.

I found that the Buddha did not concern himself with having to prove through magical, mystical, scientific, or any other means, the truth of his Dhamma.

I found that the Buddha taught an Eightfold Path to awakening that any human being who wholeheartedly engaged with the Dhamma, as he presented his Dhamma, could, and often did awaken.

Most importantly, I found a Dhamma that I could engage with and understand. I found a Dhamma that developed in a direct way understanding, without becoming confused or distracted with dogma, ritual, mutually conditioned agreement, or "spiritual" acquisition.

I found that the problem of suffering was due to my own need to establish and maintain a doctrine of self.

I found that the Buddha's Dhamma develops the understanding to abandon all views arising from a doctrine of self.

I found, through direct inquiry of the Buddha's Dhamma, a peaceful and calm mind, and lasting peace and contentment.

You can contact John via Becoming-Buddha.com

Also By John

The Truth Of Happiness A Personal Study Of The Buddha's Direct Teachings and Companion Guide to Becoming Buddha with the option to correspond with John through weekly emails and phone or video chat. Available at Amazon.com and at Becoming-Buddha.com

The Spiritual Solution. For those in the recovery community. A simple and straightforward guide to the 12 Steps.

Available at Amazon.com and at JohnH12Steps.com

Mindfulness Based Recovery to be published summer 2017

To be notified of new books, please subscribe to my newsletter at Becoming-Buddha.Com.

Made in the USA
Monee, IL
22 July 2020